HOW TO NEGOTIATE WORLDWIDE

How to negotiate worldwide

A practical handbook

Donald W Hendon, PhD

Rebecca Angeles Hendon

Published by
Gower Publishing Company Limited
Gower House
Croft Road
Aldershot
Hants GU11 3HR
England

Reprinted 1994

British Library Cataloguing in Publication Data

Hendon, Donald W.
    How to negotiate worldwide.
    1.   Business negotiation – Manuals – For management
    I.   Title II. Hendon, Rebecca A. S. Angeles
    658.4'5

ISBN 0 566 07481 8

Printed and bound by Hartnolls Limited, Bodmin, Cornwall

Contents

Preface

A book on international negotiation is a fitting response to the growing demand for 'world-mindedness' in today's global market place, where competition from foreign companies – both at home and overseas – continues to challenge the international executive. Consider the following remarks:

I intend to make international experience for our American managers a key issue.
(Richard W. Siebrasse,
President of CPC International's consumer foods division)
Decision-making is slower overseas, the nuance of dealing with governments is different.
(Carl W. Menk,
President of Candy Bowen, an international recruiting firm)
You gain a certain appreciation that there are other ways to do things than the American way, that other economies play a part in the world, that the sun does not rise and set in New York City... It is not just language and culture; these people develop a broader set of problem-solving skills.
(John R. Fulkerson,
Director of Human Resources, Pepsi-Cola International)

If you're in business, you negotiate, and you should think like a negotiator. This book will help you, especially if you deal with people outside your own country. It is a book about negotiating, but it is written in an international context. This means that we are going to be talking about how negotiating is done when people of different cultures and different nations get together.

In 1972 a newspaper reported that an American business executive from Arizona made a $2,460,000 negotiating error. In 1968 he heard that the Greater London Council was going to demolish the old London Bridge and build a new one. He thought it would be a great idea to import the old bridge, stone by stone, and rebuild it at Lake Havasu City, Arizona, a resort he was developing. He thought this would make the resort a tourist attraction that would, perhaps, someday rival nearby tourist attractions like the Grand Canyon and Las Vegas. He had seen pictures of Tower Bridge, with its twin Gothic towers and drawbridge, and assumed that that was the bridge he had bought. However, when the first stones arrived, the $2,460,000 turned out to be for a plain, five-arched granite structure, a completely different bridge spanning the Thames. He was disappointed, but he put it up anyway. And a few tourists came, but not as many as he had hoped for.

Americans are not the best negotiators in the world, of course. In fact some have taken pride in their mediocrity. In the late 1800s, J.P. Morgan bragged that he could have made $3 million more on a deal, but he was in too much of a hurry to haggle. All of us can, and should, learn from mistakes made by Americans and by other nationalities. In the London Bridge instance, the American made an assumption that was wrong – and then he believed his assumption was correct. He also assumed erroneously, that the contract he made was going to be the contract that was delivered. Often it's not. For example, one negotiator looked at 100 invoices from different hotels he had stayed at during a one-year period. He found only twenty that were correct; eighty were not in accordance with the agreement he had made with the hotels. Seventy-nine of those were wrong in the hotels' favour, and only one was wrong in his favour. Be warned by both of these examples!

Our extensive travels and international exposure – seminars and consulting in 22 nations on 6 continents – prompted us to write this book, which is a logical extension of our seminar, 'How You Can Negotiate and Win', where we teach the basic principles of negotiation. As such, the book focuses on the salient issues involved in doing business on a global scale rather than on the basics of negotiating skills. We do, however, discuss the most important basic negotiating considerations and, in addition, illustrate them within the context of the international scene, as you'll read in Part I. Part I also gives you a sweeping view of the structural changes in the global market-place that underscore the need for international negotiating skills. We shall also discuss the concession patterns of the executives from many different nations who have been participants in our seminar. Then in Part II, we'll show business executives how important cultural factors are to the success of a negotiation. Part III contains detailed information that will help everybody who negotiates after a thorough discussion of 82 tactics and countermeasures to these tactics. And in the Appendix you'll find the favourite tactics, broken down by country, that were chosen by the executives in our seminar that they like to use in five specific business situations.

We address this book to business executives in particular, but those engaged in other types of work involving international exposure stand to benefit from it as well – for instance, the diplomat, government civil servant, volunteer worker, missionary, technical expert and consultant, student, tourist, and so forth. This book, though, isn't meant to teach you *all* the rudiments of general negotiation. A basic background will help you, but it isn't essential. This book features the nuances of how to negotiate in an international setting.

You will need to learn to be an effective negotiator because *negotiating* is probably the thing we do most often in this world. It's not something done only by diplomats and trade unions: negotiating is simply the process you follow to get somebody else to do what you want them to do. That somebody else can be a business partner, a buyer or seller, a boss or an employee; it may be your spouse, lover, parent, child, friend, doctor, banker, lawyer or landlord. Negotiating is the art of making the deal a matter of persuasion rather than a crude power play. It's the art of making your boss *want* to give you that rise or promotion; of making the other person your friend, rather than your enemy, no matter how tough a bargain you strike. It's the *art* too, of choosing the right strategy for each situation, painting the right business picture, doing the right research, projecting the right personal image, asking the right questions, applying the right pressure at the right time, offering the right inducements and demanding the right extras.

In short, negotiating skills are essential to your success not only in business, but in life itself. The kinds of agreement and relationship that you have with other people and companies determine your success. Poor agreements always seem to break down, bringing continued dissatisfaction not only to you yourself, but to those you deal with in your personal and business life. And good agreements not only help you *reach* your objectives, but to *exceed* them – and, at the same time, the person on the other side (referred to as TOS throughout this book) gets greater satisfaction, instead of feeling resentful and determined to take revenge in another part of the deal. This is always true, whether you are persuading others to work with you and not against you; setting your budget; determining the price and terms at which you buy or sell; breaking or avoiding a serious impasse; closing a deal with an important customer; managing and supervising your employees; or finalizing and administering contracts.

Negotiating is not just about coming out on top. That's too short-sighted. Winning in the short term sometimes can damage long-term relationships, if TOS doesn't win, too. For example, what's terrific for your sales department can create endless problems in the factory floor. The factory has to win, too. In this book you'll learn how to achieve a win–win result as you learn about negotiating in general.

Don Hendon
Rebecca Hendon

Part I

THE NATURE OF INTERNATIONAL NEGOTIATING

Introduction to Part I

This book isn't only about general negotiating. While it *does* cover negotiating in general, it is in fact a lot more specialized than that – i.e. it's about *international* negotiating. Today international negotiating is much harder than ever before because international business itself is changing. More firms are doing business across borders. More competition means that executives need negotiating skills and the ability to forge co-operative agreements as never before if firms are to survive, let alone remain competitive in the international market-place.

Here we shall cover three important areas: the six stages that negotiators must go through; how international executives make concessions; and the profile of the ideal international negotiator.

1 As we talk about the six negotiating stages in Chapter 1 ('The six stages'), we look at how General Motors and Toyota negotiated and created the New United Motor Manufacturing, Inc. (NUMMI). This case shows up the complexities involved in creating joint ventures that are now becoming more and more commonplace.

2 Chapter 2 ('How to make concessions') features executives of different nationalities behaving in terms of their response to the give-and-take of negotiating – always at the heart of any negotiation. Through an exercise in our seminar, 'How You Can Negotiate and Win', we arrived at a well-drawn picture of

how exactly executives in many nations concede when they negotiate.

3   Chapter 3, a profile of the ideal international negotiator, was written in response to the pattern of problems almost always to be found in negotiating internationally. Use the eight points discussed in the profile as a benchmark or framework to evaluate the effectiveness of your own international negotiating style. Eventually, though, the value judgement as to whether or not you did well is yours. That's because this chapter gives you flexible guidelines, not hard-and-fast rules. The guidelines are meant to be fluid. It is up to your prudence and creativity to respond appropriately to the problems you face – so use our guidelines well!

The changing international business environment

The large multinational corporations (MNCs) are not only continuing their involvement in direct foreign investments, but they have also substantially increased their participation in the following five activities:

1   *Joint ventures* – arrangements where two or more organizations share in the ownership of a direct investment.
2   *Licensing agreements* – where one firm gives rights to another to use such assets as trade marks, patents, copyrights and know-how for a fee.
3   *Subcontracting* – an arrangement where a firm pays another company to perform part of the production process in manufacturing a product.
4   *Turnkey projects* – a contract for the construction of an operating facility that is transferred to the owner once it is finished and ready for operations; under this arrangement, the contractor is responsible for delivering the materials, equipment, workforce and managerial personnel to accomplish the entire project.
5   *Management contracts* – arrangements through which one firm provides another firm with management personnel to perform general or specialized managerial tasks for a fee.

Now, none of these forms of international business arrangements is new. What *is* different is that more MNCs from many countries are participating in these forms of business to a much greater extent now than they have ever done in previous decades.[1]

Challenges in the international business scene for the remainder of the twentieth century

You are reading this book because you're involved in international business. To stay ahead of your competitors, you need to know what to expect in the years to come. What will the future bring? Many observers have said that there is a growing tendency for companies and industries, and even nations, to engage in cross-border alliances or to locate operations abroad to survive more competitive conditions in the international market in the remaining years of this century. They foresee eight important events, each highlighting the importance of international negotiations, as follows.

1 Increased foreign presence in the USA

The USA is the biggest player in the international market. Things are changing there, though. There is much more foreign investment in that nation than ever before, and that trend seems likely to continue. The main impetus to the entry of foreign investors into the USA has been the weakening of the US dollar until the summer of 1989. Since the mid-1980s its value has plunged dramatically against the West German Mark and Japanese yen. The US stock prices were especially low after the 'Black Monday' stock market crash in October 1987. As a result of all this, some American firms such as General Motors began planning to move parts of their production processes from abroad back to the USA.

Another interesting consequence of the weak dollar is the scramble of firms in other nations to buy American companies to take advantage of the bargain prices of their assets. Europeans and Japanese have taken especially keen interest in the USA because of its political stability. Some Europeans prefer to invest in the USA rather than at home because the profit picture is brighter there. They are especially looking into the oil, pharmaceuticals, biotechnology and chemicals industries. British Petroleum bought Standard Oil of Ohio; Belgium's Petrofina is looking into US oil reserves; and Germany's Bayer purchased a Houston, Texas chemical maker in 1988. There are many more European examples.

Japanese acquisitions in the USA doubled from $2.7 billion in 1986 to $5.9 billion in 1987 – and more brisk buying is expected. One example is the $2.6 billion acquisition, in May 1988, by Japan's Bridgestone Corporation of Firestone Tire & Rubber, the number two American tyre maker. The weak dollar prior to the summer of 1989 and strong yen were just part of the story. Fears of being shut out of the American market as a result of growing protectionist sentiments and rising costs of production in Japan have also motivated Japanese purchases in the USA. The Japanese primarily prefer high-technology, biotechnology securities companies, and other firms that would help them expand their distribution systems in the USA or enhance their technology. They are looking for companies that make a strategic contribution to their own development efforts at home. The Japanese seem to be heading towards being truly multinational in a global sense – manufacturing and selling in markets worldwide, rather than just manufacturing at home and selling abroad.[2]

2   Many dramatic changes making Europe more competitive

The deregulation of Europe's financial markets has led to changes that facilitate international negotiations. Although the European Economic Community (EC) is planning to create a single, easy-to-get banking licence that would be valid anywhere in the EC by 1992, many banks are not waiting. European banks are crossing national boundaries: Deutsche Bank moved into Italy by purchasing Bank America's network of 100 banks for $603 million; and Munich-based Bayerische Vereinsbank acquired the First National Bank of Chicago's Rome and Milan branches. The banking licence also allows banks to undertake a wide range of securities activities such as underwriting, brokerage and portfolio management. Spain and

France have already allowed foreign financial institutions to purchase local brokerage firms – in effect, breaking up long-established cartels in the Madrid and Paris bourses. Swiss Bank Corporation, America's J.P. Morgan & Co., and the S.G. Warburg Group of Britain are among twelve financial institutions that have put up about $1 billion for financial acquisitions.

Structural changes that are meant to integrate Europe's financial resources are already occurring. There is already a European stock exchange centred in London, with regional exchanges in Frankfurt and Paris, where most large European companies place their paper. This exchange system makes it possible to negotiate business arrangements between and among nations in Europe and outside.

Financial deregulation has created a big demand for data networks providing card verification and services to link branch networks of banks and insurance companies. The nationalized telephone monopolies in Europe have long neglected developing telecommunications technology, and this has created a niche for American companies such as Electronic Data Systems, which is putting up its own data-processing plant near Paris, and IBM, which has formed a joint venture with two French banks, Paribas and Credit Agricole, to develop a $110 million data transmission service for financial institutions.[3]

Privatization of once state-owned enterprises is one significant change in industrial policy that has been carried out in several European nations. Compagnie Générale d'Electricité (CGE), France's second largest industrial group, was privatized in mid-1987, and the government expected a lot of profits from a dramatic turnaround.[4]

The weak US dollar in the late 1980s has adversely affected US imports from Europe, Fewer Americans bought such European-made items as Porsche motor cars, Bang & Olufsen audio equipment, Waterford crystal and Louis Vuitton luggage because of their much higher prices. To meet this difficulty of exporting to the USA, some European firms like the French pharmaceutical firm Rhône-Poulenc are opting to buy companies in the USA, and gain profits from exporting to Europe and other parts of the world. This move is also an effective hedge against the effects of protectionist policies that could shut them out completely from the American market. The advantage of this strategic move has paid off for several European firms, including the Hoechst Group; in the third quarter of 1987 its pretax profits shot up by 32 per cent, solely on account of its newly acquired American subsidiary, the Celanese Corporation.[5]

The EC is removing many nontariff barriers, principally local regulations stipulating product standards, that are restricting not only the flow of goods, but also the flow of services and capital among its member states. This is a welcome change, for companies expect to cut their production costs considerably as a result of the simplification of product standards. They won't have to make many alterations in product models to meet the regulations of different countries. The removal of nontariff barriers, expected to be completed by 1992, along with the deregulation of certain industries, is once again making Europe an attractive site for international investments.

The Japanese are responding quickly and are looking forward to locating more manufacturing plants in Europe; some of their motor car companies are considering manufacturing there. As long as they use a high proportion of European components, Japanese cars made in, say, Spain or Britain, could be sold throughout Europe just as easily as Peugeots and Fiats. Americans are also coming in: the insurance giant, the American International Group, and US insurance broker Marsh & McLennan both plan to expand their operations in Europe.[6]

3   The growing significance of Japan in international business

Following reconstruction efforts after the Second World War and rapid economic growth in the 1950s and 1960s, Japan focused its efforts on exporting textiles, consumer electronics, steel, motor cars and other products to developed countries and nearby developing countries in Asia. In the 1970s and 1980s, Japan firmed up its leadership in the world market as its industrial companies, such as Sony, Matsushita, Honda and Mitsubishi, began manufacturing in the USA to gain greater market access. Another important reason for locating in the USA was the need to secure production facilities there, as a hedge against the possible future imposition of quotas and import restrictions. Therefore many Japanese companies have become *even more internationalized* in their organization and orientation (if that is possible!) in recognition of the imperatives of survival in the global market-place. With the changing business climate in Europe, Japanese firms expect to locate more of their manufacturing plants there in the 1990s.

While Japan has stunned the Western world with its phenomenal recovery and success, some observers perceive this successful image to be exaggerated. Now that Japan is not only selling but also manufacturing abroad, the country is experiencing problems of adjustment. The Japanese way of doing business and managing isn't that easy to transplant in the West. Intercultural barriers to smooth internationalized procedures are formidable, and they are real enough to slow down the transfer of technology and know-how from Japan. They realize the need to internationalize their operations, but they are having problems finding the people with the right combination of managerial skills to oversee operations abroad. An even more serious problem is the difficulty of getting Japanese managers to locate abroad because of the significant cultural dislocation that an overseas assignment can cause.

In the meantime companies from other countries are recognizing the strategic importance of locating in Japan. Japan is the second largest market for technology-based industries, so there's a lot more competition in that market from foreign firms. In fact locating in Japan is a guarantee against protectionist policies that that country may later enforce as worldwide competition grows in high-technology products.[7]

4 Competition made steeper by industrializing Third World countries

Increased global competition has also come from rapidly industrializing countries such as Asia's 'Four Tigers' – South Korea, Singapore, Taiwan and Hong Kong – in product groups such as textiles, apparel, steel, metallurgical products and electronics. The MNCs from developing Third World nations have also begun manufacturing abroad, with scaled-down, more labour-intensive technology. They have competed mainly on the basis of price. Moving direct investments abroad has been motivated mainly by their need to maintain markets, reduce costs of production and diversify their product lines.[8]

5 Peculiar problems in developing countries

Negotiations in developing countries are complicated because of many factors. If you are from a developed country, you will find differences in levels of economic development, economic structure and national economic planning, and the mix of capitalism and socialism adopted. There are other groups external to the business transaction itself that have considerable influence on decisions – e.g. other local business executives, labour unions, consumers, intellectuals, environmentalists, international and regional organizations, such as UNCTAD and the Group of 77, and so forth. Special issues will also complicate your business transactions there: protection of national sovereignty, aspirations of modernization, transfer pricing issues, past abuses and political interference of a former colonizing nation, fears of the oligopoly power of MNCs and conflicts between the national interests of a developing country and the global objectives of MNCs.

Some developing countries, such as India and Peru, have also placed stricter requirements on foreign MNCs: severe entry-screening procedures, steeper ownership requirements, performance restrictions and limitations on the repatriation of earnings. The MNCs are particularly burdened with the difficulties of negotiating with host governments. Some inconveniences are also likely to include inconsistent and highly bureaucratic regulations, too many government offices involved in the approval process, too much power and subjectivity given to too few decision-makers, and dealing with many forms of bribery and corruption.[9]

6 The race for the lead in high-tech industries forges alliances

The growth of high-technology industries is so fast that it's too hard for one company alone to control critical elements of production. Companies in office automation, robotics and consumer electronics have the added task of overseeing rapid developments in evolving new technologies and deciding where to concentrate their research and development (R&D) resources. Even giant companies have learned that there usually isn't enough time to catch up with competitors, thus the technological patent exchange between America's IBM and Japan's Nippon Telegraph and Telephone. Similar arrangements by many high-tech firms which recognize the value of surviving through alliances with competitors are occurring. For example, American Telephone and Telegraph has arranged a partnership with Europe's Philips and Olivetti. Burroughs is packaging Fujitsu's high-speed facsimiles as part of its office automation products and is manufacturing under licence the Nippon Electric Co.'s optical character readers.

Such arrangements are valuable not only in manufacturing, but also in marketing and distribution. Take the example of video cassette recorders. While the product was at its introductory stage, Sony and the Matsushita Group (JVC, National Panasonic, Technics and Quasar) developed the Beta and VHS formats respectively. They co-operated through different consortia to gain significant market shares in the USA, Europe and Japan. Sony franchised Toshiba and Sanyo in Japan, Zenith and Sears in the USA, Fischer in the UK, Neckermann in Germany and Vega in Spain to gain sizeable shares in those markets. Matsushita franchised others for its VHS format and was quite successful also.[10]

7 Increased modernization, education and technological diffusion improve business practices

The cost of monitoring foreign operations has been reduced for parent companies if they have invested in modern computer and communications technologies. These developments have facilitated the push to internationalize business operations. And the new crop of managers produced by business schools are a lot more prepared to handle the challenges of international business. For instance, the better educated, young European managers appear to be more flexible and less affected by 'national pride', and so the new

Pan-European companies are expected to be successful – and most are. Some companies are adopting more liberal and open hiring policies: nearly half of Olivetti's payroll consists of non-Italians who are expected to understand and speak English.

Other companies have reorganized their structure to suit the demands of global operations. For instance, America's Gillette Co. changed from fifteen firms in fifteen nations, each self-contained, to a system organized along product lines which cut across international boundaries. Under the new arrangement, product managers are required to be multilingual and sensitive to cultural differences. Advanced telecommunications technology has also helped international operations by making it possible to transmit information across borders instantaneously. (Some firms are even running round-the-clock operations because of time-zone differences.) In Europe the electronic translation of documents from one language to another has also been made possible by such technological advances.[11]

8   Shift to the short-term perspective

A host of factors has prompted leading businesses throughout the world to shift their perspective more to the short term and shorten their planning horizons. Among these factors are the stagflation and global recessions of the 1970s and early 1980s, the slowdown in productivity and investments in nations belonging to the Organization for Economic Co-operation and Development, the shift to floating exchange rates, relatively high inflation and high interest rates. Uncertain world conditions, accelerated change and intensified international competition have robbed even the bigger MNCs of any sense of security and permanence that they might have had. Given the shorter period of time within which to produce results, corporate executives and business entrepreneurs are hard-pressed to negotiate the best deals possible within restricted time periods.[12]

We think the ultimate challenge to all you international negotiators is to evolve a style that will let you not only survive the challenges you will surely face in all phases of the negotiation, but enable you to stick to your 'bottom line' until the very end, in spite of modifications you may have to make. The thing, of course, is not only to be clear about your own cultural identity which eventually colours your own style (this will be taken up extensively in Part II), but to be able to observe it, to be aware of how it works and, eventually, to work with it and modify it to suit the needs called for by the changing character of the game as it's played with its many different players and settings.

1 The six stages

The epitome of international corporate co-operation involving two radically different cultures occurred in April 1984 when the US government approved a joint venture between General Motors (GM) and Japan's Toyota to manufacture compact motor-cars in the USA. The joint venture, incorporated as New United Motor Manufacturing Inc. (NUMMI), is unique, in that it isn't a merger or a partnership. Rather it is a purely co-operative arrangement between two of the world's largest motor-car manufacturers to build just one model of automobile for a limited period of twelve years. Production is done in a former GM assembly plant in the northern Californian city of Fremont. The joint venture's first baby, the Nova, began production in the summer of 1985, and they were ready for display in Chevrolet's showrooms in the autumn of 1985.

This innovative working arrangement between GM and Toyota was the product of complex and tedious international negotiating efforts with its own unique problems. In this chapter, we trace the progress of the negotiation efforts that culminated in the creation of this joint venture. You will see how good negotiating principles (shown in *italic* type) were followed at each stage of their negotiations.

The six main stages in a typical negotiation are:

Stage 1: Prenegotiation – a period of determining objectives in relation to the opportunities and problems involved in the scenario.

Stage 2: Entry – the formal sales presentation to TOS is made at this time.

Stage 3: Establishing effective relationships with TOS – this is the time for establishing trust and rapport and earning the right to learn the needs and objectives of TOS.

Stage 4: Learning more about TOS and reformulation of your earlier strategies – mistaken and inaccurate assumptions are corrected at this time to arrive at better proposals to meet the needs of TOS.

Stage 5: Bargaining and concession-making – this is the dynamic part of the negotiation when parties involved take turns giving and taking, ideally, in defence of their 'bottom line'.

Stage 6: Reaching agreement – after a period of exchanging concessions, the final round is reached when terms agreeable to both parties are made to constitute the elements of their written or verbal contracts.

We shall now see how these stages applied to the GM – Toyota negotiation.

Stage 1: Prenegotiation

At this stage, determine your objectives in relation to the opportunities presented by the environment and the difficulties posed by situational factors. List the relevant issues that affect your opportunities and constraints. Prepare a tentative list both outlining your interests and those of the other side (TOS) with an accompanying list of acceptable trade-offs. Establish the level of your best first offer. Anticipate TOS's reactions. What are your contingency plans for each possible reaction? You'll have to assemble your negotiation team at this stage.[1]

In 1982, GM and Toyota began their negotiations. Both appreciated the tremendous advantages of pursuing the joint venture; GM was motivated by the fact that the venture would produce a competitive, profitable compact car, designed entirely by Toyota to enhance its line. The final product, which was to be sold through Chevrolet dealers throughout the USA, would give GM the opportunity of winning back its share of the small-car market. Finally, GM's management and workers would have the opportunity of observing Japanese manufacturing and management methods at first hand, and learn from this experience.

From the point-of-view of Toyota, the joint venture was equally attractive because it would give them an avenue through which to establish their presence in the American market, at a time when public attitudes towards imported cars had been dampening. Two of Toyota's competitors, Nissan and Honda, had already established their own plants in the USA; it was only logical for Toyota to follow suit to maintain its competitiveness. Unlike its competitors, though, Toyota didn't take as many risks since its affiliation with GM eliminated the need to invest additional capital in a plant.

However, at this initial stage, the problems and issues faced by GM–Toyota were tremendous. The primary negotiating parties involved were the GM–Toyota group vs the American workers, formerly hired by GM at the Fremont plant. Other secondary negotiating parties with which the GM–Toyota group had to contend were the Federal Trade Commission (FTC), other American motor-car industrial giants like Chrysler and the American public in general.

First, the joint venture needed the approval of the FTC, a major regulatory agency. Chrysler, one of GM's major competitors in the American motor-car industry, was lobbying strongly against the approval of the venture and filed a lawsuit, claiming that it violated the country's antitrust laws. Toyota hired a large Washington law firm to work on getting FTC approval. Eventually, the FTC ruled that since the joint venture was to be undertaken within a limited time period, it was legally permissible.

Secondly, the joint venture was affected by the actions of GM concerning its workforce at the Fremont plant. GM shut down the plant in early 1982 but was still under contractual obligation to rehire the laid-off workers, should the joint venture with Toyota occur. Horror stories about the workers at the Fremont plant had been circulating for years. The Japanese were especially aware that the workers were notorious for drug use, sabotage, violence and high grievance rates. The plant, one of GM's worst, had a very poor history of labour-management relations. They didn't want that to happen again, and so they were quite adamant about not hiring any of the former workers for the joint venture. On top of that, the Japanese had very basic doubts about the ability of even an adequate American workforce to deliver the same quality of performance and devotion they were accustomed to seeing in Japan. Toyota strongly demanded *complete* freedom in running the Fremont plant; and GM responded to it positively by guaranteeing them a totally free hand. Meanwhile the Fremont workers who were members of the United Auto Workers (UAW) Local 1364 were pushing for 100 per cent rehiring and the recognition of the UAW as their bargaining agent.

Thirdly, there were many communication problems between the Japanese and Americans because the US team didn't know the Japanese language, and the Japanese weren't proficient in English and needed more time to grasp the fundamental concepts of American labour law. Cross-cultural 'noise' resulting from cultural differences had to be managed in discussions between the Japanese and the Americans.

Finally, in early 1983, GM and Toyota invited former US Secretary of Labor, William J. Usery, Jr, to act as *chief negotiator* between their team and the parties they had to deal with. Usery was well aware of the opposing interests involved, and he was prudent enough to first clarify his position before he began his work. When he was interviewed by Toyota, Usery said he didn't want to be called 'chief negotiator', because this implied he worked solely for Toyota and GM. He appreciated the need for him to be perceived as neutral, particularly by the UAW, in order to gain their trust and confidence. So he called himself *facilitator, catalyst, mediator* and *consultant* to improve his standing with the UAW and give him more credibility. By using those terms, he thought he would leave the impression that he was above the interests of all parties involved and would act impartially, even though he was in fact employed by GM and Toyota.

Usery knew that the timing of the negotiations for the joint venture was favourable. In 1983 the American motor-car industry was at a low point – thousands of workers had been laid off, and jobs were highly sought after.[2]

Stage 2: Entry

This is when you make your first formal presentation to TOS. It should be a strong selling proposal.

Before he started his mediation work, Usery knew that in order to be fully effective, he first had to be accepted by the UAW. So he met with the then UAW President, Douglas Fraser, and incoming President, Owen Bieber. He told them he had been retained by GM and Toyota as facilitator between them and the UAW. Fraser expressed support for the joint venture, but Bieber was noncommittal. They discussed the UAW convention that was coming up in May 1983; the UAW might condemn the joint venture at the meeting or, at least, refuse to take part in it until all Fremont workers were rehired. To prevent such resolutions from being passed, Usery suggested having a press conference before the convention to give the UAW members a clear understanding of the joint venture's intentions regarding the rehiring issue.

Here, Usery was faced with the ultimate difficulty of designing an initial presentation that would win UAW support, knowing fully well that Toyota was strongly against rehiring the Fremont workers. He knew too that Fraser's initial support for the joint venture was based on the premise that the UAW would eventually be recognized as the workers' official bargaining agent when the Fremont workers were rehired.

Before leaving for Japan, Usery met with GM executives to sound them out on how the UAW should be dealt with. Under American labour law, a firm may not bargain with a union until that union has been officially recognized. But a union cannot exist without its first having a workforce. That was precisely where the problem lay: negotiations with the UAW could not begin without having a workforce for the joint venture. GM's lawyers advised Usery to take the position of not recognizing the UAW until a full workforce had been hired. In the meantime the GM–Toyota group would take a neutral stand. It would recognize the UAW in the future and bargain with it when the UAW had the support of the majority of the workers hired by GM and Toyota for their Fremont plant. Usery anticipated that a neutral stance would be unacceptable to the UAW.

While caught in this dilemma, Usery left for Japan, where he began a series of intense educational sessions with Toyota executives. Thus he rehashed the fundamentals of American labour law and emphasized the crucial importance of recognizing the UAW and rehiring the Fremont workforce. Although the Japanese didn't budge from their initial position, Usery wasn't fazed and persisted in his campaign. He explained that refusing to hire a person on the basis of his or her previous association with the Fremont plant was illegal in the USA because it was regarded as discrimination. By refusing to hire the old Fremont workers, 'atmosphere of harmony', so important to the Japanese, would be hard to establish. He remembered that the Japanese had publicly announced they were seeking 'an atmosphere of harmony' in this joint venture. Toyota's hard line would only estrange the heavily unionized and liberal San Francisco Bay Area, where Fremont was located.

While Usery was in Japan talking with Toyota, GM announced it would have no responsibility for the venture's labour relations structure and that Toyota would be fully responsible for this task. Thus more pressure was placed on Usery to get Toyota to see things his way.

Usery finally succeeded in obtaining a concession from the Japanese by getting them to agree to use the old Fremont workforce as a 'primary source' for recruitment. Long hours were spent simply getting the Japanese to understand the concept behind the words 'primary source'. Usery intended the phrase to mean that the joint venture would first hire from the old Fremont workers, but it would not be restricted from seeking workers from other sources as well.

Usery announced the intentions of GM–Toyota to use the Fremont workforce as a 'primary source' of workers in a press conference held a few days before the UAW convention. This clarified their official position to UAW members, and there were no more serious objections to the joint venture by the UAW. Usery succeeded in maintaining goodwill with the UAW.[3]

Stage 3: Establishing effective relationships with TOS

At this point, both you and TOS have to get to know one another better. International sensitivities are varied, and different cultures perceive this need differently. For instance, Americans and West Germans don't attach too much importance to personal matters. Their 'bottom line' is the efficiency of carrying out the transaction itself, and they are impatient to get down to business immediately. Other people, such as South Americans, Mexicans, Filipinos, Chinese, Singaporeans, Taiwanese, Malaysians and Japanese, attach great importance to this phase because long-term relationships are valued and nurtured in these cultures. In those nations the efficiency of the business transaction is subordinated to the interest of maintaining smooth interpersonal relationships.

At this stage, you'll need to earn the right to learn the needs and objectives of TOS. We say in our seminars that you can't even begin to negotiate until you learn these – and they are hard to find out. Remember that your initial presentation at the entry stage has been mostly based on your perception of their needs and objectives. This is the time for you to refine your definition of their needs by winning the trust and confidence necessary to get past the level of pleasant civility to a deeper level of exchange of mutual information and interests. It is usually during the meetings at this stage that you are first able to discover the true feelings and thoughts of TOS about the issues. The 'truth' often slips out in casual encounters because we tend to let our guards down then.

Usery scheduled several informal meetings with the UAW's new President Bieber after the May 1983 convention to try to move towards a greater degree of agreement with the union. Usery was disappointed that Bieber was not as enthusiastic about the joint venture as was the previous President, Fraser. For instance, Fraser had previously agreed that old seniority rights in GM need not be observed under the joint venture, which would be considered an entirely new entity. Bieber, new in his role as UAW President, needed to prove himself, and so he went back to the old extreme demands, namely recognition of the UAW and the rehiring of all the old workers.

Although Usery wanted to establish better interpersonal relationships with Bieber after the convention, his new 'bottom line' demands got in the way. Even though there was no progress towards an agreement, at least Usery had a better idea of how deeply Bieber was committed to the stronger demands.[4]

Stage 4: Learning more about TOS and reformulating your earlier strategies

From the casual meetings that you use to establish a more comfortable level of interpersonal rapport, your focus shifts to finding out much more information about the needs and desires of TOS and about the situation. Since the 'ice has been broken', it should be easier to obtain this information. This will help you correct your initial (incorrect) assumptions in formulating both the negotiating strategies that you have used earlier and those you plan to use.

To emphasize their claims to the full recognition, the UAW maintained that Roger Smith, GM's Chairman, had once implied he would guarantee such recognition. In addition, they demanded to deal with Smith in future meetings. Any binding obligation as a result of Smith's alleged guarantees was quickly denied by GM's representatives. Toyota's legal counsel responded to this situation by drafting a letter of intent. It stated that the joint venture intended to begin, intended to hire a workforce and intended to maintain a neutral position in the matter of recognizing the UAW. Bieber quickly rejected this letter of intent. He knew it was not legally binding.

Usery realized that the next time he went to Japan, he had to be more persistent and creative in handling the Toyota executives. He needed to reformulate their side's strategy to salvage the rapidly deteriorating relationship they had with Bieber and the UAW. Once again, it is important to recall that one of the main problems of the joint venture was that it could not bargain with the UAW since GM and Toyota officials could not legally recognize it as the official bargaining agent of the plant workers until the latter were hired and had held an election. The election's result would either be a union (probably the UAW) or no union. The UAW knew it was overstepping its bounds – it couldn't legally function on behalf of a workforce that wasn't there yet.

But after talking with his side's lawyers, Usery found it was possible for the joint venture officials to start bargaining *even before* a workforce was hired, if one of two things happened: (1) if it could be shown that the joint venture had bargaining obligations as a 'successor employer' (but NUMMI was a new entity and couldn't claim to be a successor to GM in Fremont); or the only other way successorship obligations could be assumed would be (2) that NUMMI agree to hire at least 50 per cent of the new workers from the old workforce. So, armed with this knowledge on his next trip to Japan, Usery jumped at the chance to reformulate his side's strategy by renewing his campaign to persuade Toyota to agree to hire at least a majority of the old workforce.[5]

Stage 5: Bargaining and concession-making

This is the critical part of the negotiating process. We recommend you follow four steps during this stage. It's an excellent way to conduct yourself. The four steps are: (1) separate people from the problem; (2) focus on interests, not positions; (3) invent options for mutual gain; and (4) insist on using objective criteria. We shall go through each step briefly.

First, separate people from the problem. You will certainly encounter 'people problems', such as problems in perception, emotion and communication when negotiating with others, and do not suppose that making small concessions will make these problems disappear. 'People problems' are psychological problems, and as such they require psychological techniques (not business concessions) for their resolution.

Secondly focus on interests, not positions. Positions are particular courses of actions that limit the range of solutions available in a situation if you strictly adhere to them. Interests express our needs and desires, which are satisfied by the positions we take up. Take the following example of sticking to a position. A woman walks into the cosmetic section of a department store. She sees on display a designer label Italian bag accompanying a makeup kit. She decides she wants the makeup kit only, not the bag. She approaches the sales person, points to the display and says: 'Excuse me, I like the makeup set displayed with the bag somewhere up front there. I would like to buy just the makeup set. Is that possible?' Let's assume that an unprofessional and untrained sales assistant is taking this sale. What does this person do? The assistant merely says: 'No, I'm sorry, you can't have the makeup kit. That item is sold as a set.' How do you think the customer reacts? She walks out, naturally.

Now, let's change the characters and put in a well-trained sales assistant. What does this person do? After hearing the customer's request, he or she thinks carefully: 'This lady wants the makeup kit, but I can't sell it apart from the bag. We're supposed to sell these in sets. I know she needs the makeup kit to improve her looks – but she doesn't need to do so at the fantastic price we're charging for this set on display. Hey, we have a makeup kit of the same brand in our pharmaceutical section. In fact, I think it's on sale! I should let her know that.' So the customer's request is courteously responded to and she is informed about the availability of the same item in another department, while being told that she cannot buy the makeup kit apart from the bag. The result? A sure sale. With some insight, the well-trained salesperson persuaded the customer to abandon her position of wanting to buy the makeup kit from the cosmetic department apart from the bag. Knowing that the customer's interest was to get that particular makeup kit and nothing else, the sales assistant prudently redirected her away from her initial position of purchasing the item from the cosmetics department and buying it from the pharmaceutical department, where the same item was available at less cost. Not only did the sales person avert a possible loss of sale, but promoted the goodwill of the store as well.

Thirdly, invent options for mutual gain. This step is very much related to the second step of separating interests from positions. The sales assistant in the above vignette could have presented other options to the customer, including telling the customer that a very similar brand of makeup kit was available from the cosmetics department for less money. Or that she could assemble the makeup items included in the kit on display simply by purchasing individual items of the same brand from the cosmetics department. This would cost her less money since she wouldn't have to pay for the bag too. This third step, inventing options, is the natural offshoot of separating interests from positions. By doing this, then, you can multiply the possibilities of coming to an agreement by thinking of more solutions that take into consideration the interests of TOS.

Fourthly, insist on using objective criteria. For instance, you are looking for exercise equipment. How would you go about your search? Would you simply take at face value the sales assistant's opinion at the sporting goods store? Wouldn't you suspect that the salespeople are under some pressure from management to dispose of certain items? What then gives you bargaining leverage in

*negotiating with salespeople? In the USA one 'objective criterion'
you can consult is* Consumer Reports *magazine, which rates
different products according to test standards; there are similar
magazines in other countries.*

When Usery met with the UAW again, his reformulated offer –
NUMMI as a 'successor employer' would hire at least 50 per
cent of the old workforce – was rejected by the UAW, who
demanded that *all* members of the old workforce be rehired.
Subsequent proposals sent to the UAW which reiterated joint
venture demands were also summarily rejected. Each meeting
that followed ended in deadlock.

  Usery didn't give up, though. He continued to search for a
solution or some loophole that would satisfy both sides. When
everybody else was giving up on the possibility of coming to
an agreement, Usery finally realized that time had been wasted
pursuing something that simply should not have been sought
for in the first place: NUMMI did not really need a collective
bargaining agreement with the UAW. All that both sides really
needed was to come to some kind of understanding that they
were willing to work together on a co-operative basis and that
labour relations would be handled with trust. When he
realized this, Usery tried to convince both sides to sign a letter
of intent, spelling out the areas of agreement between the joint
venture and the UAW. The letter would schedule collective
bargaining at some time in the future. Usery succeeded in
convincing the UAW to sign the letter in principle. Then, after
obtaining still another extension, Usery worked on getting both
sides to agree on the contents of the letter. At this point, only
minor matters of language had to be resolved in the drafting of
the letter. Both sides were relieved that they didn't have to deal
with the pressures of concluding a collective bargaining session
with so little time left. And the UAW even made a gesture of
good faith by disbanding the former Fremont local and
revoking its charter.[6]

Stage 6: Reaching agreement

*At this stage, basic agreement over terms has been reached, and
both sides get very close to finalizing their agreement. In most
developed countries the written contract is the standard way to*

express the agreement. Some developed countries like Japan place a higher value on trust and honour which have been embodied in a personal relationship that has been nurtured and protected over a long time period. In fact drafting an extremely complicated contract in the presence of lawyers can even be insulting to people from Japan (and from countries similar to Japan). It is important for you to study the local practices, so that you will know the appropriate way to express your agreement.

A new problem cropped up after the UAW's gesture of good faith. Local 1364, the Fremont chapter of the UAW, filed a lawsuit against the national union, charging that the national union violated its own constitution and by-laws. It also asked for an injunction to prevent NUMMI and the UAW from signing an agreement. The UAW responded that since the Fremont plant no longer existed, it acted within its rights to the charter. Eventually the case against the UAW was dismissed, both NUMMI and the UAW agreed on the language used in the letter of intent and it was signed.

At this point, Usery had other parties to worry about. He still had to get the FTC's approval of the joint venture. In effect, his job was to act as a public relations spokesperson for the joint venture to win the approval of the American public as a whole. Lee Iacocca, President of Chrysler, was most vocal in his objections to the joint venture. He said this was an underhanded way for GM and Toyota to gain an unfair advantage in the motor-car industry. Chrysler filed a lawsuit charging that the joint venture violated the country's antitrust laws, but later withdrew its suit when it formed its own similar joint venture with Mitsubishi. After GM and Toyota signed a consent decree giving the FTC the power to monitor its activities, the FTC approved the joint venture on 11 April 1984, about two years after GM and Toyota started their original talks.

Before the first Novas rolled off the Fremont assembly line, NUMMI set up an interim labour relations structure at the Fremont plant. It hired a large consulting firm to create the initial wage and benefits package for the first employees. The package was modified after the plant became unionized, and the new local and NUMMI conducted its first collective bargaining sessions.[7]

2 How to make concessions

Introduction

The heart of negotiation is the way both sides make concessions to get what they really want. One of the exercises we give in our seminar, 'How You Can Negotiate and Win', captures our executive participants' natural inclinations in their concession behaviour, so we know the concession patterns of executives in 15 nations – i.e. the USA, Canada, South Africa, Australia, New Zealand, Hong Kong, Taiwan, Singapore, Malaysia, Thailand, Indonesia, Philippines, India, Kenya and Brazil.

In our seminar we made this statement: 'On the screen you see seven concession patterns (Figure 2.1). Let's assume your boss has told you that you can give away $100.00 during your next negotiation session. The other side doesn't know how much you have to give away, or even if you have anything at all to give away. We shall assume that the negotiation session lasts one hour. Four times during that hour you have an opportunity to give away all or part of the $100.00 to the other side. Let's ignore how much you get from the other side in return when you're doing this exercise.' (The reason this condition had to be eliminated was because it would introduce too many variables and complicate things too much. People concede differently, depending on their natural tendency, based on what they get from TOS, and so forth. Here, by keeping things simple, it was tried to eliminate all considerations except for the way the executive naturally concedes.) 'For example, concession pattern no. 1 means giving away $25 the first time, $25 the second time, $25 the third time and $25 the fourth time during that hour; and concession pattern no. 7 means giving away $50 the first time, $30 the second time, $25 the third time, and then taking back $5 the fourth time because you had given away $105 by the third time, $5 more than what your boss gave you (Table 1.1). Please tell us what your favourite concession pattern is and the one you dislike the most. Write down both on a sheet of paper, with the words 'like' and 'dislike' next to the numbers, and pass them up front to me. Thank you.'

Table 1.1   Which of these seven ways of giving away $100 worth of concessions do you like best? Dislike the most?

	Time periods			
No.	1	2	3	4
1	$25	$25	$25	$25
2	50	50	0	0
3	0	0	0	100
4	100	0	0	0
5	10	20	30	40
6	40	30	20	10
7	50	30	25	−5 (take $5 back)

Here is an explanation of the seven concession patterns (NB: Please understand, though, that we withheld this explanation from executives until after they had completed the exercise; we assumed that since we allowed them only a short time to make up their minds, we captured their truest and most spontaneous resonse to the like–dislike choices we asked them to make.)

1   The first is a consistent pattern of giving away $25 each of the four times. If you chose this pattern, the other side can very easily detect your predictability – if they're keeping score.

2   This pattern reflects your great generosity in the first half, and you have no more concessons to give in the second half of the session. This pattern is somewhat similar to pattern four, the extreme expression of generosity.

3   This can be called the 'hard-nosed' style, in which you concede totally and begrudgingly at the very end, only after everything else you've done has failed to work.

4   This is pattern three's polar opposite. You may call it the 'naïve' style, in that you lay all your cards on the table at the beginning, and then give no more away, because you have no more. You reveal your bottom line at the very beginning. This style should be adopted only when both sides are long-time negotiating partners and have achieved over the years a high level of trust. Here you don't waste your time playing games. It will work only if TOS does likewise (otherwise, you've made yourself too vulnerable).

5   This is an escalating pattern. If TOS is keeping score, they will stall the negotiations because they know that they'll get more and more as time goes on. It's in their interest to prolong the negotiations for as long as possible.

6   This is pattern five's polar opposite. It is a de-escalating pattern, with generosity at first, tapering off to very few concessions later – you're telling TOS that 'your well is getting drier and drier'. Again, if TOS is keen, they will detect your pattern and try to get the most from you at the beginning stages of the negotiating process.

7   This is similar to pattern six, in that it's de-escalating for the first three time periods, again making it easy for TOS's score-keepers to discover your tendency. However, at the very end, you take back $5 worth of concessions, to stay within the $100 given to you by your boss. You use this pattern to indicate

Table 1.2 Most liked concession pattern by nation (percentages)

Nation	Concession patterns						
	1	2	3	4	5	6	7
USA	1.27	0.73	34.73	4.55	33.09	20.36	5.27
Canada	2.40	2.40	26.20	–	16.70	42.90	9.50
South Africa	1.80	–	52.70	7.30	20.00	9.10	9.10
Australia	–	–	–	–	30.80	69.20	–
New Zealand	3.60	–	14.30	–	25.00	53.39	3.60
Hong Kong	–	1.12	16.85	3.37	39.33	35.96	3.37
Taiwan	4.97	3.73	11.18	1.24	14.91	60.87	3.11
Singapore	3.50	–	13.80	3.50	48.30	31.00	–
Malaysia	8.70	4.40	8.70	4.40	56.50	13.00	4.40
Thailand	–	5.00	5.00	5.00	30.00	45.00	10.00
Indonesia	12.50	–	3.10	3.10	43.80	31.30	6.30
Philippines	1.48	2.96	8.15	2.96	60.74	20.74	2.22
India	–	–	8.70	4.35	43.48	39.13	4.35
Kenya	–	–	–	–	71.40	28.60	–
Brazil	15.38	–	38.46	–	15.38	30.77	–

that 'your well is very, very dry' – i.e. you gave away far too much earlier, expecting that TOS would respond commensurately. But they didn't. So, to keep from getting fired, you have to get back the $5. Pattern seven is more effectively executed if you make some show of how pained and disappointed you are at failing to get the concessions you had expected.

Tables 1.2 and 1.3 show the concession patterns liked and disliked most by the executives in the 15 nations. Three distinct groups of nations are in agreement about what concession pattern they like most. The first group consists of executives from the USA, South Africa and Brazil. They prefer pattern three – they are the 'hard-nosed' ones who concede grudgingly. The second group, executives from Canada, Australia, New Zealand, Taiwan and Thailand, like pattern six, the de-escalating pattern – they liked to be generous at first and then taper off, perhaps sending the message that 'their well is getting drier and drier all the time'. The third group was the executives from Hong Kong, Singapore, Malaysia, Indonesia, Philippines, India, and Kenya. They prefer pattern five, the escalating pattern which is the opposite of pattern six – they would begin with a low amount and continuously increase it at each negotiating session.

After the executives completed the exercise, we discussed with them why they chose the pattern they did; and we have spent a lot of time on this in our seminar. These are the reasons the three groups of nations made the choices they did: The USA, South Africa and Brazil preferred the most competitive concession pattern. This choice fits in with the way they like to behave in the business environment – assertive, aggressive and competitive; looking at their past and present positions in the world economy confirms this. Although ranking behind Japan, the USA is still one of the leading world economies. South Africa and Brazil are leaders in their regions, and both countries were experiencing debilitating problems in the 1980s. Apartheid has created a backlash against the South Africans, and a considerable number of foreign firms have pulled out of that country. Brazil's economy has been severely mismanaged and is burdened with a tremendous debt.

Table 1.3 Most disliked concession patterns by nation (percentages)

Nation	Concession patterns						
	1	2	3	4	5	6	7
USA	3.83	0.36	2.92	64.42	5.29	–	23.18
Canada	–	–	–	51.20	–	–	48.80
South Africa	5.30	–	5.30	66.70	15.80	–	7.00
Australia	–	–	–	76.90	7.70	–	15.40
New Zealand	7.10	–	10.70	64.30	–	–	17.90
Hong Kong	–	–	7.78	65.56	5.56	–	21.11
Taiwan	0.62	–	3.70	51.23	14.81	0.62	29.01
Singapore	3.20	–	16.10	25.80	3.20	–	51.60
Malaysia	–	–	24.10	44.80	3.50	–	27.60
Thailand	27.27	–	9.09	54.55	–	–	9.09
Indonesia	6.30	–	12.50	34.40	3.10	–	43.80
Philippines	0.70	1.41	9.86	58.45	–	–	29.58
India	4.35	4.35	–	34.78	–	–	56.52
Kenya	–	–	6.30	93.80	–	–	–
Brazil	–	–	–	33.33	20.00	–	46.67

The second group of nations – Canada, Australia, New Zealand, Taiwan and Thailand – don't seem to have too much in common, except for the pattern they picked, and the fact that their economies are in good shape. We think their choice of de-escalation was the wisest choice, assuming all else is equal. We can say that the concession style in these five nations is de-escalation.

The choice of the third group of executives from Hong Kong, Singapore, Malaysia, Indonesia, the Philippines, India and Kenya is comprehensible from the point of view of their predominant negotiating style. Asians (and half of the Kenyan executives were Indian) have always been primarily concerned with creating and maintaining long-term personal relationships in business (see later). They spend a lot of time getting to know new negotiating partners, to evaluate the possibility of nurturing such relationships before rolling up their sleeves to get down to business. In some ways, they exercise a great deal of caution in the manner in which they postpone starting business activities until they feel 'right' with their new business partners, hence they conceded the way they did – very carefully at first, and then rewarding TOS by constantly escalating the amount they conceded, assuming that they are receiving feedback which supports their idea of what a 'right' business partner is.

There is greater agreement among the executives of the 15 countries regarding the concession patterns they *disliked* the most. Executives from 11 countries – the USA, Canada, South Africa, Australia, New Zealand, Hong Kong, Taiwan, Malaysia, Thailand, Philippines and Kenya – agreed that concession pattern four was the worst. In this pattern you laid all your cards on the table at the beginning of the negotiation session, in total honesty. What this seems to be telling us is that there is close to a universal agreement that being totally honest in the beginning, especially when you are dealing with a new business partner, is unwise and naive. Of course, this is not always true, particularly when dealing with a long-trusted business partner. But even so, these business executives obviously recognize that some degree of deception and competition is always involved in negotiating, even with old and trusted friends!

The other group of business executives from Singapore, Indonesia, India and Brazil formed a minority in choosing concession pattern seven as the worst. You will recall that this is a variation of the de-escalating pattern number six that involved taking $5 back. With the exception of Brazil, all the other countries in this group are Asian. The Asian preoccupation with losing face may largely account for this finding. Some Asian nations think that they stand to lose face if they go back on their word and take something back. And then, there's the more Western notion that contracts must be honoured not so much to preserve face as to uphold integrity in the business world where 'a deal is a deal'. Because of these two concepts eight other nations picked pattern seven as their second most disliked pattern, four Western nations (the USA, Canada, Australia and New Zealand) and four Asian nations (Hong Kong, Taiwan, Malaysia and the Philippines). So if you use it, most people won't like it!

How to concede – the dos and don'ts

The following are brief guidelines on how to concede (see p.128 Chapter 7, 'Tactics and countermeasures', for a more detailed discussion of concession-making:)

- Give yourself enough room by starting off with a high offer if you're selling or with a low offer if you're buying.
- Get TOS to open up first while you keep your objectives, needs and demands hidden.
- Don't ever be first to concede on a major issue. It is OK to concede first on minor issues, though.
- Give 'straw-man' concessions, or those that really give nothing away. But make TOS think that they're really valuable to you. (You need to be a good actor or actress here; for more information on how to detect lies, see Chapter 6, pages 97–103.)
- Make TOS work hard for every concession you make, so that they'll appreciate them more.
- Trade-off: get something for each concession you make. Remember that saying, 'I'll consider it', is a concession,

because it raises TOS's expectations. Say instead, 'What will you give me if I consider it?'

- Concede slowly – as far as possible; don't concede at all, if it can be avoided.
- Say 'no' often (the trouble with 'no', though, is that most people can't take a 'no' very well, and you might lose momentum early in the negotiations, so you will have to time this negative response precisely so as not to turn TOS away completely).
- Don't be afraid to take concessions back, if you haven't signed the contract yet. Remember the pros of concession in pattern seven. (You'll need to be careful about using this, however; taking back concessions could give TOS the impression that you're not dependable; you must choose the right situation to use it in – it might be OK to do so when TOS reneges on a promise, for instance).
- Keep a record of your concessions, and those of TOS, to see if there's a pattern. By studying them, you can respond to TOS's future moves more appropriately.
- Constantly keep TOS's expectations low by not giving in too often, too soon or too much.

3 The ideal negotiator

Introduction

The best international negotiators we've seen have the eight qualities, which are described below. How many do *you* have? Train yourself properly, and eventually these will make up *your* profile.

1 Ideal international negotiators understand and work effectively with the decision-making processes peculiar to the countries they're dealing with.

Ideal negotiators mesh well with the wide variety of institutional norms and practices found in different countries. They can shift their strategies radically whether they're dealing with people from developing countries, which tend to have more centralized structures, or from developed countries, where decentralized decision-making is typical. Although most Western countries' decision-making patterns tend to be more similar than dissimilar, procedural differences are still present. West Germans usually process their decisions through committees composed mainly of technical people. The French emphasize the long-range view of their objectives and give low priority to short-term decisions, which they use for unimportant goals. Also, unlike most other developed countries, the French seem to adopt a more centralized decision-making structure, and this means it takes more time for their decisions to be processed. The French don't mind introducing conflict – in fact they are comfortable dealing with a lot of conflict during their negotiation sessions. Most nationalities, such as the Americans and Japanese, are usually unnerved by the stumbling-blocks introduced by conflict. Unlike the Americans and Germans, the French don't attach much importance to factual information in their negotiations.

Normally Third World countries have radically different decision-making practices. In Mexico, for instance, decision-making is centralized, and the personality of whoever holds the position of authority largely influences the kind of decisions that are made. In fact authority tends to reside more in the person than in the position itself. People from cultures which are more used to having a certain degree of authority accompany a position are usually at a loss when they're in Mexico. Although the times of the *caudillos* (or 'macho' men on horseback) are over, their influence on styles of decision-making in Mexico still persists.

Dealing often with the host government is necessary for multinational corporations (MNCs) which are interested in setting up projects in developing countries. When negotiating with the host country's government, the MNC usually emphasizes the multiplier-effect of the project's economic benefits, such as offering constructive competition, improving working conditions, developing local resources, and providing managerial and entrepreneurial skills. While the host government will be concerned about ensuring a rate of return that is high enough to satisfy the MNC, it will try to siphon off as much as it can above the rate of return in the form of taxes, shared profits or exchange controls to keep excess money in the country. Bilateral bargaining based on such economic considerations is the usual arrangement through which host governments and MNCs negotiate.

Uninformed MNCs make weak presentations about the positive political effects of their projects. This is unfortunate because host governments are normally concerned about achieving attractive economic benefits without inviting unnecessary political attacks from rival politicians and pressure groups. In one case, an Asian government persuaded an MNC to accept no more than 49 per cent ownership along with a management contract allowing exclusive management control by the MNC. This way, the host government would not be criticized for allowing unreasonable foreign equity participation and, at the same time, the MNC would appreciate having total control over the project, even if it didn't have majority equity participation.

Quite a number of decision-makers in developing countries have been educated in the West or in Western-style universities in other parts of the world. Naturally, representatives of MNCs from developed countries prefer to deal with them, hoping they are more familiar with modern business practices and thus more predictable. Although this is partly true, Western-educated negotiators in developed and less developed nations alike are still largely influenced by the institutional pressures of their cultures. Japanese educated in Canada or Australia will still have to deal with group norms in making decisions when they return to Japan.

Delays are another area of conflict. For instance, it is generally known that it takes longer to negotiate business deals in Europe and Asia than in the USA. Negotiators from 'hurry-up' nations easily mistake delays as a sinister ploy on the part of TOS. They don't realize that, especially in highly centralized countries, decisions often have to pass through many layers of the bureaucracy.

Another area of difficulty is the lack of technical expertise on the part of negotiators from less developed countries. And it is not unusual either to find that negotiators from developed countries have only the vaguest idea about the social cost–benefit analysis that the government of the underdeveloped nation has made when studying their proposal. Ideal international negotiators gather information about how the host government evaluates proposals before they even begin their negotiations, and they spend a lot of time briefing the government about the technical content of the project.[1]

2 Ideal international negotiators are flexible enough to handle effectively even the most delicate issues, such as bribery, and manage these issues within the context of the local culture.

Gift-giving or handing out payoffs has always been a contentious issue for negotiators whose cultures deem bribery unethical, while other cultures look upon the same practices in a somewhat different context. The position of Western negotiators, particularly of North American negotiators, is to stick to the 'bottom line', playing strictly by market rules and competing in terms of quality, price and service. To them, gifts and payoffs have no place in the impersonal market system. Often the laws of their countries prohibit payoffs. Many negotiators with these attitudes will walk out of negotiations, particularly in less developed countries where various forms of what they may consider as bribery form part of accepted business practices.

Three linked traditions provide the background that will explain to readers the cultural significance of payoffs. The first tradition is that of the 'inner circle'. The more communal cultures seem to have a greater need to divide society into those who belong to the 'inner circle', or those with whom they have active business dealings, and those who belong to the 'outer circle' of strangers and aliens. Preferring to deal only with those they know, such communities restrict their social and commercial dealings to members only of the 'inner circle'. A member of the 'inner circle', for instance, may be asked to hire workers only from a particular clan in exchange for dependable labour.

The second tradition is that of preserving a system of future favours: members of the 'inner circle' enliven their relationships through an exchange of favours. In Japan this concept translates as *giri* or 'inner duty'; in Kenya it is *uthoni* or 'inner relationship'; and in the Philippines it is *utang na loob* or 'inner debt'. In this system it is assumed that any person who is under obligation to another person or group has the duty to repay the favour at some time in the future. In the process of repaying the debt, of course, the person paid for the favour now becomes the debtor. A lifelong cycle of obligatory relationships has thus been formed.

The third tradition is that of gift exchange. People from non-Western nations often value long-term personal relationships in business more than the material exchange itself. They use gifts therefore to express both their affection and willingness to maintain the business relationship indefinitely. Their logic runs thus: gifts seem to be an appropriate way of creating social ties and obligations with impersonal Westerners who generally in gatherings talk only about business. It is therefore necessary, if trust is to be cultivated in the relationship, to instil in the Westerner a sense of obligation.

International negotiators who understand how these three traditions relate work better within the 'inner circle' of non-Western business colleagues and participate actively in the exchange of favours and gifts. As a result, their companies are usually given preferential treatment in the market, and they gain access to an otherwise clandestine network of business contracts and intermediaries. At the same time, they become more trusted by the members of the local culture as they reinforce their contractual obligations.[2]

3   Ideal international negotiators possess a keen intuitive sensitivity in an intercultural situation; they are able to empathize with their local counterparts, anticipate and respond appropriately to emotional and social needs that their local hosts may have a hard time expressing.

Here there are special sensitivities to be dealt with, for example, in negotiating with Asians, who place great importance on preserving smooth interpersonal relations and the appearance of harmony. They observe society's standards of what is right and wrong, acceptable and unacceptable, rather than their own internalized system of values. In that society making the appearance of conforming to society's standards is very much the basis of their personal worth. Asians, then, invest a lot more personally in preserving acceptable appearances than do Westerners. In addition, they judge persons more on the basis of their actions rather than their words.

International negotiators who understand these sensitivities behave appropriately in Asia. For instance, they never criticize their Asian hosts in public or try to force an answer out of them when the time isn't 'right'. Western negotiators avoid making scenes in public, especially if they're angry, knowing full well that Asians have the stereotype of them as rude and arrogant. During negotiations they allow extra time for their business meetings and avoid giving the impression that they're in a hurry. Rushing about leaves the impression that the Asian host is unimportant to the visitor. They also give their local hosts extra time to arrive at business decisions. Astute international negotiators also use the concept of 'saving face' as a negotiating tactic in Asian countries, where this concept is most fully understood. For instance, they will say that they hesitate to make certain concessions which will result in their losing face. During negotiations they let TOS take the lead in determining procedures not only to give them a sense of importance, but also to understand and conform to the local ways of doing things.

Ideal international negotiators are able to attune to the sensitivities of whatever country they are in. For instance, in Latin America, they will open business meetings by discussing family matters important to the hosts before getting down to 'shop talk'. When negotiating with Europeans, they avoid using data that emphasize how the productivity of Europeans is lagging behind that of their own country. They know too that the West Germans, British and French are extremely sensitive about being compared with one another so they avoid so doing.[3]

4 Ideal international negotiators can communicate and relate effectively with their local counterparts; they are keen observers of the subtle communication clues in the verbal and non-verbal behaviour of their hosts.

International negotiators who are also effective communicators manage both the verbal and non-verbal content of the messages that flow between them and TOS. One of their verbal skills is the ability to use suitable language to summarize and test their understanding of what TOS has said, for example: 'Correct me if I'm wrong, but as I understand it right now, your company is requiring us to offer a skills training programme for both the local executives and technical personnel who will be involved in our joint venture. Is this correct?'

They also understand that when more than one foreign language is involved in the negotiations, there are greater chances of misunderstanding. The pitch and tone of voice alone, not to mention the words, can introduce communication 'noise'. The flat tones of the English make us think they're bored or sarcastic. Of course, this may not be true. When

Arabs speak English, they sound as if they're shouting. The truth of the matter is over-assertion and exaggeration is the natural way they express themselves, or else, they fear, they might convey the opposite meaning instead. The Japanese concern for preserving face and harmony compels them to say *hai* or 'yes' when they really mean 'no'. Effective communicators watch for these things. And for their part, they see to it that they use the appropriate pitch, loudness, tone, speed and rhythm associated with their intended meaning. If they're communicating in a foreign language they don't know too well, they will make sure they're assisted by an expert interpreter.

Greater sensitivity and sharp powers of observation are required in handling non-verbal communication. International negotiators who understand 'body language' have a great advantage over those who don't. Why? Because non-verbal behaviour is the most natural way we have of expressing our spontaneous and true reactions. Non-verbal behaviour acts as a safety valve through which we release our pent-up emotions and feelings, especially in stressful and threatening situations. Negotiators express their frustration with frowns, groans and grunts when they perceive TOS to be unjustly demanding, unreasonably resistant to alternative solutions presented, or just plain difficult. Research studies also show that people tend to believe non-verbal behaviour more than the verbal content of a message. We'll say more about this in Chapter 6, 'Nonverbal Communication'.

Ideal international negotiators who understand non-verbal behaviour when abroad have first understood the cues of their own culture. From this understanding they find it much easier to appreciate the nuances of the behaviour of foreigners. Take physical distance during conversations, for example. They will notice that Mexicans and Italians tend to stand closer to TOS when conversing than do the Dutch or Japanese. They also know the differences in business protocol. For instance, Americans are more informal in conducting their business meetings. They believe that creating and sustaining a relaxed atmosphere is more conducive to effective communication, so they slouch, put their hands behind their heads in a 'flying elbows' position and sometimes even rest their feet on top of their desks. When exposed to this behaviour, Asians and northern Europeans may quickly dismiss the Americans as rude and unpolished.

Effective international negotiators are flexible and able to complement the non-verbal behaviour they observe. They recognize their responsibility of changing *their* behaviour if TOS prefers to stick to their own way of behaving. In Mexico, for instance, the actions of Mexicans often strongly suggest an authoritarian mode and machismo, which they perceive to be necessary in maintaining their public image. The appropriate response of the international negotiator is to accord the Mexican the respect, deference and social distance the latter is obviously seeking.[4]

5 Ideal international negotiators have personal stability, a sense of inner security and the ability to handle stress on-the-job.

Negotiating with foreigners abroad, or in your own country, introduces unusual stresses above the normal pressures associated with a negotiation with one's own countrymen. Ideal international negotiators are secure enough within themselves that they don't have a great need to be *liked*. Wanting to be liked makes you want to give away the store, just to see TOS smile! In dealing with strangers from another country, you may have a strong tendency to be solicitous at times, to earn goodwill. In some countries negotiators may try to take advantage of this. For example, American negotiators have reported that in their negotiations with the Chinese, the latter have tried to exert pressure on them by creating guilt feelings by reminding them of past American policies that promoted the 'mistreatment' of mainland China.

International negotiators should be resilient enough to roll with the punches, especially when they are targets of the prejudice and negative behaviour of others. For instance, some British business executives have seemed at times to consider themselves 'superior' to their Australian counterparts, while the Australians who, naturally, resent this attitude have sometimes referred to the British as 'Pommy bastards'. Many French people are preoccupied with the perceived superiority of their language and culture; they think they hold a special position in the international arena on account of their culture and history. Some of them tend to ignore and lose respect for foreigners who don't speak their language.[5]

6   Ideal international negotiators use humour, with good taste and discrimination, to 'break the ice' and enhance the pleasant ambience of the business negotiations.

In a country as seemingly socially forbidding and stolid as Japan, one British visitor succeeded in making his business hosts laugh. During their meeting the discussions moved on to economic issues and someone pointed out to the group that the new trade agreement offered by the Americans was 'like a gift on a silver platter'. No sooner had this been said than the British businessman realized an opportunity for light-heartedness. He quickly reached for a small item in the shopping-bag he had nearby, and said smilingly: 'I myself have no silver platter for you today, gentlemen, but I hope you will accept this present instead.' The Japanese gentlemen in the meeting broke out in laughter, and the incident etched this foreigner's graciousness on their memory for some time to come.[6]

From the point of view of a Westerner, there was nothing particularly funny about the gesture. Nevertheless, the British executive captivated the Japanese, and he was pleasantly surprised at the response to his spontaneous attempts at levity. It is a rare pleasure indeed to be able to indulge in humour with one's foreign counterparts, considering the complexity of the cultural differences involved. Japanese humour, for example, which is based on word plays and 'twittings' at tradition, is not easily appreciated by foreigners. On the other hand, the Japanese do not find Western humour based on irony particularly funny either. Some business executives have learned that when attempting humour in Japan, they should preface their statements with appropriate warnings like, 'A joke is coming! Here it is!', simply to help out their audience. Others have suggested trying jokes without words through antics like card or magic tricks.[7]

7   Ideal international negotiators can tolerate ambiguity and are patient with TOS, even under situations of great pressure.

Westerners have the stereotype of the 'inscrutability' of Orientals, and undoubtedly there is some basis for this. Part of the challenge of dealing with Asians is their unexplored potential for verbalizing and expressing thoughts and feelings.

Societal constraints, such as the rules governing 'saving face' and the authoritarian tenor of some cultures like China's Confucian tradition, have held them back. And so the forthright and direct Australians, who always seem to be honest about what they have in mind, say that they often have to do a lot of digging to find out what the Asian really wants to say.

The negotiating situation with the Chinese presents its own unique hurdles too. American negotiators have reported that the mainland Chinese hold their cards close to their chest and refuse to reveal their own needs and objectives, even after a lot of time has been spent breaking the ice. Without any guidelines about what the Chinese really need, foreign negotiators are really navigating in the dark and are less effective in their proposals.[8]

If you are an ideal international negotiator, you will persist through ambiguous situations and wait for TOS until they are willing to share vital information, or until they are convinced that you have earned the right to know their real needs. You will also exercise deliberate patience, especially as you await final decisions by the different parties involved in the negotiations. You are also prudent enough to build a good deal of extra time into your schedule, to allow for bureaucratic delays, procrastination and extra-thorough deliberations by TOS.

8 Ideal international negotiators get involved with TOS's organization, actively seeking allies and extending their network of influence throughout TOS's company.

One observer of international negotiations remarked that negotiators dealing with foreigners miss a lot of other business opportunities because they fail to reach out, extend and cement their initial relationships. They erroneously believe that the momentum obtained from the signed contract would carry them through to winning future contracts. Take the case of an American engineering firm that succeeded in obtaining a one-year operation and maintenance contract in Asia. Since the technology they introduced was so superior, they thought their technical efficiency alone was enough to build a foundation for a long-term relationship. The locals who worked for the Asian company were highly dissatisfied with what they perceived as unfriendly, impersonal and arrogant behaviour on the part of the Americans. They kept this to themselves, though, and without letting the Americans know it, they made overtures to other engineering firms about future contract work. Eventually the Amercian firm lost out to another foreign bidder.

Effective international negotiators nurture their interpersonal relationships at all times; they take nothing for granted. They realize the value of spending additional time exchanging social pleasantries, feedback and loyalties. They study the power networks of the local community and create gestures of goodwill to penetrate these networks. They try hard to become part of the 'inner circle' normally closed to unknown aliens or strangers. They pay the price of what it takes to be socially accepted and rewarded in the local community.[9]

Part II

DEALING WITH OTHER CULTURES

Introduction to Part II

The speed of progress and the internationalization of business activities thrust people from various cultures into common work settings. Even if each person is aware of economic interdependence, still there may be much difficulty in living and working together. While there are many technologies and techniques available for those of two quite different cultures to be productive on the job together, tensions in human relations often sabotage multinational work projects. Take, for example, the case of one Japanese firm that has been set up in the USA. Asa Jonishi, senior director of Kyocera Corporation, a Japanese high-technology firm with a branch in California, says: 'Most Americans are very, very individualistic – you could almost say egotistical; they are quite different from the way we would like our people to be.' On the other hand, Robert Georgine, President of the Building and Construction Trades Department of the AFL-CIO, the leading American labour federation, says this about the Japanese paternalistic methods of managing companies: 'We're the father and you're the children. We'll tell you what's good for you, and you do everything you can to make us successful. That doesn't wash here.'[1]

A direct clash of values! International business executives of the future are going to be challenged to take a more conscious effort to rediscover their own cultural programming and stretch the range of assumptions with which they have already been programmed. All the values, attitudes, knowledge and behaviour patterns in which they are cast must be set aside every so often to accommodate a different – perhaps even strange – combination of cultural assumptions of their foreign counterparts. This constant switching between cultures will have to be a swift and automatic thing. Insight, timing and flexibility are of the essence.

Chapter 4 deals with shifting one's cultural assumptions through 21 exercises. The brief experience encapsulated in this chapter represents, as it were, only the tip of the iceberg. It will give only an inkling of the complex, indeed vague and undefinable, kind of education in cross-cultural competence that business executives must get quite apart from their own companies' overly organized and pre-defined formats of structured intercultural training programmes and international business courses.

What happens when we deal with people from other cultures?

An important part of gaining intercultural awareness is knowing what we automatically or subconsciously do when we deal with people from other cultures. This is a kind of on-the-job training when we travel overseas; – and the difficulty with that type of training is that we are often caught by surprise in situations we thought we could handle well. Self-control and a deliberateness in interacting effectively is required of us when dealing with those who belong to other cultures. This is perhaps because we more often are inclined to lose our tempers when dealing with foreigners – we assume all other cultures share our own value systems; and our value systems are buried in our subconscious. We haven't had much need to analyse these hitherto, let alone define them, unless we've been constantly exposed to people who are culturally different. Here there are a number of tendencies universal enough to define and discuss in depth.

We tend to have stereotypes of people from other cultures

We tend to have strong ideas or carry pictures about other people without either having met them or known them personally.[2] Consequently, these pictures tend to be very inaccurate. For instance, many Americans perceive the Iranians as a rather violent and unruly people; that most British people are snobbish; and that most Germans are so rigid and disciplined in their ways that minor changes or deviations from the norm must throw them into confusion. Snapshot impressions such as these are formed from many sources: what your parents and family taught you, what your schoolteachers and classmates told you, what TV, newspapers, and magazines have said, together with personal encounters, ethnic jokes, and so forth. Such mental pictures are formed quickly (almost instantaneously), with very little thought or objective analysis involved. This, then, is why they're dangerous; but these unexamined impressions are what business executives largely rely upon when they judge foreign negotiators and make decisions concerning their mutual welfare.

Psychologists say we group people, things and phenomena into categories, so that we can deal effectively with the complex world about us. In other words, we need to classify what appears to us to be similar, because classification helps us adjust to the world. Trouble arises when we refuse to abandon the stereotypes in favour of the unique reality of the actual persons we are dealing with.[3] For instance, German managers who see their Asian employees as passive or unassertive even when they're 'super-achievers' on the job may not consider them for managerial slots or promotions. Asians are unused to the Westerners' confrontation style and so the way the Asian handles conflict, employing milder methods in order to save mutual face, may be interpreted at work as inadequate. Western managers, then, need to be more aware of cultural differences in the way that Asians handle situations, and they must evaluate the performance of their foreign co-workers on the basis of the foreigners' cultural assumptions. What should matter here isn't the method used to solve the conflict, rather whether or not the participants arrive at a resolution.

We tend to classify people from other cultures into 'in'-groups and 'out'-groups

Habitually we divide people whom we meet into those that belong to our 'in'-group – i.e. our family, friends and fellow countrymen – and those who belong to the 'out'-group – i.e. strangers, foreigners and enemies.[4] We feel comfortable and secure with members of our in-group; conversely, we exclude or avoid members of the out-group; in short, they have no place in our lives.[5] The Japanese seem to have very strong in-group/out-group proclivities; they were extremely relieved, for example, when Prince Hiro returned home from Oxford University without a foreigner as his bride: 'Everybody was worried that Prince Hiro would marry a foreigner', said Hideaki Kase, a conservative Japanese writer. 'That would be a real national crisis. Personally, I would find it revolting.'[6] The Japanese are unique, in this sense: while they are internationally connected because of their economic prominence through adopting Western ways of doing business, high technology, fashion, and so on, still they are quite isolated psychologically. Very few nationalities guard the integrity of their culture and race so steadfastly as the Japanese. So Westerners who work in Japan face the rather complex problem of finding a social support system (the difficulty is not so great for the American worker in a Japanese firm based in the USA, however). Yet, at base, the in-group/out-group mentality increases the gap that divides culturally different groups.

We tend to attribute causes to the way other people behave

We can't let actions go unexplained. Whenever someone does something, we want to make judgements about that person's motivations, without knowing all the facts of the situation.[7] In intercultural interactions we may tend to assign bad motives to strangers, instead of taking the objective circumstances into consideration before making our judgements.[8] Let's suppose some Australians are working with the Japanese; they're discussing 'quality circle' concerns. Some unexpected issue arises that triggers concern over the ability of the vendor to meet quotas on time. The clock strikes 5, and one of the Australians excuses herself from what looks like an indefinitely long meeting. The Japanese quality circle leader lets her go, but one may well note a trace of disappointment among the Japanese as this person leaves the room. In their minds, they are perhaps thinking: 'There goes the lazy Australian. This thing would never happen in Japan. Everybody sticks it out back home to the very end, quitting time or not.' The Japanese, then, have firmly attributed laziness as the cause of the Australian's behaviour. They may not stop to think that work habits are different in Australia. The unmitigated devotion to work of the Japanese is uncommon in Australia. Workers there have more competing loyalties – to themselves, their family or their personal interests. Then there is the situational factor: the Australian may have had an important appointment with her doctor at that time. Studies have shown that when it comes to strangers, or people whom we consider to be members of the out-group, very often we assign bad motives or undesirable qualities. On the other hand, when we're looking at our own behaviour, or the behaviour of members of our in-group, we will more readily take objective situational factors into consideration.

We tend to think that our culture is the best in the world

The technical term for such cultural narcissism is 'ethnocentrism', or the belief that one's own culture is superior to all others. Such feelings can be triggered by statements such as the one made by former Japanese Prime Minister Nakasone, which inadvertently produced a wave of anti-Japanese sentiments in the USA. He said that Japan's racial homogeneity has made it a more 'intelligent society than that of the USA, where there are blacks, Mexicans and Puerto Ricans, and the level is still quite low'.[9] Another example of ethnocentrism may be cited as the intolerance of many French-speakers towards those who don't speak their language. In both of these examples, you may well find other factors than that of superiority – behaviours that are harsh, unkind and discriminating against a certain group. In more extreme cases, you will find too an emotional interplay involving anger, disgust and a strong desire to avoid contact with people from the out-group. This is quite obviously happening in Israel at the moment between the Arabs and Jews: whatever degree of emotional repulsion is awakened, the person's behaviour towards the foreign culture is prejudiced.[10]

It is said that prejudice has an importance: it protects the interests of the superior groups within society, it gives them enough 'ego-defence' to maintain their inflated image of superiority and protects important institutions, religious beliefs and traditions.[11] The world has many shades of prejudice. Japanese are said to be prejudiced not only against foreigners, but also against Koreans residing in Japan, and that the Korean minority is discriminated against in housing, jobs and social life. An Indonesian university student has said; 'The Japanese are nice to me, but they don't invite me to enter their circle. If I'm watching TV, they never enter. If I go towards them, they disperse.'[12] In Canada, English speaking immigrants of British descent tend to land better jobs and earn higher incomes than the French-speaking minority. In other countries, such as Malaysia and South Africa, the law enforces political, economic and social preference for certain ethnic groups. In Malaysia the government wants its Malay citizens to be economically on an equal footing with the generally wealthier Chinese minority, so it requires businesses to make sure that the *bumiputras,* or Malays, make up at least 30 per cent of the workforce. South Africa's apartheid policy institutionalizes racial discrimination by not allowing some ethnic groups to participate equitably in some political and economic activities. In Australia women are struggling to gain equal footing with men; men's spirit of 'mateship', a special kind of camaraderie that developed during pioneer times in the bush, excluded females from their social activities. That same spirit gave women an inferior position in the workplace.

It is hard indeed to get rid of these kinds of cultural prejudice. Negotiators will need to deal with this whenever different people get together. Broaden your perspective on different cultures. Change whatever prejudiced cultural assumptions you may have. How?

Look for a systematic educational programme that emphasizes cultural differences.[13] There are several training organizations that offer these educational programmes, including our own firm, Business Consultants International.

4 Exercises

This chapter features 21 problematic intercultural situations. International business executives may not face exactly those situations that we illustrate here, but when you analyse the cultural factors that complicate the situations, you will broaden your range of cultural assumptions. So do this exercise. You'll find it is a most valuable experience – and it will make you a better international negotiator.

Here's how you'll do the exercise: first, read each situation. Then select the best answer to the question posed at the end of each fictional situation. To learn the right answer – and why it's correct – turn to the page indicated.

Situation 1: A square peg in a round hole

Logistics Department Manager Edward Kindall, a Canadian, has just brought in American Lou Salinger to join a working team of ten, nine of whom are Japanese. After two months' working, Lou met with Edward privately and said, 'Frankly, I can't stand my working situation any more. Meetings take so long and my team members have to agree on each and every minute detail – all this is wearing me out. In the other Japanese firm I worked for, my boss allowed me to follow the usual American practices. Of course, that was easy because there were other Americans on my team. I want to transfer to the department's special project group A, which is an all-American group. I've met them briefly, and I think I could work well with them. Lately too I've noticed that my present team members have been rather cold to me.'

To this, Edward replied, 'I don't know, Lou. You're too new at the job to give up so soon. I don't want it to appear that you're a quitter. Let me think about this some more.' The next day, Edward met with the group supervisor, Yoshiro Fume, and asked him what he though of Lou. Yoshiro shared this: 'Lou is technically competent. We admire his qualifications and have learned a lot from him. But he is all theory and isn't much help in the actual work. He doesn't participate actively enough and leaves promptly at 5 p.m. That's just about the time the group is getting started with it. Also we can't count on him for weekend work. He's just like the rest of the lazy Americans we've worked with. Pardon me, but that's just my opinion – a sample of one.'

What's going on between Lou and his Japanese team members?

1. Lou is a victim of 'US-bashing' by his logistics team.
2. Lou is acting like a prima donna. He thinks he can afford to be hopping around because of his special qualifications.
3. There are real cultural tensions because of the different work styles of Lou and his Japanese team members.
    (See p. 112 for answer.)

Situation 2: The lady wants to be a manager

Laurie Sommers, a talented engineer, is a technical research associate in a Japanese firm located in Knoxville, Tennessee, USA. The firm makes electronic products for the consumer market. For two years her boss, Herbert Mann, acknowledged her contribution and told her that when he left, she was the most likely successor. One day, Herbert accepted a lucrative offer from a competitor and resigned. To the surprise of the entire department, the company brought in a Japanese male from another department to take his place. Laurie met with the Personnel Manager to protest. The new boss admitted she was more qualified for the job. However, the company president, who was Japanese, did not change his mind. Laurie promptly met with her lawyer and was advised to file a sex-discrimination suit. Laurie had considered resigning, but her lawyer convinced her to fight instead. On being informed of Laurie's plan, the company president was somewhat distraught and tried to persuade Laurie to stop. He did not like the publicity she had generated within the local media. Laurie went ahead with her efforts, and she won the court battle. The company was forced to offer her the job, but she refused to accept. She had gone to all the trouble merely to prove a point. She couldn't imagine herself working under what she considered to be outrageously backward company policies. What, then, was Laurie a victim of?

1. The Japanese president really just didn't like Laurie.
2. The president preferred all managers to be Japanese. Herbert Mann was an exception because of his rare skills.
3. The Japanese don't regard women – Japanese or non-Japanese – as equals in the work world.
    (See p. 113 for answer.)

Situation 3: The designer from Paris

The Japanese buyer of a women's clothing-store chain phoned the Paris headquarters of a French clothing manufacturer to send a representative to Tokyo to present its autumn collection. The two companies had done business often over the past few years. The Paris firm sent designer Christine Beaumont to Tokyo to make the presentation. She knew the Japanese firm invited representatives from competitors, so she had a big selling job to do. She had never been to Japan before. Two days after she arrived, the company scheduled her presentation. Christine assumed she could get right down to business, considering her company's long-time relationship with this Japanese firm. And so Christine glossed over social pleasantries and immediately proceeded to her slide presentation. Then she discussed the pricing of the clothes and how they could be marketed. Christine met with a rather bland reaction to her presentation from the company president and representatives. After a long silence, the Japanese president took over and abruptly shifted the focus to Christine herself. He questioned her about her training in the fashion world, previous work experiences, the fashion schools she had attended, her hobbies, how long she's been with the Paris company, and so on. At first, Christine was taken aback because of the sudden switch, but she quickly recovered and answered the questions. The president then talked about how successful his firm's relationship had been with the Paris company, the profitable projects that both companies engaged in, using names of high-ranking executives who had visited Tokyo and their out-of-town trips together, and so forth. Christine was then told by the president to remember all that information because she would need it when meeting the other company executives. Later she made a phone call to her head office and told the boss how uncertain she felt about the results of her presentation. What went wrong in that business meeting?

1. Christine was not thoroughly prepared for this business trip and had a mistaken sense of priorities.
2. The Japanese audience found Christine's presentation boring, and so the Japanese president changed the subject-matter of the meeting.
3. Christine should have used live models instead of slides in her presentation.
    (See p. 113 for answer.)

Situation 4: A matter of discretion

Ted Miller, head of the Japanese branch of a British pharmaceutical company, was excited about the completion of the testing of a drug that rapidly cures gonorrhea. His office just telexed him that the first shipment is to arrive in two weeks. Ted has excellent contacts in the local industry and thought he wouldn't have any problems in marketing the new drug. Ted contacted the president of the biggest local distributor of drugs in Tokyo. They agreed to meet next day in the distributor's office. Ted broke the news about the drug and asked the president if his company would be open to distributing it. The president first congratulated Ted's firm, and after a silence, carefully expressed his reluctance to market a product that would make the Japanese appear promiscuous. Although Ted was disappointed at the results of his meeting, he was determined not to let the event get him down. He still plans to market the product, but next time he may have to modify his targets. Ted still thought that the Japanese executive should have reacted more rationally to the new product. He didn't understand why his reaction had been so personal; here are three possible reasons:

1. The president was just close-minded and didn't like the product.
2. Ted didn't do a good job of selling the drug.
3. The Japanese made a decision that was a face-saving gesture for his country.
   (See p. 114 for answer.)

Situation 5: The 'velvet glove' approach

Carlos Garza, a citizen of Argentina, is the Division Manager of a Swiss cosmetics firm operating in Japan. He wanted more support by large Japanese department store chains to supplement his marketing efforts in areas outside the main cities of Tokyo, Nagoya and Osaka. Carlos came up with a plan and asked his marketing *bucho* (department head) to contact one particular Japanese department store chain and discuss it with middle- and lower-level managers. Gaining a preliminary consensus at the working level, he thought, was a necessary step to take in order to obtain the approval of top management. The *bucho* reported positive reactions, so Carlos made an appointment with the store's top management. At the meeting, Carlos was surprised to hear the president say that it was the first time he had heard about the plan; he said it would take time for his subordinates to evaluate it. Carlos followed up a number of times, but he continued to hear the same message. He was so sure his plan would be accepted that he had informed his head office in Geneva that this chain would distribute his product. Why do you think that here Carlos was getting the 'run-around'?

1. The president was so busy that he didn't recall being briefed about Carlos' proposal.
2. The company wasn't really interested in Carlos' proposal. The middle- and lower-level executives were just trying to please him by sending positive signals.
3. The executive was just testing Carlos' resolve in selling his proposal.
    (See p. 114 for answer.)

Situation 6: It's a matter of principle

At this stage of the game, Rutger Siemens, negotiator for a West German manufacturer of coalmining equipment, had already reached substantial agreement with a Chinese firm for the importation of equipment from Germany. In the final round of preliminary meetings, Rutger and top Chinese executives agreed, in principle, that the Chinese company needed to have its technical personnel trained in the use of coalmining machinery and equipment. They agreed to meet at a future date for the final drafting of the contract. Meanwhile, Rutger had to fly back to Frankfurt to iron out final price concessions with his boss.

One month later, Rutger flew back to Beijing for the drafting of the contract. The set of company officials he met with this time was different, save for one person who appeared to be the head negotiator. As they went through the terms of the contract the Chinese head negotiator said that since they had already agreed, in principle, that the German manufacturer would train their personnel in the use of the equipment, they should also be trained in the use of one particular unit – the new model of the X-ray spectrometer unit, a machine used for mineral analysis, which Rutger had talked about in one of his earlier technical seminars. Rutger was caught by surprise because he had clearly mentioned in the seminar that this machine was not yet available for use outside Germany because of maintenance difficulties; he checked the recorded minutes to make sure, and he was right.

The Chinese head negotiator insisted that excluding training on this machinery was contrary to the spirit of the principle they had earlier agreed upon. He also pointed out that no other company they knew about made such a machine, all the more reason that Rutger should agree to sharing the technology. Rutger tried to clarify that the machine in question was clearly not included in the list of machinery they intended to make available to any Asian country. He said it would take at least another year before it could be distributed outside Germany. The Chinese regretted this disagreement over an important item and moved to adjourn the meeting temporarily. Why were Rutger and his Chinese counterparts on different wavelengths?

1. The Chinese firmly believe that negotiations should be anchored in agreed-upon broad principles rather than in details of contracts.
2. The firm Rutger is representing was discriminating against certain customers, in this case, Asian countries.
3. The Chinese negotiators were being deceptive, leaving certain points vague in order to extract concessions later on.
   (See p. 114 for answer.)

Situation 7: Please, send back the white flowers

Wolfgang Renger had just arrived in Singapore from West Germany, accompanied by his wife, Annemarie. He was to meet with exporters of metals. Wolfgang has been referred to one particular exporter by friends back home who had had dealings with them. Wolfgang and Annemarie were invited for dinner to the home of Joe Wu, the firm's president. Annemarie brought some white silk flowers as a present – one of the few inexpensive things she usually takes along with her on business trips. Joe Wu and his wife met the Rengers at the front door. Their faces fell when they were given the white flowers. They quickly recovered after seeing the puzzled looks on their guests' faces. Meanwhile, Wolfgang and Annemarie aren't quite sure what went wrong.

1. The Chinese couple were disappointed that the Rengers didn't bring their children with them.
2. White flowers have a negative connotation in Chinese culture.

3.   Joe Wu and his wife were expecting a much older-looking couple, judging from Wolfgang's deep voice on the phone. (See p. 115 for answer.)

Situation 8: You can do it

Peter Go, an assistant technician in a steel mill, has just been assigned to train under Canadian Dudley Wadsworth, resident expert on steel processing. Dudley requires Peter to hand in weekly reports on the work he has done after his training sessions.

One day in a department meeting, Dudley reported on the performance of his apprentices. Dudley profusely praised all of his apprentices and said he was confident they would complete their training in six months. All this catches Peter by surprise because he knows he isn't doing well. If fact, in private talks with Dudley, he achnowledges his weaknesses, including his poor English and lack of comprehension of highly technical terms. After the meeting, Dudley called Peter to his office and reassured him that he had his support if he worked extra hard. He suggested that he take English lessons at weekends. He said if he could show a drastic improvement in two months' time, he could stay with the group. Why do you think Dudley covered for Peter in the meeting?

1.   Dudley was new in the firm and was trying to impress his boss.
2.   Dudley was expressing sincere support for Peter without unduly embarrassing him during the meeting by admitting publicly that Peter may need more help.
3.   Dudley was trying to win the favour and acceptance of his trainees.
(See p. 115 for answer.)

Situation 9: Questionable procurement

Richard West, a New Zealand executive in the Taipei, Taiwan, branch of a South African agricultural technology firm, was assigned to team up with two Chinese managers, one from purchasing and one from the agricultural machinery department, for an equipment procurement project; all three contacted vendors they knew. Within one month they had offers from many different vendors throughout the world. After the preliminary evaluation procedure, they decided to choose between a French maker of excellent machinery and a South African manufacturer. They didn't know anyone from the French company, but it sent them references they could check, sales brochures and documents bearing benchmark test results. The South African manufacturer was contacted by one of the Chinese managers through a friend. After an objective discussion comparing the products of the two companies, Richard and the two Chinese managers were in agreement that the French products were far superior both in quality and performance but more expensive than the South African products. They agreed to decide by a majority vote. Richard wanted to give the contract to the French firm, but he was outvoted by the Chinese managers. Mainly because of their contacts, they favoured the South African company; they figured they would get better attention, service and maintenance. Richard was very disappointed because the South African machinery didn't have the features that they would need within a year. Why did the Chinese managers decide on the South African firm?

1. The Chinese managers were expecting a commission from their friend in South Africa.
2. Richard was outvoted because he is from New Zealand.
3. The Chinese managers were strongly influenced by the existence of personal contacts in South Africa.
   (See p. 116 for answer.)

Situation 10: Going a bit too far

Henry Li is assistant manager in the Chinese branch of a European shipbuilding firm that is helping the Chinese people update their technology and methods. The branch is based in Guangzhou. Henry has a reasonably amicable relationship with his boss, Leonard Glass, of British descent, who has been with the firm for a little less than a year. On the job, Henry has never been reluctant to approach Leonard about things he needs to know. Leonard has been only too willing to serve as a mentor. One day, Henry approached Leonard about his cousin – also an employee in the shipping industry, but in a competitor's company. His cousin wants to go to London to study and needs recommendation papers to present to the British Consulate. Henry asked Leonard to write a recommendation for his cousin, even though he didn't know him. Leonard was appalled by the request and said 'no'. He made up a story that the British Consulate double-checks such recommendations. Not knowing Henry's cousin would therefore put Leonard in jeopardy. After that meeting, Henry's relationship with Leonard became distant. A month later, Henry resigned. How would you account for Henry's behaviour?

1. Henry found a better job elsewhere and simply quit.
2. Leonard let Henry down. Henry expected Leonard not only to be a mentor, but also a friend in a case of personal need.
3. Leonard became less friendly with Henry after that meeting because he began to be more concerned about being taken advantage of.

(See p. 116 for answer.)

Situation 11: Watch your agent

Robert Conway, an American engineer, wanted to set up a company selling pumps and similar equipment in Saudi Arabia; he contacted a Saudi agent recommended to him by a friend. Robert met with this agent many times. The groundwork for putting up his business has been set, approvals have been won through different government agencies and contracts have been drafted and signed. One day, his agent, who claimed to be well connected, promised Robert to have the warehouse built in six months, just in time for the arrival of the first shipment of inventory. Robert was excited by his agent's enthusiasm and left the construction entirely to him. Three months passed and nothing substantial had taken place beyond the paper plan for the warehouse. Robert became upset and impulsively decided to meet his agent. In that brief meeting, Robert became quite angry. His secretary could even hear him banging on the table. After the banging, the agent walked out of the office briskly; he looked very embarrassed. Since that day, Robert never saw his agent. Finally, he cancelled their working contract. Why do you think the agent took so long to execute his plan?

1. There was difficulty getting construction materials for the warehouse.
2. The agent had many competing responsibilities and couldn't attend to the warehouse project; all these other activities were part of 'God's plan' for him.
3. There was miscommunication. The agent thought that Robert would take the lead responsibility in the construction of the warehouse.
(See p. 116 for answer.)

Situation 12: Unexpected visit

Gerald Sullivan, vice-president of a British office equipment manufacturer, had just suffered a stroke. The next day, the company sent the next highest-ranking executive, Kathleen Anderson, to Riyadh in place of her boss. This important meeting was held to finalize plans for the introduction of the company's latest line of microcomputers and word processors in Saudi Arabia. Kathleen arrived there on the second day of the month of Ramadan. The Saudi executive, Adnam Beg, a traditional businessman in his late fifties, decided to meet Kathleen in the circumstances of a *diwaniyah* or the ritualistic visit held in the home of the host. She went from the airport directly to his home. She was famished and the Saudia flight had been a bad one. She assumed she'd make up for her lost meals at Mr Beg's house. Everything went well at first. Adnam was obliged to serve food to his guest, even if it was Ramadan. Kathleen liked what was served and ate heartily. She was quite surprised that her host wasn't eating and so she urged him to eat with her. In between gulps, she asked Adnam if she could meet him in his office. She said, 'I'm very curious about your local setup. I'm very excited about making my sales presentation here.' Although Kathleen is generally a relaxed person, she tends to wiggle her foot with legs crossed as a nervous habit! Adnam notices this behaviour, even catches a glimpse of the soles of her black leather shoes! The enthusiasm of the earlier stages of her visit is lost. What happened?

1. Adnam Beg was put off by the sound of her chewing food.
2. He thought Kathleen was too assertive for a businesswoman when enthusing about the new line of office products.
3. Beg thought Kathleen lacked consideration by suggesting that he eat with her. He also thought she was too forward by asking to be invited to his office.

(See p. 117 for answer.)

Situation 13: A most unusual meeting

André Martin, a French civil engineering contractor, was invited to visit a Saudi Arabian engineering firm involved in a government project. André is well known for his work in urban traffic-control engineering. He never had projects in the Middle East before. Most of his projects had been in Europe and North America. When André arrived at the office of the president of the Saudi Arabian firm, he was asked to sit down on any of the cushions on the floor. The president was busy meeting other people, but he was in full view of André, who seated himself comfortably in a big cushion along the wall. There were about seven other executive guests awaiting their turn – this is the typical Saudi Arabian *majiles* system of receiving business visitors. After half an hour had passed, André asked the secretary when his turn will be. The secretary didn't know exactly.

André started to feel uncomfortable when more people came in and interrupted the president's discussions. The president obviously didn't mind the interruptions and attended to the walk-ins briefly. After another full hour, the secretary fetched André and led him to the guest's chair opposite the president's desk. They talked in English. After prolonged social pleasantries, the president asked André to make a presentation to a group of company engineers, including the president's cousin, an executive vice-president. They came in, and André enthusiastically lectured in English on his traffic routeing plans. While giving his talk, André notices puzzled looks on the faces of some of his audience. He realizes he has forgotten to have some terms and concepts translated. It seems only the president's cousin, graduate of the Massachusetts Institute of Technology, understood him well. André concluded his presentation on a positive note, in spite of the lack of response from the group. As he rested in his hotel, André wondered what went wrong and thought it one of the strangest business meetings he had ever attended. What was André unaware of concerning Saudi Arabian business meetings?

1. Saudi Arabian executives have no sense of priorities; they entertain anyone who walks in.
2. André didn't prepare himself for his presentation. His visual aids were inadequate.
3. André should have been accompanied by an interpreter; his English was heavily accented because of his French background.
4. Saudi Arabian businessmen take time in conducting their discussions and give priority to people close to them.
(See p. 118 for answer.)

Situation 14: For men only

Natalie Bouchet, single, was sent by her office in Brussels to their Australian branch in Sydney. She was to spend two years in training groups of sales representatives in operating networking systems using minicomputers. After a hectic three weeks in producing a training programme and giving lectures to the trainees, Natalie decided to give herself a break and visit a well-known club. She thought that joining such a club would make her life a little more interesting. As she entered the main lobby, Natalie noticed that most of the guests were men, except for two women who were seated in a far corner. Then she spotted a colleague, Terrence Layton, one of the computer specialists.

Natalie: 'Hello. Fancy meeting you here!'
Terrence: 'Hi, Natalie, how are you doing?'

Natalie: 'Terrence, this is my first visit here. I want to find out more about some of the executive groups I could meet if I join this club. I wonder if you could help me?'

Terrence: 'I'm sorry, Natalie. Most of the executive groups here are all-male groups. There aren't many females. Oh, excuse me, Natalie, my friend here is picking me up for a meeting that happens to be going on now. Sorry, I wasn't much help. Bye.'

Natalie wanted to have a drink anyway and proceeded to the nearest bar in the club. When she was seated, the bartender approached her and politely requested her to leave. He said all function rooms in that club were for males only. Women, he said, were allowed in one of the lounges, but that lounge happened now to be closed. Natalie went to the manager's office and complained. The manager repeated the same explanations and made her no exception. Natalie went home very disappointed; she was now quite concerned about her social life for the next two years in Sydney. Why was Natalie treated this way at the club?

1. Natalie obviously looked like a foreigner, and the club's personnel didn't want to cater to her.
2. She happened to step into a strange club, with strange rules.
3. Natalie, unknowingly, entered the kind of society where males are dominant, and this prejudice is still expressed in the policies of some social clubs.
   (See p. 118 for answer.)

Situation 15: Third World 'cronyism'

Henri Deneuve, a Frenchman, has owned for the past three years a medium-sized firm in Indonesia which manufactures consumer products; it has been profitable throughout that period. The plant there imports all its plastic components. One day, the government announced that a state trading firm would handle all importations of plastic. The government said that this would indicate for the first time the volume of imported plastic; it also said that it would save local manufacturers money because it would bargain for lower prices from international suppliers. Six months later, Henri thinks the new system has only made plastic much more expensive to purchase, and the delays in delivery are much longer than before. His trade association wrote him and the rest of its members the following letter: 'We will petition the government to get rid of the state trading company. The fees it charges have made imports much more expensive, and their inefficiency causes delivery delays. Many manufacturers who rely on imported plastic raw materials have had to shut down due to the dramatic increase in production costs.' The trade association also said that the head of the state trading company is a nephew of one of the top government officials. Even so, it would still go ahead with its lobbying efforts.

That night, Henri looked at his financial statements and was alarmed by the trend of increasing expenses. He felt frustrated about the local political setup and started to think about transferring his operations to another nation in south-east Asia. How would you view the situation?

1. Henri's perceptions are mistaken. He is blaming the government when world prices for plastic have risen.
2. Henri and the trade association want to be able to import directly once again and have some leeway in earning price concessions from their suppliers.
3. Henri and the trade association are correct in thinking that the local business environment is dominated by special interests protected by political backers.

(See p. 119 for answer.)

Situation 16: A fish out of water

Roger O'Leary, an Australian, was sent by his firm, a manufacturer of rubber products, to replace one of the expatriate managers in its Kuala Lumpur, Malaysia, branch. Staffing the firm was the prime concern at present, and a comprehensive 45-day recruiting programme had been launched to obtain the best local talent available to hire to the firm. Roger was assigned to head this recruiting project and briefed about the local laws concerning hiring *bumiputras* (Malays, or 'sons of the soil'), Chinese and members of other ethnic groups. Roger participated in all phases of the hiring process, particularly at the interviews; at night he pored over many application forms. After a month, Roger had a good picture of the quality of people available and keenly eyed certain candidates for specific positions. He had a problem in staffing the new products department: he wanted to hire a Chinese male, who was a highly skilled and experienced chemical engineer; no one else could match his qualifications. He talked to the Head of Personnel to try to find ways around the government requirement to hire a *bumiputra* for that position. Roger was disappointed that the rule could not be changed. Before coming to Malaysia, he thought the laws would be simple to follow there. He had not realized how strongly ingrained his bias towards egalitarianism was until now. He didn't like the prospect of having to contend with these restrictions in the future. So he asked his head office for a transfer. How would you explain the way Roger reacted?

1. Roger was over-reacting to a government guideline that was simple and clear.
2. Roger was starting out on the wrong foot by trying to alter government regulations.
3. Roger didn't fully appreciate the government's rationale for the law governing hiring practices.
4. Roger's inner values were challenged by this assignment.
   (See p. 119 for answer.)

Situation 17: Sweeteners can be bitter

Trevor Sutton, born and reared in London, has for the past five years been a top-ranking financial officer in the Hong Kong branch of the Standard Chartered Bank. One of his main responsibilities is to evaluate applicants for corporate loans. The bank has been a significant contributor to the development of Hong Kong, and it has supported a number of successful business ventures. One firm whose fate was turned around after the bank gave them a loan is owned by a prominent Kowloon family. It produces polyester-cotton and polyester-viscose yarn. It was January, and the time was drawing near for the Chinese New Year. In Hong Kong this is a time of great commercial activity and gift-giving. Trevor unexpectedly received a letter from the owner of this firm, expressing gratitude for the bank's support. Their annual report showed large profits. The letter said that as a token of the firm's gratitude, he had purchased a Jaguar motor car for Mr Sutton, and he hoped he would accept the gift. The keys were enclosed in a separate envelope. Trevor thought this was an outstanding present, but to accept it would be outrageous. He quickly typed up a letter declining the gift, and called on his special assistant to handle the matter discretely. How would you interpret the motivations of the Chinese owner in offering the car as a present to Trevor?

1. The Chinese owner was, in effect, offering Trevor a bribe in case his good offices would be needed in the future.
2. The Chinese owner was acting out of genuine gratitude; the car had nothing to do with future dealings.
3. The Chinese owner was so rich that the cost of the motor-car meant nothing to him. It was just a small gift in gratitude as far as he was concerned. It is common practice to give gifts to significant partners in business during the Chinese New Year celebrations.
   (See p. 120 for answer.)

Situation 18: The roundabout ways of smooth interpersonal relationships (SIR)

Renato Tolentino, president of a Philippine trading firm, had requested a representative from an American agricultural producer of grains to meet with him to discuss the possibility of importing selected grains. Ronald Parker was sent on a short visit. The preliminaries went well. On the second day, Parker talked about the price ranges that were acceptable for certain grain groups. In one of the breaks, Tolentino met with his executive assistant, Joe Mijares, to tell him that the price ranges were way out of line even if the American firm took off the 20 per cent discount allowable. The prospects of dealing with this company looked dim. However, since the representative had been personable, they would not spoil his trip by giving him a negative decision right away. Perhaps they could compensate his efforts by introducing him to other executives in the industry, who might be future business prospects? Tolentino instructed Mijares to invite to a dinner party the next night several business executives, so that Parker could meet them. Parker enjoyed the party. He felt that all signals pointed to positive business prospects with Tolentino's firm. A week after he arrived in the USA, he received a letter from Tolentino telling him that the price range was way beyond what the firm's budget allowed. He was puzzled about why he was not told this while he was still in the Philippines. How would you explain the situation to him?

1. The president of the trading firm was just using the letter as a ploy to gain more price concessions.
2. Filipinos aren't confrontative in certain occasions. They may give out 'yes' signals, even if they mean 'no'.
3. Tolentino didn't want to spoil a good relationship with Parker as he found him personable. He thought he could soften the blow by saying 'no' in a letter instead.
   (See p. 120 for answer.)

Situation 19: No better way of doing things

The Tres Estrellas Co. markets electronics products through retail stores in Mexico. Tom Hanan had just moved from Dallas, Texas, to assume the duties of national sales manager. He became especially concerned when he found that sales in one of the Mexico City stores dropped dramatically. He phoned Ambrosio Gomez, general manager for the Mexico City area. Gomez suggested that he, Tom and Felipe Farias, the manager of the store, meet that afternoon. The three met at Tom's office. Farias explained that the sudden drop in sales was accounted for by the unexpected entry of a new line of Japanese-made electronics products that were sold with rebates and 'money-back' guarantees at a nearby competing store. He thought that a 'buy-one-take-one' offer on old stock and small discounts on the new stock would help them recover. Gomez quickly objected. He said a buy-one-take-one deal had never been used by the company before and that it would only lead to losses. He reminded Farias that, in cases such as this, the company had for the past ten years always spent more on advertising. Gomez decided to spend more on TV advertising, particularly on the local channel where electronics sales had been successful in the past. Hanan was mostly an observer at this meeting; he merely asked a few questions. Since he was new to Mexico, he thought he'd leave most of the responsibility to Gomez. Farias went ahead and advertised on TV. No price reductions were made; after two months of advertising, sales had declined even further. What can you say about the decision-making process that went on here?

1. Gomez was adopting a 'macho' or authoritarian stance to warn the newcomer Hanan not to step on his turf.
2. Farias was too weak, he should have argued more for his ideas.
3. Gomez simply followed the Mexican way of observing traditional guidelines when faced with problems.
   (See p. 121 for answer.)

Situation 20: Caught in the middle

Pedro Ortiz, an accountant, is a promising management trainee in a Mexican management consulting firm. His immediate boss, Emilio Juarez is Vice-President for Finance. Ortiz is being trained to provide management services. Andres Gonsalves, a Brazilian, is the firm's resident training consultant. He is on a two-year contract. His job is to train professionals such as accountants, auditors, financial analysts and personnel administrators in delivering professional management consulting services to client companies. Ortiz has learned to please his boss, Juarez. He never confronts his boss in cases when they have strong disagreements. Occasionally he would take issue with some of Juarez's ideas, but only when his boss was in a good mood. Ortiz always implemented his boss's plans unquestioningly. When Ortiz started working with Gonsalves, he was exposed to an entirely new style of interaction. Gonsalves always coached him to be candid, spontaneous and honest when he evaluated his training techniques. Ortiz was uncomfortable with this, he wasn't used to it. Gonsalves noticed Ortiz's reluctance to share his thoughts and confronted him about this one day. Ortiz resented Gonsalves's prying efforts. Since that afternoon he avoided having snacks with Gonsalves. How would you account for Ortiz's behaviour?

1.   He is naturally introverted. He hates probing.
2.   He is caught between two directly opposing management styles – the traditional authoritarian mode of Emilio Juarez, his boss, and the open, democratic style of Andres Gonsalves.
3.   He resented Gonsalves's approach, which he thought went beyond professional boundaries.
     (See p. 121 for answer.)

Situation 21: Time off for a vacation

An American electrical equipment firm located in Denver, Colorado, hired West German Rolf Leyendecker, an expert in equipment design, to work in its Fort Worth, Texas, office. He spent the first two years working hard. He finally produced innovative equipment designs that were better than the latest line of products of their major competitor. Rolf got along well with his design group, which consisted mostly of Americans and a few Japanese. In the third year, Rolf was beginning to become burned out. He talked with his boss, an American, to arrange for a two-week European vacation the following month. Tentatively his boss agreed. However, next month, Rolf's boss received word that three top executives from Denver would visit Fort Worth to see the prototypes developed by the design team. The proposed date of the visit coincided with Rolf's intended vacation. His boss tried to persuade him to change his vacation dates, but he failed. Rolf said that apart from his air fare and hotel reservations, his wife and daughter, both working, had already made arrangements with their respective offices. He tried to convince his boss that the rest of the team knew enough to conduct the presentation themselves. But his boss told him he wanted to make Rolf the main presenter because the group used his basic designs. With Rolf's participation, it would be easier to increase the budgetary support for the department. Rolf wasn't convinced and took his vacation anyway. His boss wasn't happy with the group's presentation, much less with Rolf's hard-headedness. He hated to think of problems in the future because of this incident, but the possibilities were there. How would you view Rolf's behaviour?

1. Rolf acted irresponsibly by abandoning a timely opportunity to win budgetary support.
2. Rolf acted like a prima donna because he knew his talents and accomplishments were rare.
3. Rolf really just wanted time out. He was burned out. Besides, he believed in his group's capabilities. He felt they'd do a good job on the presentation.

(See p. 122 for answer.)

5 Cultural self-awareness

This chapter will help you create your own inventory of personal values. This will help you to understand your own cultural assumptions. Many of these are already probably operating on a subconscious level. We strongly feel that the more you are aware of your own cultural assumptions, the greater control you will have over your reactions. You'll be able to do a better job of planning your cross-cultural interactions in the future.

Your cultural baseline

Gaining an increased awareness will *not* occur automatically. A lot of work and self-examination will first have to be done by you. You can start by filling out these blanks:

Full name: _____

Country: _____

Nationality: _____

Ethnic group: _____

Language: _____

Religious affiliation: _____

Your formative years

Our parents, family members, schoolteachers and friends, and even a few mere acquaintances, have influenced us a lot in the earlier stages of our lives. One of the things they may have taught us was how to deal with strangers, including people from other countries. Try to go back to your earlier days and recall what you've been taught:

Their nationality: _____

What you were taught about them: _____
_____

What you were supposed to say to them: _____
_____

How you were supposed to behave towards them: _____
_____ *(Repeat this process if you've encountered several nationalities)*

Your current cultural profile

Now, let's take a look at your cultural assumptions at the present time. Here is a list of 39 concepts that probably influence your behaviour in the business world to a great extent. In the blank, write down what you think about each concept (don't think too much about it). Try to capture your immediate thoughts and answers: there are no 'right' or 'wrong' answers. In this exercise you will learn much about yourself and about your cultural assumptions. It doesn't matter where your cultural assumptions have come from; you may even discover that your values and attitudes are the complete opposite of those of your culture – but that's all right, just write them down:

Emotion _____
Time _____
Power _____
Success _____
Self-realization _____
Fulfilment _____
The future _____

Planning change _____
Wealth _____
Achievement _____
Material consumption _____
Risks _____
Authority (how to act towards your boss) _____
(how to treat subordinates) _____
_____
Individual initiative _____
Body language _____
Uncertainty _____
Freedom _____
The decision-making process _____
_____
Decision-makers _____
Groupwork vs individual work _____
_____
Bureaucratic procedures/red tape _____
_____
Foreign managers _____
Foreign workers _____
Foreign procedures/work methods _____
_____
Negotiating _____
Trust _____
Honesty _____
Co-operation _____
Competition _____
Social interaction in general _____
_____
Compromise _____
Business ethics _____
Corruption _____
Bribery _____
Goals _____
Profit _____
Tasks vs people _____
Pragmatism vs tradition _____

Now, do the same thing for other cultures – especially those with whom you negotiate. The grid of cultural assumptions below shows how four cultures differ in regard to seven of the 39 concepts. That will give you an idea of what you'll be doing. Don't worry about leaving blank some of the concepts. You probably don't know much about these other cultures. But the more often you negotiate with people from a different culture, the more you'll know about that culture. So watch TOS carefully. After several years, you'll probably have all 39 blanks filled out accurately. The important thing, though, is to compare *your* culture to TOS's culture. Ask yourself the following three important questions: (1) what do we have in common?; (2) what are our potential areas of conflict?; and (3) what can I do about making my next negotiation a successful one?

Grid of cultural assumptions

	Japan
Concepts	
1 Emotion	Emotions are important but must not be shown
2 Social interaction	Feelings of harmony and formality are important to establish; Japanese people display much politeness and complimentary behaviour, there is great concern for mutual 'saving face'; rituals may complicate introductions – you'll need proper instructions to perform a bow, for example
3 Body language	Japanese people don't approve of physical touching; because they are cramped together in a small space, they value their physical and psychological privacy
4 Time	Time isn't money in the Western sense; it is more important to be cautious; they *will* delay a decision, they want to make sure it's the best decision or solution to a

problem; the Japanese, though, are punctual for meetings

5 Power

Connections are not essential, but helpful; it's good to know a well-placed banker, industrialist or public official, they can help you; government linkages are especially important to speed approvals – government bureaucrats, through their system of *amakudari* ('descending from heaven'), assume senior positions in the private sector upon retirement

6 Negotiating

The Japanese value building long-term, personal relationships rather than just getting the contract signed; they appreciate gentle negotiation tactics and repetition of the points that need to be clarified; silence is used for deliberation; detailed minutes of meetings must be kept; good recall of past agreements and details of meetings impress the Japanese

7 Decision-making

The *kacho,* or second in command, to the *bucho,* or general manager, initiates the decision-making process and seeks consensus of all members of the department concerned through the process of *ringi-sei.* Top management approves and re-confirms the consensus decisions of lower levels and co-ordinates their activities

People's Republic of China

1 Emotion

Feelings of ambivalence towards foreigners (some distrust and aloofness pulling against their attraction for material things which developed countries can offer); they can be enthusiastic about proposals and foreign products one moment and then turn defensive about Chinese superiority the next

2	Social interaction	Sensitive to 'losing face', this is a matter of prestige, dignity and self-esteem
3	Body language	A poker-face hides volatility of emotions, the Chinese tend to look passive; physical intimacy isn't displayed, even if at times the Chinese have to be huddled in a cramped space; during negotiations they prefer to sit opposite TOS's team
4	Time	They don't hurry decisions; Punctuality is valued as part of modernity, they take their time when there's no urgency; negotiations take longer than in the West
5	Power	Personal connections aren't essential, since the Chinese are very well-informed – having friends, though, is still helpful; connections are hard to establish, except through introductions from joint trade councils or well-known suppliers
6	Negotiations	Circular negotiating methods, with many questions are much used; discussions can be tiresome, the Chinese are up-to-date with market facts and pay great attention to details; foreign negotiators may tend to feel they're being tricked when dealing with the Chinese
7	Decision-making	The Chinese are trying to change their ways by being anti-bureaucratic and by speeding up decision-making through channels. Committee consensus is the managerial mode

North America (USA and Canada)

1	Emotion	Impersonalism and non-emotionalism are the rule
2	Social interaction	Directness and frankness are valued rather than face-saving
3	Body language	Personal space is larger than that required by most other nationalities, privacy and space are highly guarded and respected; physical closeness is uncommon, occasional body contact may be observed if they are making a point or expressing a feeling
4	Time	Time is money – a scarce commodity not to be wasted
5	Power	Patronage is not essential in North America, where fairness and equal opportunity are valued; in big organizations, power is dispersed; nepotism is very rare, accomplishment and achievement matter more than pull
6	Negotiations	Directness and being well-informed about your offerings are highly valued; a great deal of effort must be spent in giving first-rate presentations, the image projected is critical; issues are resolved promptly since efficiency in the organization is a paramount concern
7	Decision-making	Highly rational and objective, assisted by the tools of high technology; consensus is unimportant; decentralization is typical in organizations; top-level involvement is observed only in rare cases involving unusual decisions

Saudi Arabia

1   Emotion   When dealing with foreign business
                       executives, formality, politeness and some
                       emotional restraint characterize the Saudi
                       executive – especially the older, more
                       traditional businessman; in private, though,
                       they don't hesitate to curse when angry

2   Social   Face-saving is valued; matters concerning
    interaction   family, friends and countrymen are given
                       high priority; business is often set aside to
                       attend to personal matters; local women
                       are excluded from business situations;
                       God's will governs all their activities and is
                       mentioned often in their business and
                       personal relationships

3   Body   Saudis stand close to people, physical
    language   touching may be involved; they look into
                       the eyes of people they're dealing with to
                       find out the extent of TOS's interest (if
                       TOS's pupils are dilated, TOS is interested)

4   Time   Time is governed by the will of God; Arabs
                       don't hurry – they figure that activities will
                       be accomplished in God's good time

5   Power   Getting help from important people, such
                       as members of the ruling family and senior
                       government officials or local agents, is
                       essential; try to make them your agents –
                       this may be difficult, for there is a complex
                       system involved in finding local agents;
                       their direct involvement in making
                       business arrangements for you is very
                       important

6   Negotiations   Building personal relationships and trust is
                       needed; Saudis don't hesitate to haggle; use
                       of interpreters and local agents smooth out

		relationships; Saudis take time to reconsider matters
7	Decision-making	Highly centralized control, senior government officials and members of elite families hold the power reins; recently more highly educated middle managers, comprising an emerging group, are using less traditional and more decentralized methods of decision-making

When you have studied the grid carefully, you will understand how important it is for you to make up a similar grid for the executives with whom you'll be negotiating. At first, it will be hard for you to be totally accurate. Over time, however, you will become more so. Make a start today: looking at the cultural assumptions of various nationalities in a comparative grid, will make it easier for you to evaluate international differences more effectively. This method is in fact best used whenever you negotiate with people of different nationalities; a clearly defined list of cultural assumptions will help you to devise the right strategies and tactics to use in dealing with each nationality.

6 Nonverbal communication

Consider this scene in a typical Singapore office: an American expatriate concludes his presentation of the coming year's sales programme with a typical American expression of gung-ho enthusiasm – perhaps making a fist and hitting it against the open palm of his other hand. Initially, his staff is excited by his line-up of concepts and acknowledges this by continuously nodding their heads during his presentation, a signal, he supposes, that he has effected a coup. But shortly after he hits his fist in his other palm, he notices how the faces of his team members fall, and this is accompanied by a mysterious silence. Then they simply walk out of the conference room.[1]

Scenes like this are typical for workers and executives thrust into an intercultural setting without preparation. If the American executive had been briefed beforehand, he would have been spared the embarrassment he has brought upon himself by simply not knowing that he has just made an insulting gesture before his entire staff. Miscommunication can be extremely costly; narrow-minded ethnocentric minds are unforgiving; and an untimely *faux pas* is difficult to recover from.

Chapter 4 made it clear how complex international communication is, especially when it's nonverbal. Here we explore in depth 'international body language' – i.e. the social rules governing nonverbal communication in different societies. We'll look at faces, eyes, touching and hand and other body gestures; office layouts; how to tell when TOS is lying to you; and how to influence TOS with *your* body language. Then we give some guidelines on how to make you a better judge of what is actually on TOS's mind, without them knowing you already have this valuable information.

We do not talk about the basics of body language in this book; we assume you already know most of the fundamentals, for if you're an experienced negotiator, you do have some knowledge of body language, and you can sense already if TOS is accepting or rejecting you. You might even be able to guess when TOS is lying to you. But when abroad or talking to a foreigner in your own country, you may not necessarily have this facility. More often than not, you are unfamiliar with the body language of foreigners, even if many gestures mean the same in most countries. In the absence of this familiarity, you find yourself relying heavily – perhaps more than is justified – on what the foreigners are *saying*. But if you are unfamiliar with the language, or clumsy with its nuances, you will fumble over patches of data and information and proceed blindly, with uncertain feelings about the new business and social relationships that you are forming along the way.

There are a few areas in which people of different cultures overlap in their understanding and use of nonverbal communication. Many researchers have found that most people understand the expressions we have on our faces when we're sad, happy, angry, surprised or afraid; the basic emotions aroused by situations that result in these facial expressions are pretty much universal. Cultures, though, vary in the rules their societies impose regarding the manner in which emotions are displayed in public.[2] For example, Filipinos, Thais and Malaysians are quite effusive about their smiles as they try to maintain smooth interpersonal relations. The Americans, British and Japanese, though, aren't as generous with such positive signals and are much more restrained in their facial expressions. Yet there are differences even among the second group of countries: the Japanese are considerably more restrained than the Americans, for instance. An expert once said that if you observed a group of Japanese watching a highly stressful movie without their knowledge, you would see many emotional facial expressions – much as the Americans would. But should an authority figure step into the room, you'll see those facial expressions instantly disappear. The social rules in Japan prohibit the public display of emotions.[3]

Here we cover six specific peculiarities of body language in many countries: face, eye and touch behaviour; movements of the entire body; space management and office layout; and lying gestures.

Facial behaviour

North Americans and Europeans, who are used to formal and restrained behaviour, might find the smiles that come so readily to Filipinos, Thais and Malaysians a bit disconcerting. These Asians value keeping smooth and harmonious interpersonal relationships, which they think their smiles facilitate.[4] The French also use their faces a great deal in person-to-person interaction, but in a different way. Basically, they practice restraint in their expressions, however, they won't hesitate to use facial movements to help emphasize what they're saying.[5] Meanwhile, North Americans, and to a greater extent the British and Japanese, tend to exert a greater control over their facial expressions of emotions than most other cultures: Indonesians smile or giggle while giving bad or tragic news to a friend to assuage the hurt that the message may evoke;[6] Japanese may laugh not so much to respond to something funny, but to give way to emotions of confusion, embarrassment and dismay.[7]

Casual movements like blinking and winking are taboo motions in some countries: blinking in Taiwan and winking (especially at women) in Australia are considered impolite. What might appear to you as an obscene gesture, such as using your index finger to make a screwing motion into the centre of your cheek, is in fact a gesture of praise in Italy![8] A somewhat similar gesture, the 'head screw', using the screwing motion of your index finger this time to your temple means 'You're crazy!' in Germany. A circular motion of your finger around your ear means 'crazy' in most European and some Latin American countries.[9]

You will observe many interesting facial motions in business meetings: pulling the end of the eyelids tells you that a person is on the alert or that he or she wants *you* to be alert in Europe and some Latin American countries. To show that highly confidential information is being discussed, a British business executive may tap his or her nose; the same motion will indicate a friendly warning to Italians.[10] Brazilians and Paraguayans flick their chins to tell you they don't know something; Italians use the same motion to tell you they're not interested in what you're saying or to get you out of their sight! Argentinians tap their heads to show that they're thinking. Paraguayans tilt their heads backwards to show that they've forgotten something.[11] Certain signals, in some countries, are interpreted in reverse. Bulgarians and Greeks nod their heads to mean 'no',[12] while Yugoslavians and South Indians shake their heads to mean 'yes'.[13]

Eye behaviour

Americans think that keeping direct eye contact is a sign of openness, honesty and assertiveness.[14] Other cultures that appreciate consistent eye contact are Saudi Arabia, South Korea, Thailand and Scandinavia. In business meetings, South Koreans maintain eye contact as a sign of courtesy, attention and a means of keeping one's relationship with another.[15] Saudi Arabians are even more intense in their involvement with eye contact: they look closely 'behind a person's eye' to search into the soul and evaluate TOS's inner qualities.[16] The Arabs know that dilated pupils are an indication of interest, and so they observe the person they're dealing with for such signs. Conversely and cleverly, they're fond of wearing tinted eyeglasses even indoors to conceal the extent of *their* interest, just in case the party they're dealing with is as shrewd as they are. Meanwhile the Thais use eye contact in order to facilitate their daily activities: if you're taking a bus ride in Bangkok and have inadvertently been skipped by the conductor who collects tickets, all you'll have to do is catch his or her eye and raise you eyebrows to be attended to![17]

Scandinavians appreciate eye contact, which they consider to be a sign of sincerity.[18] There are differences, though, in the way they express eye contact. Swedes, in particular, look less frequently at their partners in conversation than do the

Americans and British, but they hold their look for longer periods of time.[19] Pursuing this a little further, the British and Americans also differ in their manner of eye contact. The British tend to look away from you as they talk, while the Americans keep their full attention on your eyes and words. The British turn-yielding signal is when they look back at you – this indicates they are through with what they have to say. Furthermore, the British give the appearance of looking directly at your eye without really doing so – they try to look at an angle rather than directly. This is quite unlike the Americans, who look directly but alternately between your left and right eye.[20] People in Mexico, Japan and Puerto Rico consider direct eye contact an aggressive gesture. A Japanese boss who looks a subordinate in the eye is considered punitive, while a subordinate who looks the boss in the eye is seen as hostile or somewhat insane.[21]

These few examples of the nuances of eye behaviours only underscore the delicateness of intercultural interaction. Chances for even more extreme misunderstandings occur when two people's interpretations are diametrically opposed. A North American would be offended by the behaviour of the Vietnamese, who are taught to look at a person directly in the eye while keeping their arms folded across their chest. This sign of humility and respect to the Vietnamese suggests arrogance to the North American. Take another situation, this time involving a Puerto Rican. An American high school principal in New York City misconstrued the eye behaviour of a Puerto Rican girl. She was accused of wrongdoing, and he called her into his office. Because she was unable to look the principal directly in the eye, he suspended her. The principal was ignorant of Puerto Rican culture, and so he concluded she showed signs of guilt. He didn't know that Puerto Ricans do not look their superiors in the eye out of respect.[22] Koreans' approach to eye behaviour is embodied in the concept of *nuichee*. This approach actually helps them save face. Highly conscious of status differences, Koreans look at your eyes for answers to their questions instead of directly asking for an answer. This saves both parties some embarrassment.[23]

Touch behaviour

There is a whole spectrum of touch behaviour around the world. 'High-contact' cultures include the French, Brazilians, Spanish (among those of the same class), Russians, Indonesians, Filipinos, Mexicans and other Latin Americans, Saudi Arabians and the Thais.[24] Friendly touch behaviour is a sign of warmth and acceptance in Indonesia, the Philippines and Thailand – but only among locals and not with foreigners they don't know very well. Touch behaviour is acceptable even in business situations for Saudi Arabians, Mexicans and Thais. Arabs shake their hands with business colleagues and visitors frequently, using both hands. Among themselves, Arab men don't hesitate to walk hand in hand, arm in arm in public. During discussions they may tap another person gently or rest their hand or arm on the other person's arm or shoulder to express a feeling or emphasize a point.[25] Similarly, Mexicans, who are close business colleagues, express mutual support and friendship through the *abrazo,* or embrace. This is frequently used as a greeting.[26]

The Thais may not be as demonstrative as the Mexicans, but they will occasionally move close to and touch each other to emphasize a point.[27] In business encounters the French are ordinarily a 'non-touch' culture.[28] However, on social calls and at gatherings, the French, just like the Brazilians, will publicly kiss enthusiastically.[29] Spaniards of one social class keep their distance from people of other social classes; however, when with members of their own class, they may be uninhibited in touching each other during animated conversations.[30] Touching is essential in Latin America. Friends don't just greet each other or wave their hands, they shake each other's hand then hug with both arms, or squeeze each other's upper arm. When conversing, they tend to tap the other person's lapel with their fingers or tap their shoulders, or squeeze their arm to bridge the emotional gap or to stress what they're saying.[31]

Non-contact cultures include the British, Americans, Scandinavians and certain Asian groups, especially the Japanese, Indians, mainland Chinese, Taiwanese, Singaporeans and Koreans. Physical contact between the sexes in public is especially taboo in these Asian countries. There physical contact, such as holding each other's hand or arm, or holding on the waist and shoulder, is usually interpreted in amorous or sexual terms. Although there is a great deal of physical crowding in larger cities in Asian countries, the people don't seem to mind huddling together in buses and don't feel this crowding is a violation of their personal space.[32] A peculiar taboo in Thailand, Malaysia, Singapore and Taiwan is touching the top of TOS's head. This is a violation, because the top of the head is a sacred spot of wisdom and spirituality.[33]

Scandinavians are unique in having seemingly widely contradictory inclinations. Although they are basically a non-touch culture, the physical privacy that they staunchly protect is abandoned once a social gathering takes place in a sauna. Here Scandinavians unabashedly go naked and invite their guests to do likewise. Being invited to the sauna is a sure sign that the road to friendship has been taken.[34] Americans are also basically a non-tactile culture, and their personal 'buffer zone' is a distance of about six to ten feet. They sit that far apart when seated during negotiations. However, don't be surprised to find them touching one another sometimes when they wish to emphasize a point.[35] Finally to end our discussion of touch behaviour, touching the ear is a sign of sincerity and repentance in India.[36]

Hand and other body movements

Be careful when you move your hands in foreign countries! Be especially careful when you point your finger, pass food or articles with your left hand, gesture, beckon and put your hands in your pockets or on your hips. These movements are of special concern because of the wide variety of intercultural sensitivities regarding their meanings.

Pointing at people and things with your fingers, particularly your index finder, is considered rude in the Philippines, Korea, Singapore, Indonesia and the Middle East. Malaysians and Indonesians will tolerate finger pointing if you use your thumb with your other fingers folded into your palm. The rules are somewhat more complicated in Thailand, where pointing with your finger isn't as rude as pointing with your foot. The Thais' tolerance is also greater if you point at objects (but not sacred objects) rather than at people. If it really is necessary to point at somebody because you can't identify him or her verbally, then move your chin slightly upward towards the person you're identifying.[37] Filipinos like to point at persons, objects or locations by pursing their lips; you will notice this happening often in casual conversations.

Don't use your left hand to pass objects or food in Singapore, Malaysia, South Korea, Saudi Arabia, Indonesia and India. People in these countries generally consider the left hand unclean because it is the one used to clean oneself after going to the bathroom.[38] This is a very important rule: don't break it, even if you're left-handed!

Italians, Saudi Arabians and Latin Americans use their hands a great deal. They make lively gestures to emphasize or support what they're saying. Male Italian speakers will use both arms, making broad and sweeping symmetrical movements. Arabs use their hands and heads when expressing themselves. If their message is 'yes', they will shake their heads from side to side; and if it is 'no', they will tilt their head upward and lightly click their tongue. The Arabs are largely uninhibited, so they think the more exaggerated is the gesture, the more effective they will be.[39]

The hand-beckoning gesture is another source of confusion. When you beckon by hand, you hold all four fingers close together, with your palm facing upward or downward: hand-beckoning with the palm up is acceptable in England, Holland, the USA, France, and many other places: however, the opposite is true in Japan, Singapore, Thailand, Portugal, Spain, Latin America, Italy, Sardinia, Malta, and Tunisia – and it is considered rude to beckon with your palm facing upward.[40]

Don't put your hands on your hips: many people will think you're challenging them. This holds true in such widely dispersed countries as Mexico, Saudi Arabia, Singapore and the Scandinavian region.[41]

Don't show the soles of your shoes or feet to Indians, Arabs, Taiwanese, Malaysians and Thais. Feet and shoes are considered unclean, and keeping them out of sight is a matter of social courtesy. Indians even apologize to one another when they accidentally touch with their shoes.[42]

Watch your posture too. Koreans, Indonesians and Taiwanese are sensitive about the crossing of legs. Generally they feel it is rude because they think whoever does it is presuming a premature familiarity. Indonesians consider sitting erect with feet flat on the floor as proper behaviour in the presence of elders. This same posture impresses the Japanese and Koreans. These Asians and northern Europeans share this bias for the 'proper' posture, which is both upright and more formal. Americans are the complete opposite, in that they prefer to be relaxed at meetings and naturally slouch in their chairs. Sometimes this leaves the impression thay they are rude and arrogant, but they don't mean to appear that way. They don't know any better![43]

The next point is touchy: when you can't control your bodily functions, you may tarnish the pleasant relations you are trying to establish. For example, be careful with Koreans and Saudi Arabians, they are sensitive about guests who sneeze, blow their nose, cough, cluck, hiccup, and so forth. You may be more relaxed with Americans, who are more at home with such exigencies. But don't fart loudly in public anywhere! Burping is also taboo in most countries.[44]

Expressions of salutation using hand gestures are also important to know about. The ceremonial formalism of Asians is reflected in a variety of greeting behaviour using a bow. Thais are extremely elaborate in their use of the *wai,* which is a way of distinguishing between those who belong to the higher and lower echelons of society. People of both the higher and lower levels incline their heads until they meet the thumbs of both hands, the palms being held up together, with fingers pointed upwards. The person in the inferior social position initiates the *wai* when meeting with a person of a superior level, and then the superior person reciprocates. Historically the *wai* was used by weaker men to prove that they were unarmed; in addition, they lowered their eyes and heads to emphasize that they were harmless. A person in a very superior position, such as the king or queen, does not have to perform the *wai* in return, but most people in a superior position will return the gesture to be courteous. Thais also offer the *wai* to monks and to sacred objects and places like temples or to the elephant god. Male visitors unfamiliar with the social rules covering the *wai* should merely shake hands with male

Thais and offer female Thais a courteous half-smile. If you want to use the *wai*, here are a few rules you should know about: do not use the *wai* on lower-status people such as servants, labourers or children; if the high *wai* is offered to you, respond with the low *wai*. It would be safe for you to offer the *wai* to monks and older Thais. The proper way of showing respect is to lower your head and body rather than raise your hands.[45]

Malays in Singapore and Malaysia practise the *salaam* ritual, which is performed with a member of the same sex. It is similar to hand-shaking. Usually Malay men and women do not shake hands with one another, but Malay women greet Malay men with a *salaam* only if the man's hand is covered with a cloth – a sign that he has ritually cleansed himself before praying. You execute the *salaam* by offering both hands to your friend, lightly touching the friend's outstretched hands and then bringing your own up to your breast. This translates as: 'I greet you from my heart.' The procedure is slightly more elaborate among women in the rural areas.[46]

You should not hazard an encounter with the Japanese without some briefing beforehand on how the bow is correctly done. Greater respect, gratitude, sincerity and humility are indicated by a bow that is lower and held for a longer period of time. Usually the Japanese use three kinds of bow. The 'informal' bow is used for casual occasions or when people of equal rank are dealing with one another. Here you bend you body at a 15-degree angle while keeping your hands at your sides. With the 'formal' bow, you bend your body at a 30-degree angle, hold your hands together, palms down, touching your knees. Normally you keep this position for about two to three seconds, then once again stretch to your upright position. Bows are usually repeated several times, and a practical problem arises when you don't know when to terminate the constant reciprocation of bowing. It would be safe for you to bow about three times only, making your first bow the deepest and gradually raising your head to the last bow. You probably won't ever use the third or 'deep' bow; more properly called the *saikeirei*, it is the traditional form of bowing as commonly used by the elderly who wish to preserve their heritage.[47]

Less ceremonial forms of bowing are practised in India and Taiwan. Indians exchange greetings with the *namaste* gesture.

You hold your hands together, palms touching, and fingers pointing upwards; this is accompanied by a nod of your head. The Taiwanese appreciate a simple and slight bow to indicate politeness during business meetings.[48]

Other than the bow, enthusiastic handshaking and kissing of the cheeks are also used for greeting in many parts of the world. Saudi Arabians extend their left hand to the vistor's right shoulder and kiss both the cheeks, after which they hold the visitor's hands for a long period of time to show friendship. Latin Americans enthusiastically offer double handshakes and warm hugs, together with a light buzz on both cheeks, even among mere acquaintances; the hugs are known as *abrazos*. North Americans, incidentally, feel that using both hands in a handshake is a phony gesture.[49]

Most Europeans and North Americans shake hands lightly as a form of greeting. They don't quite take as long, nor are they so frequent, as the handshakes given by Latin Americans, but nevertheless they are friendly. An exception is the West German who shakes hands vigorously and frequently; one study showed the average West German employee spent 20 per cent of the time shaking hands. When meeting a group, it is customary to shake the hands of the most senior in position or the oldest member first. In addition, you should shake hands with *everyone* at a gathering; if you miss somebody, this is considered rude.[50]

Space management and office layout

International differences are very apparent in the use of the environmental space within which people work and live. Here our main interest, of course, is the workplace, so we won't talk about what people's homes are like.

Americans associate higher status with larger spaces. The person with the most power in a company is the president, and his or her office is usually the largest and most private one; it is often in a corner of the building, high up, with a nice view. This office is followed in size by that of the vice-president, then the division managers and finally departmental managers. Countries such as Taiwan, Singapore, Thailand and the Philippines also associate larger office space with higher rank and status. Americans, though, seem to appreciate space and privacy the most. This is probably because of the country's enormous size. Businesses there have traditionally used incredible amounts of space to construct their offices and buildings. You will also notice that Americans like to place their desks near walls. The center of the room is usually left open for traffic and human interaction.[51]

Europeans arrange their offices quite differently. Authority flows from the middle of the room outwards, not from the corners inwards, as in the USA. Usually desks are placed in the middle of the room. Top executives and managers in France, Latin America and Mediterranean Europe have their desks situated amid open departmental areas. They feel it is easier to exert control from the middle. Following their traditional management rules, these managers prefer to keep an eye physically on their subordinates. Britons and West Germans, though, are highly protective of their office space. Often they keep their office doors shut, entering without a previous appointment is considered very rude.[52]

Higher-level Japanese executives have office suites of their own. The size of the office space usually is in direct proportion to the power the executive holds. At the departmental level senior managers are usually located near windows, if there are any, but they will also have full view of the entire department. Junior personnel are usually situated in the middle of the department's office.[53]

Offices of the most senior Saudi Arabian officials are enormous and luxurious, but they are also crowded with official guests, friends and relatives. The crowding becomes acute in the smaller, cramped offices of lower-level officials and executives of smaller firms. This may be confusing if you are unused to seeing a crowd of people over which the receptionists exercise little control. The *majiles* system in Saudi Arabia allows friends, relatives and countrymen of the top official to enter at almost any time. These people have higher priority, and Saudis will interrupt ongoing business meetings just to attend to the needs of their nearer kin; guests already in the office simply have to be patient. Those waiting outside will have to be even more patient – and be prepared for people walking in ahead of them.[54]

How to tell when somebody is lying to you by reading their body language

A higher-level body language skill is that of the ability to detect lies. Paul Ekman and his colleagues compiled concrete guidelines for detecting lies in their recommendable book, *Telling Lies*. Detecting lies is a somewhat elusive task, complicated by the fact that there may be really no signs of deceit. You must be able to select and piece together clues from a barrage of information revealed by the different parts of TOS's body simultaneously. Your knowledge of TOS and the context of the situation within which the lie or truth fits will help you reach the correct conclusion. A good way to begin is to look at the face, listen to the words and look at the body movements (emblems, illustrators and manipulators) of TOS.

The face

Most people are unskilled in the art of detecting lies. We pay more attention to people's words and faces, but both of these are highly manipulable.[55] And words are easier to falsify than the face. It's confusing to interpret the face because it expresses both voluntary and involuntary movements. Unlike words, the face is connected with parts of the brain directly involved with emotions.[56] For instance, facial movements for the emotions of sadness, sorrow and grief are very hard to act out. To express these emotions, you have to pull the corners of your lips downwards without moving a chin muscle.[57] Try it in front of your mirror – you will find that this is hard to do. Here we discuss six facial 'leakages' that will help you to detect lies.

Smiles are one of the most unreliable signals to interpret because people use them so often to mask their true emotions. What is more, there are more than 50 different kinds of smile, and dozens of other expressions for one particular emotion can accompany a smile.[58] These expressions are hard to detect because they don't last very long; they are referred to as 'micro-expressions'. These facial movements, then, reveal the true and concealed emotion, but they flash on and off in less than one-quarter of a second; it's easy for an untrained observer to miss such expressions. One hour's training, though, will sensitize you to them. Ekman tells the story of a psychiatric patient who told her doctors that she was no longer depressed and then requested a weekend pass to enable her to visit her family. The truth in fact was that she wished to get away in order to commit suicide. How did the psychiatrist find this out? She was filmed when talking to her doctor, the film was played in slow motion and a micro-expression of complete sadness manifested itself for a fleeting instant, with a quick smile following this micro-expression. They didn't give her the pass.[59]

The second facial leakage is the 'squelched expression'. This happens when you become aware of an expression that's emerging on your face that you do not want to show, so you quickly interrupt it and cover it with another expression or mask, such as a smile; the squelched expression is usually an incomplete expression, but it lasts longer than the micro-expression and is consequently easier to spot.[60]

The third facial leakage is an asymmetrical, or crooked, facial expression. This happens when you try to fake an emotion and you're not very good at it. When you do this, it appears on both sides of your face, but it's much stronger on one side of your face than the other. These asymmetrical or crooked facial expressions indicate that you aren't genuinely feeling the emotion that you are attempting to represent.[61] One study asked one group of people to smile deliberately to express happiness. A second group smiled spontaneously and genuinely. There were many more crooked or asymmetrical smiles in the spurious group than in the genuine one; and right-handed fakers had stronger expressions on the left sides of their faces, and vice versa.[62]

The fourth facial leakage has to do with how long the facial expression lasts – i.e. both the time it takes to appear and to disappear. Most facial expressions that last longer than four to five seconds are phoney ones. However, extreme emotions last on the face for much longer – ten seconds or more. Expression of less extreme emotions won't last that long. You can be almost certain that your subordinates are feigning amusement at one of your jokes if they continue laughing long after the punch line is over.[63] Look out for smiles that are dropped too abruptly – they are almost always false.[64]

The fifth facial signal of falsehood appears in relation to the body movements, voice changes and flow of speech: it is really easy to tell when you're falsifying anger. If the angry expression appears on the face only after saying: 'I'm fed up with your behaviour', or after the fist is banged on the table, there's a reasonable basis to suspect faking. When telling the truth, they appear simultaneously.[65]

The sixth signal of facial deceit concerns movement of the eyes. Ordinarily, the eyes can be easily used to deceive. Watch out for blinking and pupil dilation. Both of these occur involuntarily when you are emotionally aroused. Here the only difficulty is that these two movements don't tell you which particular emotions are being felt – just that they are being experienced strongly. Watch out also for tears. They are hard to fake, even for experienced actors and actresses. Our autonomic nervous system produces them involuntarily whenever we're distressed or sad or relieved or laugh uncontrollably.[66]

Words

You can tell if a person is lying to you with words by looking out for slips of the tongue, tirades and the voice itself. Freud believed that the ordinary errors we make in our daily life, such as slips of the tongue, forgetting of familiar names and mistakes in reading and writing are symptoms of internal conflict within us.[67] Speech errors and pauses occur when you're caught in a situation where you feel compelled to lie but are unprepared to do so. It happens, for instance, when somebody asks you a question that you didn't anticipate, and you didn't rehearse your lines ahead of time. Or even when you've prepared amply, for just the simple fear of being found out will produce such errors.[68] A tirade is an outpouring of information that takes place when you're carried away by some emotion; in the process you may well unknowingly reveal damaging information.[69] Watch for tirades: they are valuable sources of honest information. The voice is also a rich source of clues to deception. Listen to the pitch of the voice. It increases whenever you lie. But a high-pitched voice by itself is not a reliable sign because it also accompanies genuine expressions of fear, anger and excitement.[70]

Body movements – emblems

You must also closely watch body movements for clues. Pay attention to 'emblems'. These are movements that have specific meaning within a particular culture. Examples are the shrug when Americans want to say 'I don't know', 'I'm helpless' or 'What does it matter?'; the head nod indicating 'yes'; the 'come-here' beckoning gesture; the hitchhiker's thumb; and so forth. We have already referred to some of these emblems.

An emblematic slip is an excellent sign of the concealment of information. There are two ways to detect this slip. First, look out for a *fragment* of an emblem – for instance, a complete shrug is usually performed by (1) raising both shoulders; (2) by raising the eyebrows, drooping the upper eyelids and shaping the mouth into a horseshoe; (3) by turning up both palms; or (4) by tilting the head sideways. Any combination of these emblems may also occur. When you show only a fragment of an emblem, you are usually lying. For example, you only turn up *one* of your palms; you push up only your lower lip; or you only raise one shoulder; and so on.[71] The second way to detect a lie is to look for an emblem that is performed outside the ordinary position – for instance, when medical students were subjected to stressful interviews, one of them gave the interviewing professor the finger from her knee instead of thrusting her finger right in front of her face, which is the usual spot from which this obscene gesture is done.[72]

The second group of body movements that you should keep an eye open for are known as 'illustrators' because people make these movements to illustrate what they are saying – examples include tracing in the air your flow of thought or drawing a picture in space to emphasize what you are saying. The clue to deceit is simple here: look for a significant decrease in the number of illustrators that TOS would usually use (obviously, you must already know TOS's usual body movements to use this clue effectively). Here is why a decrease in the number of illustrators usually means that TOS is lying: (1) the decrease shows a lack of emotional investment in what TOS is saying – e.g. people tend to be less animated when they are bored, disinterested, depressed or saddened; and (2) people don't use the same number of illustrators when they aren't quite sure what to say, and deceit may or may not be involved in this case – e.g. the sales rep making a pitch for the first time before an unfamiliar and hostile audience may be so cautious about the verbal content of his/her canned presentation that he/she leaves out all hand gestures, in other words, this is not lying, but caution.[73]

Body movements: manipulators

'Manipulators' are those movements where one part of the body touches, rubs, picks, scratches or seeks some other kind of contact with another part of the body. Pay *very* close attention to them too. Here we talk about them not so much because they indicate deception in themselves, but rather because it is all too easy to impute deception when these movements are made. Remember, you may be wrong. People use many manipulators both when they are relaxed and when they are tense. Therefore manipulators are unreliable clues to deceit. One such manipulator gesture that almost always indicates lying, though, is talking with your hand in front of your mouth.[74]

Lying: eight guidelines

Detecting lies is the hardest part of interpreting TOS's body language. If, however, you follow these eight general pointers, and practice a lot, 'you will eventually get better at it.[75] But you'll never become an expert at detecting lies unless you make it your life-study. Start with these guidelines, but don't stop there. (We go into this subject in more detail in our seminars. You might want to attend one of them, or read some of the books and articles we've cited.)

First, analyse your reasons for suspecting that TOS may be lying. This will help you weed out unsound preconceptions and biases that you may have.

Secondly, be open to the possibility of committing the two most common errors in lie detection – not believing the truth, and believing the lie.

Thirdly, the absence of clues to deceit in TOS's body movements does not mean they are truthful. Conversely, the presence of some of these signs is no guarantee that TOS is lying. In the early 1970s, John Dean, a former aide to US President Richard Nixon, gave a remarkable performance during the Watergate hearings held by the US Senate. This was due, in part, to the absence of emotion in his voice. Dean was a gifted actor, and his own words let us know this: 'It would be easy to overdramatize, or to seem too flip about my testimony ... I would, I decided, read evenly, unemotionally, as coldly as possible, and answer questions the same way.... . People tend to think that somebody telling the truth will be calm about it.'[76]

Fourthly, re-examine yourself and see if there are any other factors that may cloud your judgement. Are you jealous of, or angry at, TOS? If you are, it's going to be easy for you to have an overemotional reaction to whatever TOS does.

Fifthly, keep an open mind about TOS's signs of emotion. These may not actually be clues for reading deceit, but rather the reactions of TOS to being suspected of lying. Make sure you're certain TOS knows you suspect him or her in order for you to make a valid judgement.

Sixthly, if you have good reason to believe TOS is lying, you may want to use Lykken's Guilty Knowledge Technique, together with a polygraph test. (You can't do this with a business partner; often you can't do it even with an employee, for the law may not allow it.) The polygraph is a machine which shows if a person is under stress; it does not indicate a lie *per se,* but people are usually under more stress when they lie than when they tell the truth. The Guilty Knowledge Technique uses a battery of questions. It assumes the person who takes the test is covering up a lie, and it investigates further into the person's knowledge of the details of the situation that it is supposed is being lied about. The psychologist who devised this technique found that changes occur in the autonomic nervous system of persons who are lying and are confronted with the one correct alternative to the question they are answering at that moment.[77]

Seventhly, never consider as final the conclusion you reach about whether TOS is lying or telling the truth, based on the behavioural or body clues you notice. Always look for further information because you may have missed some important clues. Put all the clues you gather into clusters to see if they all point in the same direction. Some clues may contradict others. Look at *all* the clues within the context of the situation in which they were detected in the first place.

Eighthly, it is hard enough to tell if somebody within your own country and from your own culture is lying to you. As we have said; this is the hardest part of body language. But imagine how much harder it will be to tell if somebody from a different country and culture is lying to you, or telling you the truth. In short, you must watch TOS even more closely when they are from other parts of the world. The 'guru' of lie detection is Paul Ekman, and his findings are based on scientific research that was carried out mostly in the USA. Elsewhere the art of detecting lies is still at an early stage of development. (We are looking into this subject ourselves, as are other researchers. We'll report it in a future book.)

Guidelines for increasing your sensitivity to body language

Before turning to our final checklist of pointers which will help sharpen your ability to read body language across cultures, remember the following seven guidelines about body language in general:[78]

(1) First of all, strive for self-understanding at all times. Although this does not absolutely guarantee that you'll interpret TOS's body language accurately, it will at least establish an attitude of maintaining mental openness and patience when observing others. This attitude is most important to developing your skills.

(2) Persevere in your efforts to be more and more observant of detail when you analyse body language. You'll often be confronted by a barrage of data, and it will be hard to sift the relevant information from all of that.

(3) Always interpret TOS's body language from their own cultural perspective. Learn the body language code of the particular culture you're dealing with. Don't assume from what you may have read in popular literature that body language is universal. There are many differences, and we've pointed out only a very few in this chapter.

(4) Always look for a *cluster* of gestures, and consider them within the situational context in which they take place. Do not try to read the body language clues you observe as you would a dictionary, that is looking up the meaning for one word or

gesture at a time. It doesn't work that way! Interrelate the gestures as you observe them; and observe a person's gesture clusters over a certain period of time, to make sure you interpret them accurately. The following is an example of what we mean.

Look at this distinguished-looking woman executive. She is apparently chairing a department meeting. She appears to conduct herself professionally – she is sitting erect, nods at her subordinates' suggestions, echoes some of their mannerisms and smiles sparingly to give the impression that she's in command. So far, all her gestures indicate that she's a competent and credible boss. However, she occasionally covers her mouth with her hand, especially when the group breaks out in laughter. Occasionally she does this too when she speaks. If you took a 'cookbook' approach in interpreting her movements, you would think she was trying to cover up something or isn't completely trustworthy. (Remember covering you mouth when you speak is a manipulator gesture.) If you stopped there, though, you'd be wrong about this executive. Watch her more closely, talk to her a little. You'll discover after talking to her that she's candid enough to admit that she recently had orthodontic work done on her teeth. The dental wiring, she explains, prevents her from laughing freely and once in a while she feels the need to cover her mouth when she talks. With this new piece of information, your interpretation changes completely. Thus a more accurate and fairer picture of her performance in the department meeting emerges. All her gestures in the meeting, save the minor detail of occasionally covering her mouth, indicate that a professional executive is in charge. Knowing the context – the fact that she had just recently had orthodontic treatment – means that your initial suspicion that she may be lying or covering up something was wrong.

(5) Our own cultural biases colour and complicate the way we perceive and interpret the actions of people from other cultures. We also often project our *own* qualities on to the people we're observing, especially when we lack a frame of reference from which to interpet what they are saying or doing. Thus you should consult someone from the culture you're observing; compare notes and clarify your first interpretations.

(6) Be greedy for knowledge about TOS. The more you know

about them, the more powerful you are when you negotiate; the less you know about them, the less powerful you are. *Knowledge is power.* Get your knowledge by observing TOS. Knowing how to interpret body language is a skill, and as with any skill, you must practise it often to stay skilful. Practise by watching people all the time, even when you're *not* negotiating. Try to guess what's on their mind. If you watch people often enough, you will eventually become skilled in accurately reading body language.

(7) Never let TOS know that *you* know how to read body language successfully. That will frighten TOS so much that they will 'freeze up' whenever you are around. This promotes dishonesty, not honesty. And honesty, on both sides, is crucial for the success of any negotiation.

Cross-cultural body language checklist

Here is a simple checklist you can use to sharpen your observational ability, and your ability to interpret cross-cultural body language. We need to emphasize that your most important job, in this respect, is actually to learn the body language code of the specific country you are interested in before you can hope to interpret accurately what TOS's gestures mean. Thus the checklist is a simple means for sensitizing you to the nuances of gesture used in another culture. After you have answered all the questions on the checklist, you will still need to consult with experts to see if you have accurately interpreted the meanings of the observed gestures. In other words, we present the checklist in order that you can make up your own comprehensive list of what gestures mean in a particular country and culture. You will find it difficult to find ready-to-use, comprehensive cookbook guides to cross-cultural body language, however, so you'll have to make up your own guides, using the checklist as a starting-point. It will be a rewarding challenge to compile your own dictionary of 'dos and taboos' in your country of interest, backed up, perhaps, by the first-hand interpretation of natives of that country, or of expatriate residents, who know the culture well.

The scene

Where were the people meeting? What was the ambience or atmosphere of the location? Did it look clean, efficient, business-like, private, crowded, well-decorated or modern-looking or traditional-looking? How did the surroundings affect the tenor of the meeting? Was there a lot of space available for people to use? Why do you think they chose this particular place? What kind of behaviour did this particular location seem to inspire?

The subjects

Who were these people at the meeting? Their sex? Occupation? Race? Age? Educational attainment? Social class membership? Were they people of some status or reputation? If so, how did this affect the meeting? How did they look? Were they well-dressed – e.g. in business suits, expensive informal wear or faddish wear? What were their hair styles like? Their accessories? Did their clothing affect their behaviour? Was their interaction pleasant? Were they having a good time? Did the meeting appear to be accomplishing its goals? Was it a business meeting or a social meeting, or both? Did the people look satisfied? Relaxed? Tense? Uneasy?

Touch behaviour

Did you observe any form of deliberate physical contact when these people met? Did they shake hands, hug, embrace, kiss each other's cheeks or kiss on the lips? If so, for how long and how often? Did their bodily contact seem to serve some purpose such as expressing friendship, emphasizing support or reinforcing a point? Were all the parties comfortable about the physical contact? Did any one of them flinch or back off? Were they all from the same culture? Who initiated the bodily contact? What was the effect of their bodily contact? Even after the initial salutation, did they continue to engage in some form of bodily contact? If so, of what kind? If there was no bodily contact, how did they conduct themselves and facilitate their meeting?

Facial messages

Did these people use their faces much to help express the verbal content of the conversation or meeting? Who was more expressive? Who was less expressive? Why? Did you notice the momentary 'flicker of truth' in their faces – i.e. fleeting signs of disgust, anger, boredom, annoyance, and so forth? Or perhaps a minor droop of an eyelid or a slight motion of the eyebrow? How often did these micro-expressions take place? What do you think they meant? Did smiles come easily to their faces? Did their facial expressions vary in intensity throughout the conversation? Did you sense that the people present were sincere and honest towards one another, given their facial expressions? If a superior and a subordinate were meeting, did you notice any peculiar way the superior looked at his/her subordinate – e.g. did the superior acknowledge the subordinate with an abstracted glance or perhaps a minuscule smile or an open smile followed by a handshake? Did you sense that the emotional climate of the conversation changed as the facial expressions changed? How?

Eye movements

Did the people at the gathering look one another in the eye? Did they gaze at one another? If so, how often and for how long? Do you think they were comfortable doing this? How do you think their eye behaviours affected the atmosphere of the meeting? Or if there was little eye contact, what did the people look at most of the time? How did they look at one another on the few occasions that they did? Did they blink much? Did a lack of generous eye contact seem to undermine the meeting? Was anybody uncomfortable with the consistent gaze or intense eye contact of TOS? Did they belong to the same cultures? If not, can you explain the differences in the eye behaviour you observed, based on their different cultures?

Their postures

What postures were assumed by the people at the meeting? Did each person stand and sit? Or was one standing while the other sat? Why? Were they relaxed or tense? Was any person's body held upright and rigid or was there a general looseness in the way they carried their bodies? Did their postures reflect their degree of comfort? What effect did their postures have on the atmosphere of the meeting? Did they change posture during their conversation? Were they leaning back or forward? At what angle did pairs face each other? Were they positioned in such a way that others were excluded from their space? How did they position their arms and legs? Did such positions communicate openness or closedness? Were the postures of one person echoed by others? What do you think was the effect of copying the postures?

Space and body movements

How did these people handle the physical distance between them? Was there a large or small distance between them? Approximately, what was the conversational distance between them? Who approached whom? Who backed off? Why do you think this happened? How did they enter the space within which they met? If it wasn't a public space, but an office, did they knock and wait to be asked in? How did they shake hands? Did you see a 'limp fish' handshake, a firm handshake or a 'heavy-duty' hand grip? When they shook hands, how far did they extend their arms to reach for TOS's hands? Did you notice other peculiar hand gestures? Was there a lot of bodily movement? What were these? Did you notice any signs of being ill at ease such as tugging at the ear lobes, chewing a lip or playing with the hair, beard or moustache? Did the gestures communicate sincerity and truth? Did you detect any other gesture that might indicate lying? What were these gestures? Did they occur frequently? What were their 'turn-taking' signals in the conversations? How did they indicate to TOS that it was time for them to go?

A final word

Continue working on the above checklist, change it, add to it, subtract from it. Include details that are more pertinent to the situations you observe. Always remember, though, that it is important to find an expert in the culture that you are investigating who can interpret these gestures for you. The best arrangement is for you to work with an expert while you're observing people. Take the expert with you. Experts will be able to interpret the gestures most effectively if they witness the actual context within which the gestures take place.

After you have developed you own detailed checklists, one for each nation you deal with, try to summarize body language behaviours of each nation by making up a chart like the one in Table 4.1. This chart is taken from my book *Battling for Profits* (Don Hendon); it doesn't really oversimplify this complicated subject, it just may prove a succinct aid to help you to remember which are the gestures which show interest and which show hostility. That, then, is really the essence of using body language: divide up each gesture you see into 'interest' and 'hostility' gestures. If TOS responds to your negotiating tactics with many 'interest' gestures, keep on doing what you're doing, it's working. But if TOS responds with

Table 4.1 The basics of body language: how to read the other person like a book

Show negative feelings	Gestures	Show positive feelings
Crossed	Arms	Open
Crossed	Legs	Open
Lean back	Overall position of body	Sit forward
Turned away from you	Position of head	Turned towards you
Doodling	Writing during your presentation	Taking notes
Always very straight	Back	Curved, more flexible
Far away	Distance from you	Fairly close
Left on top of right	Positions of thumbs when hands are together	Right on top of left
Raised high	Shoulders	Normal position
Rubbing the nose	Hand-to-face gestures	Patting the head

many 'hostile' gestures, change what you're doing because it's not winning TOS over to your point of view.

Notice we have said, 'gestures', not 'gesture'. That is because you should *never* judge what is on TOS's mind based on just *one* gesture. That may be really misleading. Wait until you've seen several gestures. Put them into 'interest' clusters and 'hostile' clusters. If most of TOS's gestures fall into the 'hostile' cluster, you can be pretty certain that TOS's attitude is negative. When this happens, you should start to change your tactics. Not only that, you should also start making a lot of positive body language gestures. Even if TOS doesn't know the nuances of body language – and the chances are that TOS does not – your positive gestures will usually lead to positive body language gestures on the part of TOS. And since our body language echoes what is going on in our mind, TOS's new positive body language will probably lead to positive thoughts and a probable acceptance of your viewpoint.

We talk about this in the body language section of our negotiating seminars, and those who have attended were usually sceptical at first; you may be sceptical too. To prove to yourself that your positive body language gestures will lead to positive thoughts on the part of TOS, and that your negative body language gestures will lead to negative thoughts on the part of TOS, try the following exercise.

Get together with another person. Pretend you're the seller and have TOS pretend that he or she is the buyer. Tell the buyer that no matter what you do, he/she should make all the negative body language gestures he/she can think of – i.e. lean back, cross arms, make both hands made into a fist, cross legs, frown, etc. Then tell the buyer that neither one of you will talk – each of you will just stare at the other. For the first 30 seconds you will make all the negative body language gestures that you can think of. Then say, 'I'm going to change now'. At this point, make all the positive body language gestures you can think of – e.g. open arms, open legs, lean forward, smile, etc. Continue your positive gestures for another 30 seconds. Then stop and ask the buyer what went on in his/her mind when you were making negative gestures, and what went on when you were making positive gestures. Most buyers will say they felt *even more* negative when you were echoing their negative body language, and that they felt *very positive* when you made positive body language gestures. In fact they may well find it hard to continue their negative body language gestures during the second 30 seconds.

Then exchange roles – i.e. you become the buyer, and TOS becomes the seller. Do the same thing. You, the buyer, continue to make negative body language gestures throughout the one-minute exercise, no matter what the seller does. For the first 30 seconds, the seller echoes your negative body language gestures, and for the next 30 seconds, the seller makes nothing but positive body language gestures. Now that you're the buyer, see how you feel as you notice negative and then positive body language gestures. You will probably feel as TOS did when they were role-playing the buyer. The chances are that you will no longer be sceptical after this exercise is over about the great, yet subtle, power of body language. It is one of the most powerful tools a negotiator uses. We know it's helped us a lot over the years in our negotiations and in our daily lives.

But heed this warning: *Never* let TOS know you can 'read' their body language. If you do, TOS will immediately tighten up and won't trust you. Always keep your knowledge a secret and use it to your advantage. If TOS knows that you know what is going on in his/her mind, TOS will become even more secretive, and your negotiations will deteriorate steadily. And neither one of you wants that to happen!

Appendix to Part II: Answers to exercises

Situation 1: A square peg in a round hole (page 55)

1 This is incorrect. From the account, there is no indication that Lou's team members felt any trace of racial discrimination against him.
2 This is incorrect. Again, the story does not indicate this.
3 This is the best answer. A direct opposition in work styles is involved here. Although trained and experienced in teamwork, Americans are used to 'going it alone', while the Japanese think and move as a group. Americans watch the clock. When it's quitting time, it's time to leave. In this respect, the lives of Americans are more compartmentalized. Their philosophy is different – there is a right time for work and a right time for leisure activities. To the Japanese, work takes a number-one priority in their lives, and they would be embarrassed to leave their work before their boss. Working overtime and at weekends is common practice. Lou's teammates don't perceive him to be as involved as they are, and so they think Lou doesn't feel like he's part of the team.

Situation 2: The lady wants to be a manager (page 56)

1 This is incorrect. Although the president had a good working knowledge of his key people, he didn't have any special feelings of liking or disliking towards Laurie.

2 This is incorrect. Japanese firms with plants in the USA realize that managerial positions should be open to all Americans in order to foster harmonious relationships and attract talented people.

3 This is the best answer. Japanese women still hold inferior jobs such as serving tea. The perceptual stereotype held by Japanese men is that women aren't equal to men in the working world. Although Laurie is an American woman, her status is still undermined by this perception. Japanese executives still aren't too comfortable with the progress and career-mindedness of American women.

Situation 3: The designer from Paris (page 57)

1 This is the best answer. First of all, her Paris office should have prepared her better for this business trip. Of course, she is also largely responsible for her behaviour, and so she should have taken it upon herself to get some kind of training before she left. The Japanese value personal relationships, and under the concept of *ningen kankei,* such personal relationships should first be nourished before getting down to business. Christine's obvious mistake was to discuss her presentation right away without first spending more time personally relating to her audience. She relied completely on her firm's past relationship with this Japanese firm and thought that she was spared the necessity of going through the process of establishing relations again. This, then, constitutes a serious mistake in Japan, where the obligation to refresh relationships is even greater where such relationships are ongoing.

2 This is incorrect. The story didn't indicate this.

3 This is incorrect. Her slide presentation should have been adequate.

Situation 4: A matter of discretion (page 58)

1 This is incorrect. The Japanese president didn't say anything about disliking the product *per se.*
2 This is incorrect. Ted did a thorough and enthusiastic selling job.
3 This is the best answer. The Japanese president acted out of group loyalty. In this case, he considered his role as a Japanese citizen. To express his loyalty to Japan, he thought it was best not to distribute a product that made his people appear promiscuous. Here saving face is a strong issue as well.

Situation 5: The 'velvet glove' approach (page 59)

1 This is incorrect. Japanese executives are usually well prepared before meetings. The president was surely briefed that his subordinates had already studied the proposal.
2 This is the best answer. The Japanese approach is not confrontational, and they have great difficulty saying 'no'. In this case, since Carlo's company has an ongoing relationship with this chain, it was even more difficult for the executives directly to turn him down. They sent positive signals, mistakenly thinking this was the better way of treating Carlos which, of course, it was not.
3 This is incorrect. The Japanese weren't really interested in selling the product.

Situation 6: It's a matter of principle (page 60)

1 This is the best answer. The Chinese believe in establishing trust by agreeing on principles first, rather than contractual items – these come later. Such principles are also anchored in good faith that the parties involved will meet the pressing needs of the other. The Chinese firm felt slighted when, by their perception, Rutger wasn't following, in principle, the spirit of their earlier agreement. Of course, there are a number of complicating factors here: Rutger claimed that the particular piece of equipment they wanted wasn't covered in the list of items involved in this transaction. His mistake was that when

he gave the technical seminar, he talked about all his products, including those not yet available for export to Asia. The Chinese misunderstood this and thought that *all* products which they really needed would be made available to them, in keeping with their agreement in principle. Of course, Rutger had extra difficulties back-tracking, because his second audience was different except for one person – i.e. the negotiation leader.

2   This is incorrect. The X-ray spectrometer wasn't available in Asia because of the difficulty of maintaining the equipment in countries where workers aren't highly skilled. It was merely a matter of time before it was to be made available.

3   This may be partly correct. But then, leaving certain terms vague in order to extract concessions later on, is a common practice everywhere.

Situation 7: Please, send back the white flowers (page 61)

1   This is incorrect. Besides, children aren't usually included in business meetings, not even in informal business/social gatherings.

2   This is the best answer. The Chinese custom is to display white flowers on the occasion of someone's death or during a funeral.

3   This is incorrect. The story does not indicate this.

Situation 8: You can do it (page 62)

1   This is incorrect. There is no indication of this in the story.

2   This is the best answer. Dudley was apparently well prepared for his job, in that he had full understanding of the Chinese need to save face. If he admitted Peter's inadequacy in the meeting, he would have lost Peter completely. He thought it was more productive to make Peter look good and accomplish two things: encourage Peter, and commit him to the goals of the training group.

3   This is incorrect. Dudley had an effective managerial style. He didn't need to resort to flattery to get the support of his trainees.

Situation 9: Questionable procurement (page 62)

1 This is incorrect. However, in real life, relationships between friends in such a situation could easily lead to mutual financial benefits.

2 Again, incorrect: Richard's nationality had nothing to do with the decision.

3 This is the best answer. The Chinese value personal relationships in business. Personal contacts are an assurance that TOS can be trusted and that special service will be delivered. In this case, the two Chinese managers valued their personal contacts *(guan-xi)* over and above the rational consideration for the future benefits the French machinery would have given them.

Situation 10: Going a bit too far (page 63)

1 This is partly true, but it doesn't tell you why Henry resigned in the first place.

2 This is the best answer. The Chinese *guan-xi* relationship at work calls for the person in the superior position to act not only as one's boss on the job, but also as one's helper in personal matters. In this case, Henry expected Leonard to assist his cousin by writing the letter of recommendation. In Henry's eyes, that was a small favour to ask of his boss. To Leonard, who is British, such a request is highly improper and unethical, especially because deception is involved: how can he recommend someone he doesn't know?

3 This is incorrect. There was no indication in the story that Leonard became distant (or desired to be) to Henry.

Situation 11: Watch your agent (page 64)

1 This is incorrect. There's no indication in the story that the agent had this problem.

2 This is the best answer. Agents in Saudi Arabia often over-commit themselves, and foreign clients need to follow-up quite actively. Often an overenthusiastic agent will promise to get the job done in an unrealistically short time. This creates a

frustrating situation because the client's expectations are inflated. Meanwhile the agent gets tangled up in a number of simultaneous commitments and doesn't really feel too guilty about neglecting certain clients because interfering responsibilities would merely be seen as being 'part of God's plan'. It is imperative that you study the organizational setup of your prospective agents and observe their 'track record' in fulfilling their commitments.

3   This is incorrect. Agents usually take charge of and oversee projects such as the construction of warehouses. It is also quite clear, in this example, that this was the agent's responsibility.

Situation 12: Unexpected visit (page 65)

1   This is partly true. Eating enthusiastically and chewing loudly are offensive to Saudis (and other nationalities too) – especially during Ramadan, the Muslim month of fasting.

2   This is incorrect. She is expected to be proud of her company's products.

3   This is the best answer. Kathleen should have been briefed that Saudis don't eat or drink in daylight hours during the holy month of Ramadan. It is true, though, that the circumstances of the assignment gave her little chance to be prepared for this business trip. Also, since she is a woman, Adnam Beg received her in his house instead of in his office under the setup of the *diwaniyah,* which is still practised by older, more traditionally minded Saudi businessmen. Obviously, Kathleen didn't know this, and if she did, she wouldn't have put Adnam Beg in an embarrassing position by asking to visit his office premises without an invitation. She should have waited for him to invite her to make her presentation in his office. A minor but jarring detail, of course, was the fact that Adnam Beg had a view of the soles of her shoes – a petty breach of etiquette, true, but nevertheless annoying to a Saudi and to other nationalities such as the Thais.

Situation 13: A most unusual meeting (page 66)

1 This is incorrect. Saudi Arabian executives have a very ordered sense of priorities: they value their family members, friends and countrymen above all others. Should they walk in during a meeting (which they're allowed to do), they will be given priority over whatever business matters are being discussed.

2 This is true. André should have had all his visual aids translated into Arabic not only because many technical terms were used, but also because Saudis read from right to left.

3 This could be true but is a minor consideration.

4 This is the greater part of the answer. Obviously inexperienced in doing business in the Middle East, André didn't understand and anticipate the Arabian *majiles* system of receiving business visitors in which simultaneous meetings with various people are conducted. Walk-ins aren't at all ignored, especially if they are family members or friends of the visited party. André was also unfamiliar with the fact that nepotism thrives extensively in Saudi Arabian businesses.

Situation 14: For men only (page 67)

1 This is incorrect. It is true, though that there is some racial discrimination in Australia. Most of it is directed against non-whites and southern Europeans. So there would be little reason for the club to be prejudiced against Natalie.

2 This is incorrect. There is no indication in the story that this club was unusual in this respect.

3 This is the best answer. Male dominance in Australian society stems from the practice of 'mateship', or sticking close together with the boys only. In former days when men had to depend on each other to survive the harsh conditions of the bush, the concept of 'mateship' evolved. It denoted close companionship or a helping relationship with fellow males. In contemporary Australian society there are still strong traces of valuing mateship, expecially among members of the working class. Excluding women from male activities, though, is one of the surviving consequences of mateship in the larger society.

Situation 15: Third World 'cronyism' (page 68)

1 This is incorrect. There is no indication in the story that the world prices of plastic raw materials have increased.

2 This may be partly true, but it is tangential to the best answer.

3 This is the best answer. Instead of saving the local business executives money, the state trading company has been making money out of each transaction. Processing of imports has taken longer because of the artificial bureaucratic procedures that were imposed. The dominance of the extended family in the political élite in Indonesia is a well-known phenomenon – not only in that country, but also in other developing countries, such as the Philippines, particularly during the Marcos era. This kind of 'cronyism' is a reality Henri will have to learn to accept and live with if he is to continue working in Indonesia.

Situation 16: A fish out of water (page 69)

1 This is only partly correct. The law did strike a sensitive emotional chord in Roger.

2 It is true that Roger was trying to bend the rules to suit his views, but he wasn't really trying to reform company policies. So this is incorrect.

3 This is incorrect. The rationale for the law very clearly favours *bumiputra* participation in the Malaysian economy. This was plain to see, and Roger understood.

4 This is the best answer. Roger didn't really expect himself to react negatively to the government's employment guidelines. In fact, Roger had been briefed about these hiring conditions in Malaysia before he arrived. He thought it would be easy to comply with the rules after he was on the job. Until he took this post, he didn't realize how much he valued equality and fair treatment. The hiring situation clearly created a clash of values. Finally, Roger's sense of rationality was violated by a law that prevented him from hiring the best-qualified person.

Situation 17: Sweeteners can be bitter (page 70)

1   This is the best answer, although the Chinese wouldn't refer to it as a 'bribe'. They often offer presents as a sign of gratitude, but more often, as a form of insurance against some future need that may arise. It is 'grist for the mill', so to speak, to keep the mills of favourable relationships turning.

2   The possibility of this being true cannot be disregarded, but it seems more probable that this is not the case.

3   It may have been true that the cost of the motor-car was nothing compared to the means of the giver, and, as a result, it was just a small token. It is certainly true that the Chinese give business gifts, particularly at the time of the Chinese New Year.

Situation 18: The roundabout ways of smooth interpersonal relationships (SIR) (page 71)

1   This is incorrect. If the Philippine company were really interested, its negotiators would have bargained hard while Parker was still in Manila.

2   This is part of the complete answer. Filipinos may be construed as hypocritical by Westerners because of the great difficulty they have in responding frankly. They don't mean to mislead, however. They usually take more time to find more socially desirable ways to handle conflicts of interest and rejection.

3   This is the best answer. Filipinos value maintaining SIR. In dealing with foreign executives and negotiators, they use very positive body language such as smiles. They don't hesitate to invite guests to their home or to exclusive clubs for dinner. They roll out the red carpet, no matter what is in the offing. Foreigners who don't know this may easily misinterpret these signals and think that agreement is imminent. It is easier for Filipinos to express conflict of interest or disagreements in writing. Occasionally they solicit the representation of a third party to iron out the rough edges of a relationship that has floundered.

Situation 19: No better way of doing things (page 72)

1 This is incorrect. Gomez wasn't challenged by Hanan's entry, even though he was now accountable to the foreign newcomer.

2 This is incorrect. Farias was a direct subordinate of Gomez and could not disregard his orders.

3 This is the best answer. Gomez isn't used to non-traditional ways of making decisions. Other executives before him and above him have perpetuated the idea of following company policies in situations such as the one they face. The Mexican branch of this company didn't train its managers to conduct analytical evaluations of situations and experiment with new solutions. Mexicans are tradition-oriented executives.

Situation 20: Caught in the middle (page 73)

1 This is incorrect. Ortiz has healthy professional and social relationships in the company.

2 This is the best answer. Ortiz is caught in a conflict between two different managerial styles, and he can't articulate his dilemma to Gonsalves. He has not developed the level of trust required to make it comfortable for him to be completely honest with Gonsalves. Anyway, Ortiz is a typical Mexican employee subject to the controls set by his culture's authoritarian figure – in this case, his boss. The paternalistic approach of his boss is an extension of the father figure in an office setting. In Mexico fathers hand down policies at home and punish their children for deviating from these policies. This approach has been extended to the office. Therefore subordinates perform to avoid punishment rather than to contribute or express themselves freely.

3 This is also correct but is only part of the full answer. The story indicates that Ortiz resented Gonsalves's efforts to 'pry him open'. Since Ortiz wasn't used to this level of openness, he was uncomfortable interacting with Gonsalves who, in turn, was introducing him to new ways of dealing with a boss. Gonsalves should have tried methods that would gradually dissolve Ortiz's defences and prevented the latter from feeling threatened.

Situation 21: Time off for a vacation (page 74)

1 This is partly true. This was a crucial moment for him in the company. He could have used the opportunity to showcase his talents and raise the department's budget allocation, but he didn't. He had other priorities.

2 This is incorrect. There were no signs in the story that he was flaunting his rare qualifications.

3 This is the best answer. Europeans value their vacations highly, especially during times when they really need it, both physically and mentally. Although the presentation to the visiting executives was a rare opportunity, Rolf's perception of the situation was altered by the fatigue he was feeling. He thought he had put in his best efforts for the last two years. It was time to take a break.

Part III

A COMPENDIUM OF TACTICS AND COUNTERMEASURES

Introduction to Part III

The word 'tactic' usually brings to mind thoughts of manipulation, belligerence, and taking advantage of another person. We want to dispel this misconception. The intelligent use of tactics is the result of thoughtful preparation and a workable system that seeks to evaluate the major factors operating in a situation that has a potential for negotiation. In the early stages of the negotiation, before you commit your energy to the conduct of the negotiation itself, you study the situation, the problems involved in attaining the goals of all parties concerned, your and their comparative strengths, weaknesses, and downside risks. Before determining the tactics you'll use in a negotiation, you must first identify your strategy. In my book, *Battling for Profits,* (Donald Hendon), I define strategy by saying it answers the question, 'What should I do'? Tactics answer the question, 'How should I do it?'

In other words, your strategy determines the direction you and your organization will take, while tactics are the specific actions you choose to implement your approach towards the goals of your strategy. So many books are devoted to the subject of strategic planning that we decided to exclude it from this book. But it's important to point out the relationship between strategy and the consequent exercise of determining which tactics to use. On a smaller scale, you, as an individual negotiator, perform actions parallel to that of your company when you plan your own negotiations.

Another important thing you need to know about is the proper conceptual place to put your tactics. Having a complicated list of tactics to use in your efforts to second guess TOS is no substitute for the fundamental task of establishing rapport and trust at the outset. Tactics, alone, no matter how clever and well-thought out they are, will not carry you through the negotiations. Tactics should *articulate and not replace* your primary concern of seeing to it that both you and TOS get the best deal out of the situation as it is, with all its current constraints. When you use tactics mainly as toys for power games, they lose their purpose and potency.

You must also see that your tactics are consistent with chosen strategies. Your tactics should have the cumulative effect of materializing the goals your strategies have set forth. It's easy to slip into the error of choosing tactics that sabotage your strategy. Take this case, for example.

SuperByte, a manufacturer of computer hardware parts is soon coming out with their version of a super computer for university students. The hardware's design is superb and stands an excellent chance of competing favourably with current and forthcoming computers of other companies, but SuperByte has a problem – it lacks the software that's needed to run the hardware. The hardware will soon come out of the production line, but the software line needed to demonstrate the power of the super computer hasn't been produced yet. SuperByte also has a limited line of software products it has produced and marketed in the past five years. This line consists mainly of hardware utilities and competes with similar products among the bigger software companies in the industry. The company's top managers think they can solve the problem of no software by inviting their competitors to write the software themselves, and so they decided to make this their strategy.

After making this decision, they announce this innovative entrepreneurial opportunity to their competitors in the software industry. In the meantime, though, the middle-level marketing manager in charge of selling SuperByte's software utilities decides to compete even more fiercely in the market. He tries to dislodge competing products by drastic price cutting and lethal comparative advertising to severely discredit the capabilities of all competing products.

What's wrong with this situation? This aggressive plan of SuperByte's software marketing manager completely undermined the strategy the company's executives had laid out for the launching of their super computer, as this plan alienates its competitors, the very companies SuperByte is trying hard to attract to produce the software they need for their super computer. The marketing manager should have used tactics that would support the firm's strategy, such as: pulling their utilities out of the market completely especially if it created only marginal income; or lowering their profile in this segment of the market by raising prices or stopping their advertisements for the utilities software line.

As you choose your tactics, please be aware of several side issues that deal with ethical questions that particular tactics may raise. Later on in the chapter, we make a statement regarding the use of 'dirty' tactics; in effect, we say, 'don't use them'. A thoughtful use of tactics considers not only the overall goals of strategy, but also anticipates the countermeasures that TOS may take.[1]

7 Tactics and countermeasures

The tactics and countermeasures featured in this part are those chosen most often by participants in our seminar, 'How You Can Negotiate and Win', which we have presented in many different countries. In the seminar we found out what specific tactics (out of a list of 186) our participants chose for five typical business situations: asking the seller for a lower price; asking the buyer to pay more; asking the boss for a rise; asking the boss for a promotion; and asking the boss to change holiday dates.

Here we discuss each tactic in two parts: first, we describe how you can execute the tactic; and secondly ('Countermeasures'), we give tips on what you can do in cases where TOS uses any of these tactics on you. We've grouped the tactics into three categories: professional (or fair); aggressive; and downright dirty (or unfair) tactics. There are cases where it is perfectly all right to use a downright dirty tactic. If you bought an expensive computer from TOS who refused to stand behind their product according to stated guarantees and warranties after you've discovered some defects in the machine at home, you have a right to raise hell and act crazy. You'll notice that we have also cross-referenced by page numbers all the tactics in the countermeasures that we suggest for each tactic that is used against you. Professional (or fair) tactics are the ones we would like to see practised more often at the negotiating table.

However, when we deal with aggressive and dirty (or unfair) tactics, we especially recommend the use of selected professional tactics, or when all else fails, complete disengagement. Certainly, there may be those exceptional cases when you may not walk away easily from the negotiation after TOS has sprung dirty tricks on you. In these cases, even though the temptation may be great for you to fight fire with fire, we are convinced that the use and defence of the professional approach creates better chances of raising the negotiations to an acceptable level of civility. Only under such conditions can the best interests of both parties be reasonably protected.

Professional/'fair' tactics

Big pot

Most negotiation experts agree that coming in with initial high demands will help you get the most out of any deal. For instance, Sperber gives five reasons why this is so:

1. High initial demands take more time to settle and give you more time to find out more about TOS.
2. They indicate you expect at the very least to be treated fairly.
3. They show your persistence to pursue your goals.
4. They lower TOS's expectations.
5. They give you more room for real – or even 'straw-man' – concessions to give to TOS, while giving them a feeling of being able to influence the negotiations. 'Straw-man' or phoney concessions are those which don't give anything of value anyway.[1]

In addition:

- Don't be loose-lipped about your objectives and expectations. Let TOS reveal what they're willing to settle for first.
- Don't make concessions too easily – especially on important matters.

- Many negotiation experts view the concession-making process similarly, even if they use different terms to describe it.

Fisher and Ury (1983) debunked the popular concept of the 'bottom line' and replaced it with something they called 'Best Alternative to a Negotiated Agreement' (BATNA). The traditional notion of the 'bottom line' is the attainment of only *one* person's goal (usually the more assertive one), rather than the reconciliation of interests of all the people involved, which is what BATNA is all about.[2]

Schatzki suggests using two guidelines for your settlement range: your 'Least Acceptable Result' (LAR), or the point at which you'll accept and come out of the deal with benefits, and your 'Maximum Supportable Position' (MSP), or the highest point in the whole range at which you expect to meet *all* your goals.[3]

Karrass's definition of the settlement range is one that highlights the difference between the buyer's estimate of the seller's minimum and the seller's estimate of the buyer's maximum.[4]

In the midst of the heat of concession-making, don't forget to keep a tally sheet not only of the concessions you make, but also those that TOS makes. Make sure you write down the *real* value of these concessions - i.e. total cost, not percentages. Try for equity and a genuine balance in every exchange. Always distinguish real from straw-man concessions.[5]

Some people prefer to play a tougher game. They leave maximum room for making future concessions. They may even refuse offers that give them benefits way above and beyond what they really need or want.[6]

What is an 'equitable' exchange of concessions? This totally depends on several things: your needs and those of TOS, both your levels of aspiration, and both your own private sense of what is fair. Naturally, experts also differ in their advice: Oskam and Calero think that it is reasonable for the conceding side to expect TOS to *match* their concession as closely as possible in working toward an agreement.[7] Karrass is somewhat tougher, and thinks that after TOS has conceded, you don't have to respond in equal measure. He sees *any* kind of response as being valid, including making a major concession or a minor concession, promising everything or granting nothing, and responding either clearly or obscurely.[8]

Countermeasures Having a clear outline of your BATNA, settlement range or 'bottom line' protects you at the outset from selling yourself short on a deal, particularly if TOS is a competitive negotiator.

An impasse is very likely if both you and TOS are running this tactic into the ground. When you're locked in an impasse, try these tactics:[9]

* Emphasize how your *mutual* interests may be jeopardized by an impasse. Play on TOS's fears – suggest that certain negative consequences may happen to TOS, a situation they'll definitely want to avoid. Reach for an agreement, in principle, by highlighting your common interests.
* Take brief recesses, which may well refresh your minds and bring in new alternatives.

One way of dissolving opposition on an important issue is to talk about a hypothetical situation and discuss both your and TOS's responses to it. Make it clear that, at this point, neither of you is committing yourself to any solution yet. In the process of exploring the hypothetical situation, both of you may discover positive points in the proposal that were previously disqualified.

Check if you're merely experiencing superficial miscommunication, or if substantial differences are dividing you. Do this by recapping the issues on which you're having trouble.

Temporarily defer settlement of the issues giving you the most trouble. Both of you should shift your focus to lesser, or 'bridge', issues. If you're able to agree on the lesser issues, the chances are better of settling the bigger issues.

Come up with a few contingency concessions you could offer to TOS on the condition that their acceptance will be the basis for the settlement of the impasse. Other countermeasures you may use are discussed elsewhere in this chapter:

Keep the pressure on

Use your leadership. Take the initiative by doing these things before TOS does: clarify your objectives, outline the issues relevant to those objectives, identify potential problems, handle challenges to your position, and suggest solutions in the direction of your objectives.

Your internal disposition directs your performance. Assertive negotiators make things happen, but they don't ignore TOS's needs in the process. Their persuasiveness gets people to see things their way. They are persistent, not hard-nosed, and won't concede easily. This does not mean they're inflexible; they can ride out unexpected changes and present advantageous compromises.[10]

You become significantly more self-assured when you trust yourself: prepare thoroughly.

When problems exist, don't ignore or deny them. Instead use these barriers to create alternatives that still favour your objectives. Then make sure the discussion moves towards your favoured direction, even if you're working out compromises with TOS. Continue to aim high and expect the best results for yourself.[11]

Co-operate first with TOS before you can expect them to co-operate with you. Because you are already aware of TOS's needs, show TOS the benefits of co-operation. Follow up on your offer and be certain to keep your lines of communication open, so that TOS can accept your suggestions and respond in ways favourable to you.[12]

Prepare for challenges to your position when you make your presentation. Don't allow argumentative comments to disturb the flow of your presentation. Resolve all questions only at the end of that presentation. Avoid being in a debating mode as you respond to questions. Once in a while, TOS may heckle you as a way to dislodge you from pursuing your cause. Strong as the temptation may be, don't meet them at this low level of repartee. Instead calmly deliver objective answers with the same dignity and courtesy you would expect for yourself.[13]

Be alert to the ways TOS may try to divert you from the entire course of your negotiation strategy to serve their purposes:

1. Attacking your proposal to get you on the defensive and have you convince them of its merits (even if they're already basically convinced).
2. Pretending they have the authority to sign the contract when they don't.
3. Putting off the final signing of the contract with demands for a few more minor concessions while you are concerned about the prospect of finally closing the deal.
4. Cornering you to accept their proposal by saying 'it is one of the few chances left, if not the last, to keep you from a worse situation'.
5. Stirring you to jump in on a proposal that promises to earn you big bucks though an extraordinary opportunity.
6. Delaying the course of the negotiation and pacifying you meanwhile by pretending to co-operate.
7. Sweeping you off your feet with impressive credentials based on past performance to get you to sign.
8. Doing you small favours for free, only to play on your sense of obligation later on when they ask you to concede on major items in their proposal.[14]

Your self-presentation is a critical factor in keeping the pressure on in a situation where TOS is bent on keeping you off-balance. First of all, check on your own sense of self-respect and *know* that you're as worthy as TOS. From the way you treat yourself, make sure TOS knows that you expect no less than the kind of fair treatment that respects your dignity as a human being. Make sure, though, that this projection is consistent with the way *you* treat TOS. It may happen that TOS may try to give you a hard time, anyway, so brace yourself for handling hard-line tactics.[15] Also educate yourself in the basics of conflict management.

Basically, keeping the pressure on is another way of describing persuasion. At the heart of persuasion is reckoning with TOS's needs and letting them know that you have the desire and capacity to meet these needs:[16]

- Show that you understand TOS in order to get them to listen to your sales pitch.
- Find ways to hold TOS's attention throughout your presentation.
- Follow up TOS and get their commitment, without trapping them.
- Questions and objections are bound to arise; use them to change the way you sell your proposal, emphasizing its benefits in more relevant terms.
- You probably won't be able to satisfy *all* of TOS's needs; acknowledge this early, and remind them that risks are inevitable – reassure them, though, that you'll take these risks into consideration to minimize their impact in the future.
- Admit your mistakes where appropriate – this will enhance your credibility with TOS.
- Don't expect the facts of your case alone to talk to TOS: make sure TOS knows how emotionally convinced you are about the benefits of your proposal.

Don't subject TOS to such unreasonable time pressure that they are unable to explore fully all the issues involved. Don't forget this – the consequences of an unwanted decision made under unreasonable pressure will *always* backfire on you.

Countermeasures Your best defence against TOS's pressure tactics is having complete knowledge of all the issues involved and staying very firm in your position without being unreasonably closed to positive suggestions. Keep the basic principles of assertiveness in mind.

Be well-informed about the tactics that may be used against you and learn to recognize them during the negotiation, even when TOS tries to disguise them.

Check TOS's position closely and often. Make sure their proposal addresses your needs and objectives.

What can you do if you're against the wall and must find a way to get through to TOS about concessions you feel are essential to you? You need them and will give up a lot to get them if doing so doesn't totally burn you. Re-read what we have discussed earlier about making concession under the 'Big Pot' (see pp. 129–32). What we have pointed out are the social skills that we all need in making compromises. Learn them and implement them. And, of course, never let TOS know how important their concessions are to you.

Whenever TOS puts pressure on you, this gives you the opportunity to test how open and flexible they are to your counter-proposals. Use these occasions to size up TOS under conditions of heavy, stressful bargaining.

Choose what is appropriate from this list of tactical responses depending on the situation you're facing.[17]

- if TOS is presenting an unquestionably beneficial proposal and the conditions are right, accept it;
- if, on the other hand, TOS is taking their chance on a proposition that is an obvious 'lemon', reject it outright;
- ask as many questions about TOS's proposal as you can;
- ignore TOS's proposal;
- postpone any consideration of their proposal;
- make TOS justify their proposal;
- take TOS's proposal apart, weeding out undesirable features;
- if TOS's proposal shows some promise with a few modifications, offer to revise it yourself;
- compare TOS's proposal with one offered by another party to get TOS to improve their terms dramatically;
- as a way of avoiding an adversarial atmosphere, try agreeing hypothetically to TOS's proposal. Then point out problems that may work against your interests. As you

both consider the bad consequences that arise from the proposal's original terms, TOS may be a little more responsive to a few remedial suggestions that will benefit both of you.

Conflict adds a great deal of pressure to an already tense situation between you and TOS. The following practical reminders could help you cope with the steam:[18]

- avoid being a 'chicken' or an 'ostrich' by trying, at all costs, to avoid any conflict that comes your way;
- solving problems gives you a certain kind of power over TOS. It makes you aware of the subtle issues involved. It also makes you less susceptible to TOS's pressure tactics;
- sometimes, TOS becomes a 'steamroller', who'll press you to give in to their terms no matter what. They may even be so skilful that they'll get you to make an inadvertent statement which supports their contention that you've been inconsistent or 'out-of-order'. Don't let TOS put words in your mouth. Refuse to be bulldozed, re-state your own objectives calmly and persistently uphold those objectives.

TOS may put pressure on you by pre-empting you on deadlines. Make sure you accept deadlines that allow you to outwait TOS. Your needs shouldn't be so urgent that you'll find yourself accepting just any kind of settlement. Of course, the long-term remedy for this sort of thing is to plan way ahead of time.

If you are negotiating as a team, watch your members closely. Don't allow TOS to infiltrate your ranks and diffuse your collective energy through 'divide and conquer' tactics. Caucus often with members of your team to maintain your cohesiveness.[19] Other countermeasures you may use are discussed elsewhere in this chapter:

Deadlines

The setting of deadlines is a very effective technique to keep matters from sliding in your negotiations. When time is truly scarce, deadlines lend a sense of urgency, create a pressure to settle and impress upon TOS the need to make concessions. Your job is to make TOS believe your deadlines are genuine. Ask yourself the following questions before setting a deadline:

1. What self-imposed or organization-imposed deadlines am I under that make it harder for me to negotiate?
2. Are the deadlines imposed on me by myself (or by my organization) real ones?
3. Can I negotiate an extension with my own people?
4. What is my 'bottom line' if TOS does not heed my deadline?[20]

Compelling deadlines – those that make TOS take notice – are those based on phenomena that are both objective and easy to verify. For example, the expiration date of a contract, a date in court or even the date of an important football game are all compelling deadlines.[21]

Deadlines which sound like a unilateral threat usually backfire, thus: 'My boss gave me another week's extension within which to conclude this deal. If no agreement is reached with your company, we'll have to consider discontinuing business relations.' It is better to collaborate with TOS over mutually acceptable dates, thus: 'It would be a great help to me if we were able to conclude this meeting in time for me to catch the 11.30 plane. Would it be all right with you if we try to move at that speed?'[22]

There are times when announcing the real deadline could work both for you and TOS. Let's suppose you are a department chairman in a university. You have a certain amount left in your budget, but if you don't spend it before the end of the fiscal year, you lose it all. It would benefit both your department and your computer supplier to work out an agreement well before the end of the year.[23]

Don't *ever* shift the balance of power to TOS by revealing the kind of pressure you're under: 'You'll have to make an offer by Saturday because I've got to make my mortgage payment on Monday.'[24]

Learn how people in other nations deal with time. Always be on time when you're negotiating in North America or Europe, where time is valued as a precious commodity. On the other hand, if you're in Latin America or the Philippines, you may relax just a little and, perhaps, don't take things too seriously when TOS doesn't show up promptly or when a little socializing is used to break the ice. For example, when Belgian executive Maurice Van der Kuylen first met his joint venture partner from China's Post Office, he said, 'Mr Fong, time is money'. Mr Fong replied, 'Mr Van der Kuylen, time is eternity'.[25]

Countermeasures   Know TOS and their organization as well as you possibly can. Check if their deadlines are real or arbitrary ones.[26]

Always ask for extensions if they work in your favour.

If you have other alternatives, refuse TOS's deadlines.

Suggest alternative deadlines; if necessary, make adjustments elsewhere.

Don't give in to TOS when they pretend to be hurried and under tremendous pressure – they may be doing this to get you to concede quickly on certain issues without exploring them as much as you'd like to; don't allow yourself to be rattled by TOS's plight – let them know you realize the situation they're in, but keep your focus clearly on your own objectives.[27] Other countermeasures you may use are discussed elsewhere in this chapter:

Let's look at the record

Useful facts and information always enlightens a relationship, often promoting a consultative one, so show TOS you have the answers to their questions and objections. Information represents objectivity and paves the way to a more honest transaction. Arm yourself with documented information. Knowledge is power. Information gets you through the front door.[28]

A comprehensive source of information is indispensable to a successful negotiator. Make sure you have ready access to TOS's internal history file and track record. Know the status of all issues and activities covered in the negotiation. Document the tactics, proposals and suggestions made by TOS for your future reference. You'll be surprised just how predictable they may turn out to be![29]

Information alone cannot always effect a coup, however. Let your emotional convictions carry the force of your arsenal of information. TOS responds both to the validity of the objective facts you present to them and, more important, to the emotional impact of your delivery. The 'bottom line', however, is that *you* negotiate; the facts can't negotiate for you.[30]

Countermeasures   Keep your own data bank and *maintain* it.

Re-examine TOS's data closely; weed out the 'bullshit' factor. You might want to hire experts to look over TOS's data, especially if your negotiations involve highly technical data.

Agree with TOS on acknowledged experts whom you both respect and can consult with from time to time.

Establish a joint data bank with TOS, which you both can look at in times of conflict.

Observe TOS's emotional involvement when they deliver their facts to see if they are really convinced they're right.

Check to see if both you and TOS have exchanged data and information on a equitable basis.

Keep an account of TOS's negotiation moves to guide your selection of tactics.

Don't let TOS off too easily. Make them do the job of convincing you with arguments, in addition to the facts. Other countermeasures you may use are discussed elsewhere in this chapter:

We're the greatest!

Cite your accomplishments to impress TOS and get them to accept less since they're dealing with 'superstars'. Have your paraphernalia ready: that impressive résumé, books, brochures on your company and products, certificates of awards, etc. – heavy up your presentation!

As a negotiator, you're selling TOS not only on the merits of your proposal, but more important, on the worth of dealing with *you*. If you truly believe in yourself, you'll probably have very little trouble getting TOS to do likewise because the signals of self-assurance are unmistakable, displayed in a sense of being at ease, an alertness artfully combined with a relaxed attitude, a smooth and organized flow in movements, an ease in getting along with others and honesty of a kind that doesn't have to cover up for insecurities. These, then, are just some of the ways you communicate to TOS that you do indeed like yourself.[31]

Remember, though, that your past accomplishments alone aren't enough. TOS will want to know, 'What have you done for *me* lately, and what will you do for me in the future?' Your actual performance in the present must be consistent with what you have said about the past. Your credentials merely get you through the door. You mustn't back down on the amount of work required to defend your proposal.

Countermeasures   Make sure you're not dazzled by TOS's self-presentation, even if their long list of credentials is a genuine one. Don't forget either to cross-check their claims.

Always negotiate on the basis of *issues,* not on the razzle-dazzle of *presentations*. It helps to know past accomplishments, but what counts is TOS's present and future capacity to meet your needs.

This tactic is often used to give a raise or promotion. Subject TOS to other tests or to a panel interview to validate the claims they make based on their credentials. Other countermeasures you may use are discussed elsewhere in this chapter:

Trump TOS's ace

Let TOS think they're going to get their way. Then, at the last minute, come up with such an attractive counter-proposal that they'll accept it and drop their previous demands. Don't make an early open commitment to TOS's demands. Merely keep an open mind and make them see that you'll consider their proposal.

Here are some tactics you can try in order to persuade them to change their proposals:[32]

• Say, 'I will double the size of the order if you sell at the price I've asked for.'
• Say, 'I'll make this a three-year rather than a one-year contract'.
• Offer to smooth out their production by accepting delivery in their slow season.
• Offer reciprocal buying arrangements where they are legal: 'If we can get a good deal on your product, we'll sell you our product at a discount.'
• Advance payments and accelerated terms of payment can swing the vendor who is short of cash.
• Offering other services, such as storage facilities, trucking, special processing, packaging according to special specifications and generous return policies, can often produce concessions.

Countermeasures   Examine TOS's counterproposal closely and check to see if it fits in with your priorities and objectives.

If the counterproposal isn't good enough, remind TOS of the previous arrangements you've had with them and re-state how firmly committed you are to your plans.

Always push to get TOS committed to those important things in your own proposal which you *must* have. Make sure they know that backing out of previous commitments they may have made will act against the smooth reconciliation of both your interests. If TOS tries to trump your ace, here are more countermeasures you may use:

Don't give in

Don't give in to TOS when they make unreasonable demands. Take a firm stand, but do *not* brag about taking that stand. Define your position in reasonable terms. If you do not, TOS may feel they can manipulate you.

Never participate in a negotiation unless you're very well prepared: know your settlement range, the BATNA ('Best Alternative To a Negotiated Agreement') and the 'bottom line'. (See the guidelines for the 'Big pot' tactic given on p. 129.) It will be more difficult for TOS to sidetrack you if you know what you want.

Learn to recognize all the high-pressure tactics that can be used to 'soften you up' or penetrate your defences.

Never be pressured into giving in just because you're almost at your deadline for acquiring that office equipment or clinching that deal. Protect yourself by planning for your needs, and the needs of your firm, way ahead of time.

Countermeasures If you're a professional negotiator, you won't have imposed unreasonable or unfair demands on TOS in the first place.

Know TOS's settlement range, BATNA and 'bottom line', and try to find alternatives that will more likely be accepted by TOS.

Emphasize the benefits TOS will gain from your proposal.

Use co-operative and professional tactics rather than aggressive or dirty tactics in persuading TOS to change their minds and eventually accept your proposal. Other countermeasures you may use are talked about elsewhere in this chapter:

The power of powerlessness

If your position is weak, show TOS how much they have to lose by demanding too much or by taking advantage of you. Examples are: 'If I go bankrupt, you won't get anything from me.' 'I can't afford to pay you what you're asking to repair my transmission. Just put it back into my car, and I'll call somebody and pay them to tow it away to the junkyard, where I'll sell the car for its parts.'

Don't ever underestimate your ability to negotiate for better terms, even in situations where you appear to be the underdog. Negative thinking casts its own tailspin to failure. It becomes a self-fulfilling prophecy.[33]

Countermeasures Sometimes you are at a disadvantage when TOS claims they're powerless because you may not have any way to check on TOS's credibility. You have to know enough about them and their organization's resources. If you can't find out, it might be better to look for someone else who can give you more for what you're offering. Make sure you always have a number of alternative sources for the goods you want.

If you badly need what TOS has and they've run short of what they can offer you in return, trim down your offering in exchange for what TOS can give you. Other countermeasures you may use, discussed elsewhere, include:

Remind TOS of the competition

If TOS is smart, they'll assume you're also looking into offers from their competitors. At first, to keep at least a semblance of co-operation, you may not want to mention this fact to TOS.

Negotiators often find themselves deploying this tactic when TOS starts to play tough, or when the negotiations threaten to wind up in an impasse. In a way, reminding TOS of their competition is a threat, but a very mild one – and it is quite acceptable, especially if the tenor in which it is made is agreeable. And some threats are effective.[34] One good thing about this kind of minor threat is that it keeps TOS on their toes and lets them know that your options are quite wide. They'll be motivated to be more negotiable about terms that are important to you.

Try to find alternative parties to negotiate with, and come home with, even better offers for your firm. The more alternatives there are, the more leverage you have over TOS.

Countermeasures Be confident in what you have to offer, but be aware of your real competitors – know their strong and weak points.

Maintain your excellent service and performance, so you'll stay ahead of your competitors.

When TOS openly confronts you about your competitor, respond by emphasizing your company's or product's good points instead of saying bad things about your competitors.

Redesign your incentives to TOS based on your knowledge of what your competitor is offering them.

Don't let TOS intimidate you. Let's say you modify your proposal several times to match your competitors and TOS still refuses to make concessions that will make the transaction worthwhile for you and your firm. What should you do? Simply pull out. Don't scale down your objectives and goals. Pulling out should be your last resort, though. Before you do this, make sure you've used all your creativity – and your colleagues' creativity – to strike a deal that will satisfy your interests and those of TOS. Other countermeasures you may use are:

Get an ally

This tactic is slightly different from 'Divide and conquer', in which you look for allies within TOS's company. In the tactic we're discussing here, the ally can come from within TOS's firm *or* from the outside.

To locate an ally, learn as much as you can about the influence system affecting the decision-making of TOS. There may be people somewhere in their organization, not necessarily in TOS's immediate team, who are used as sounding-boards by TOS or whose opinions are usually sought by them for major decisions. An example of an ally is the systems analyst or senior programmer in a data processing centre. This person is competent but isn't a part of the formal acquisition team formed by the data processing centre manager. You might even want to draw a formal interaction grid made up of all decision-makers, links to known influencers and the flow of decision-making.[35]

A coalition you form makes it harder for TOS to bargain, increases the time it takes to reach an agreement and tends to produce more favourable results for you, the party strengthened by the coalition.[36]

Countermeasures Be sure you know how much TOS knows about your organization and whom they know. Assume that they've made up and are using an interaction grid, mapping out the flow of influence and decision-making in *your* organization.

Make sure you have more control over information leaks precisely because of the way the interaction grid works. Be especially cautious in letting out information to people in your firm who you know are in active communication with TOS.

If you're negotiating as a team, you're more vulnerable to TOS, especially if they have good contact and rapport with other members of your team. Keep a very tight sense of unity in your team. Caucus often, and make sure you have all the issues thoroughly thrashed out. Make sure each member of your team comes out of these caucuses crystal-clear about their roles and script for future negotiations.

Find your own allies too. Other countermeasures may be referred to in this chapter:

Get a prestigious ally

The ally can either be a prestigious person or a project – as long as TOS perceives the ally as prestigious. You try to get TOS to accept less because the person or project they'll be involved with is prestigious. Ads with celebrities' testimonials use this tactic.

Countermeasures Don't be dazzled by the people or projects TOS brings in just to impress you. These new entities may be solid in terms of background and reputation, but their presence shouldn't detract you from staying with your high aspirations and expecting more from TOS. Other countermeasures from this chapter you may use are:

1.   Big pot   129
2.   Control the agenda   153
3.   Deadlines   137
4.   Keep the pressure on   132
5.   Let an expert negotiate for you   155
6.   Let's look at the record   139
7.   Nibbling away   156
8.   Turn the tables on TOS   158
9.   Trump TOS's ace   142
10. We're the greatest!   141
11. You've got to do better than that   160
12. Don't give in   144
13. Get a prestigious ally   150
14. Remind TOS of the competition   146
15. Stick to your plan/be committed   167

Make promises

Be careful about the language you use when you make promises.[37] Sometimes, of course, people will say things in order to make it appear they have the intention of doing something for you when really they aren't serious. This happens whenever people don't want to appear disagreeable, or in public when they are trying to please you. It is best to qualify the things you say you'll do for TOS. Tell them you'll do it *only if you have the time, authority or resources.* Honesty is always the best policy. Being honest gives you a sense of self-esteem. If you know for a fact that you can't do certain things for TOS, admit it and let it go at that. Don't even *hint* that you'll try because that will raise their expectations.

Once you *do* make a clear promise, though, the thing you need to watch out for is to make sure you consistently fulfil all that you've promised to do. Watch out especially for poor follow-up, priorities that change and sheer forgetfulness.[38]

Always allow room for future changes in circumstances surrounding the promise. Insert clauses in your agreement with TOS that allow for adjustments in case certain events take place. Give yourself alternative options.[39]

Countermeasures Carefully record the manner in which TOS keeps, or forgets to keep, their promises. Use this record as reference material in the future or as a bargaining tool when you're dealing with TOS again.

As much as you want to build a climate of trust with TOS, maintain a healthy scepticism, especially at the early stages of your acquaintance, until they have proven their ability to keep promises.

After each negotiating session, make sure you've accurately recorded every position and commitment made. Follow-up on TOS's committed positions. Have all major concessions recorded and signed.[40]

If you're not sure about whether a promise is casual, implicit or one made with a strong commitment, recheck with TOS. Tell them what you heard and that you're not sure. Ask them to clarify things for you.

Responding to TOS's promises is directly related to concession-making. Watch how TOS fulfil their small concessions before tying yourself to bigger promises from them in exchange for major concessions on you part. Other countermeasures included in this chapter are:

Communication limits

If you're negotiating as a team, make sure all members of your team know what they can't talk about, and with whom they can't talk.

Take the lead in determining the issues to be discussed on the agenda.

In a team be clear when you divide the responsibilities and establish the channels of communication. If you're the head of your negotiating team, use your authority to limit the decision-making power of members of your team.

Caucus often with your team. Make sure you and everybody else on your team are up-to-date on everything about TOS and the general environment. That will happen if everybody exchanges information freely at these caucuses.

Use a secretary or a tape recorder in meetings to record proceedings. Control over information can be exerted only if you know what's going on.

Don't discuss matters you're not prepared to discuss or those that might undermine your position. If TOS asks about these matters, say no – or at least, stall for time.

Countermeasures   Make sure TOS doesn't gain the upper hand in setting the agenda. If you have to, divide the responsibility equally between both sides.

List all the issues that are important to your team. If you find TOS hedging or neglecting to discuss any of these issues, bring the matter into the open and ask for an explanation.

Thrash things out with the head of TOS's negotiating team. Remember, some members of TOS's team may plead limited authority, so they won't have to discuss certain matters.

Befriend members of TOS's team. Try to get information from them without being underhanded. Some other countermeasures are:

Control the agenda

See the six pointers on 'Communication limits'. They apply here too.

Do your homework – be clear on your goals, define the issues, establish your settlement range and take the lead in all the negotiation sessions. Highlight the issues that'll gain advantages for you without jeopardizing the interests of TOS. If you're negotiating as a team, make sure your members discuss only those issues you approve of.

If TOS isn't assertive enough or is rather 'muddy' about their objectives, setting the pace of the discussions should be no

problem to you. If, however, TOS is at least as headstrong as
you are, it will be difficult to agree on the agenda. Try to divide
the rights fairly as you both design the agenda.

Countermeasures　　At best, when TOS is controlling the agenda,
it means that they know what they want. At worst, they want
the biggest slice of the pie. In either case, thorough preparation
and an assertive approach is your best defence.

　　Insist that significant issues supportive of your objectives be
included in the agenda. Watch out for attempts to dominate
discussions. Don't hesitate to ask for time out. Other
countermeasures you may use include:

1.	Big pot	129
2.	Communication limits	152
3.	Deadlines	137
4.	Keep the pressure on	132
5.	Let an expert negotiate for you	155
6.	Let's look at the record	139
7.	Nibbling away	156
8.	Turn the tables on TOS	158
9.	Trump TOS's ace	142
10.	You've got to do better than that	160
11.	Anticipate TOS's objections	162
12.	Counterattack	211
13.	Don't give in	144
14.	Get an ally	148
15.	Get a prestigious ally	150
16.	Stall for time	164
17.	The power of powerlessness	145
18.	Rely on policy	163
19.	Secrecy	165
20.	Remind TOS of the competition	146
21.	Stick to your plan/be committed	167
22.	Buy time	173
23.	Learn when to leave well enough alone	174
24.	Divide and conquer	177
25.	Listen well	181

Let an expert negotiate for you

You will need experts when your transactions involve a high degree of technical knowledge such as when you're involved in a court case, or when you're dealing with real estate or insurance matters.[41]

Here are some of the advantages of using experts: they give you credibility in the eyes of TOS, especially if TOS respects your expert. You can use your expert as your buffer in establishing a settlement range with TOS.[42] The settlement range your expert recommends will usually be more realistic and closer to what the market will bear based on your expert's experience.[43] If you make it appear that your expert's power is limited, you may even succeed in getting TOS to demand less of him or her and perhaps be more negotiable as a result.[44]

Be aware of your expert's biases[45] and the nature of his or her own interests in your case. You should expect all experts you use to act in their own interests too. Therefore watch their moves closely. It's best to limit their authority – give them only the power to recommend, not the power to decide.[46]

Once your expert has established your initial power base, take over. Don't use your expert as a crutch for very long. Remember, *you* are still responsible for maintaining the momentum of the negotiations.[47]

Countermeasures Know as much as you can about TOS's experts. Don't be overwhelmed by the experts' credentials, even if in fact they are solid. Don't hesitate to put the experts' knowledge to the test. To do this, though, you will need your own set of experts who are, at least, as good as TOS's.

Find out immediately the extent of their experts' authority. It probably will be limited. In that case, insist on dealing directly with TOS. Use your contact with TOS's experts, though, to learn more about TOS.

Get TOS's written assurance that the terms of the contract will be implemented, even if they're dealing with you through a third party. Other countermeasures you may use are:

Nibbling away

Always aim at getting concessions from TOS, especially in areas that won't hurt them. If TOS isn't sharp enough, they won't even notice.

This tactic will work for you, especially if TOS is the kind who avoids major commitments up front without first testing the waters. In the early stages of the negotiation, present small proposals that will make it easy for TOS to sample your ability to deliver. Such proposals also don't ask too much from them – they'll be comfortable in giving them their attention and time. To make this work, though, you'll need to evaluate your resources carefully and see if you can really afford to make several small trial runs without running up your costs.

You might want to present TOS with two alternatives: (1) get them to try your proposal as one small test run as an independent sampling event; or (2) offer them a series of interlocked proposals.[48] Perhaps, after a number of successful independent runs, you may succeed in getting TOS to accept the second arrangement.

Countermeasures Scrutinize your contracts, especially if they involve numerous technical details and many figures. These kinds of contract are prime targets for hidden nibbles.

Extra-generous concessions or terms from TOS are always suspect. Look at other terms in the proposed contract from which they may recoup whatever losses were first incurred from their initial outward concessions to you.

Make sure that the results of the test trials proposed by TOS relate directly to your goals and objectives. If they don't, entertaining them is a waste of time. Don't commit yourself to the 'big' contract just because you agreed to a few trial runs with TOS, because these trial runs may not relate at all to the objectives and results of the 'big' contract.

Record every small concession you give to TOS. Track your 'pattern of vulnerability'. How does TOS get you to give in? Did you even know you gave in to this or that? Was your concession *really* that small? Mentally review every negotiation session with TOS in this way. Other countermeasures you may use may be looked up in this chapter:

Turn the tables on TOS

This tactic will work well for you if you're not under any time
pressure to find the right client to deal with. This tactic works
best in a seller's market. Instead of trying to convince TOS of
the desirability of what you have to sell, put them on the
defensive by getting them to prove why they deserve what you
are offering. Don't be presumptuous or arrogant, though. This
isn't very logical, but it can be very effective. Here's an
example: 'I'm interested in taking out a loan. Can you tell me
why I should deal with you and not the bank across the street?'

This tactic is also appropriate when you are hiring people.
Don't forget that when you are an applicant, you can use this
tactic to find out what the company you are applying to has to
offer you.[49]

This tactic has the same effect as reminding TOS of their
competition, namely a good way of putting them on the
defensive.

Countermeasures Whether or not you think it is worth your
while to be subjected to this tactic is your own personal

decision. If you have a good item, and TOS's account isn't that promising for you, you probably don't want to go through the motions of proving your worth to them. If you have numerous other alternatives, simply refuse to extend the interview and leave. Forget about TOS as a client.

On the other hand, if TOS's organization is well worth the effort, then anticipate this scenario and use this opportunity to showcase your best talents. Most interviewers use this ploy to evaluate your manner of self-presentation.

You can also remind TOS that you're evaluating them along with other prospects – this gives you added leverage to counterbalance the defensiveness TOS may by trying to evoke in you. Other countermeasures you may use include:

1.	Let's look at the record	139
2.	Reposition TOS	159
3.	We're the greatest!	141
4.	Anticipate TOS's objections	162
5.	Get an ally	148
6.	Get a prestigious ally	150
7.	Remind TOS of the competition	146
8.	Go beyond the call of duty	178
9.	Make TOS look good	183
10.	Make TOS an ally	184

Reposition TOS

You'll need this tactic especially when TOS has the tendency to dominate and exhibit their accomplishments or resources. Don't threaten TOS by boasting of your own credentials or by questioning their claims – that's counterproductive.

Instead make it appear that you still have something to learn from them. Distance yourself, try to see them objectively. You may in fact learn a thing or two from this encounter. If *you* have a tendency to dominate, be aware of this inclination and muster enough self-control to put yourself in the humbler position of student.

Using this tactic gives TOS the feeling that they have succeeded in establishing an image of strength. Somehow this may help to defuse the initial competitive atmosphere in the negotiations. Other countermeasures are:

You've got to do better than that

To execute this tactic effectively, you've got to believe in the power of setting high aspirations, enhanced by the positive influence of having a high self-esteem. A large number of people have difficulty demanding more because they simply don't like to bargain, or they think they are needlessly delaying negotiations or creating obstacles to an agreement.[50] Are you in that number?

To use this tactic effectively, you have to know TOS's 'bottom line' and their resources. This knowledge comes from good preparation – thorough research and investigation prior to dealing with TOS. The good thing about having accurate knowledge of what TOS can deliver is that you can set a realistic range of alternatives within which you can negotiate. If you carry this too far, though, this tactic can block an agreement because you're making unrealistic demands.[51]

Buyers use this tactic often when they ask for a better price from the seller. Companies usually anticipate these kinds of request from buyers, and so they have built-in cushions so a price cut won't hurt them. Buyers always figure there's a cushion, so they keep pushing for still more price cuts. Here are four specific situations where you can use this tactic to your advantage: (1) when you give all qualified bidders a second chance to improve their bids; (2) when a severe budgetary limit exists; (3) when there is doubt as to whether the bids reflect a true market sample; and (4) when you need to determine whether certain seller services are, or are not, included in the price and whether they are worth paying for.[52]

Countermeasures As a seller, you'll always have to face buyers who want more for less. When buyers ask you for more, you should ask them whether other vendors are offering the same product and service mix at the same price. As a seller, you're aware that different prices in the market reflect the different ways in which products and services are mixed. Argue from this point of view.[53] Here are other countermeasures you may use:

Anticipate TOS's objections and defuse them

Before you go out into the market, you'll have to study the strengths and weaknesses of your product or service. Do your homework by following these suggestions: have a list of benefits and disadvantages of your product or service vs its nearest competitors. List every conceivable objection you may get. Conduct a brainstorming session in your company, where you try to answer each objection. Practice getting TOS into a 'yes' mode – by rephrasing the objection and getting them to agree with your paraphrase. Don't reinforce their objections by focusing on the obvious weaknesses of the product. Highlight other compensating features that are useful to them.[54]

Ask TOS what it would take to satisfy their needs after you briefly recapitulate their objections.[55]

Some buyers may use objections which have no substance at all just to gain leverage. Watch out for these empty objections, and don't let them reduce your bargaining power.

Make an in-depth probe to uncover reasons why products are returned to improve your future sales efforts.[56]

Welcome the objections you get. Objections are useful feedback for a company that untiringly seeks to improve the quality of its products and services. At least when you get objections, you know what you have to work on. The worst kind of person to sell to is somebody who just sits there impassively. You don't know if you're getting your message across to TOS or not.

Countermeasures Buyers should always ask for warranties and guarantees on products they purchase. Some defects show up only after active use of the item. If no such written warranties exist, get the sales manager (not the sales rep) to stand behind the company's product. Make sure the sales manager signs your receipt to this effect.

Make sure the solutions the sales rep gives you in answer to your previous objections really solve your problems; reject placebos or excuses. Bring your case to the sales manager if you have to.

Deal only with companies that will let you return their product whenever you're not satisfied with it. Big and reputable firms usually have a policy like this. Other countermeasures include:

Rely on policy

Initiate a policy which imposes *artificial* limits on your settlement range. This creates a barrier as to how far you can be pushed, and how much TOS can hope to gain from you. You thus limit your room to negotiate on purpose. The visibility of this tactic gives it high credibility in TOS's eyes, but only if they perceive the artificial limits as reasonable.

Countermeasures Before you even begin your negotiations with TOS, find out the extent of their authority. While you're doing your research, don't forget to learn their pattern of handling transactions similar to the one that concerns you now.

Make it *your* policy to negotiate only with the decision-makers. Find ways and means to divert their underlings to the wayside. Don't waste your time on messengers.

Highlight the merits of your proposal with the aim of showing how you deserve to be treated as an exception to their policy. Let TOS know you're willing to make concessions if your case is treated as an exception to the rule.

A history of precedent-setting cases and actual exceptions to the rule TOS has allowed could be used at this point in the negotiations. Some other countermeasures are:

164 COMPENDIUM – TACTICS AND COUNTERMEASURES

Stall for time

Lower your profile by leaving the negotiation completely for a while. Come back when things are getting better and try to renegotiate then. The time period involved can be long (say you're going out of town) or short (go to the bathroom to think). Do this when TOS is trying for a showdown and you want to avoid a battle in which one of you would win and the other would lose, and there is no other alternative.

Use this time out to come up with a new proposal TOS can't refuse (see 'Trump TOS's ace', p. 142). Some people stall for time because they anticipate more favourable conditions such as new legislation supporting their case.

Countermeasures   Requests for a time out period can be dealt with in different ways. You could grant it and use the time to improve your position and create buffers in the weak areas of your proposal; or you could refuse to grant it creating an artificial sense of urgency in reaching a decision if you sense that further delay will seriously jeopardize your goals. To be able to refuse a time out, you should control the agenda or be in a position of enforcing deadlines. Other countermeasures include:

Secrecy

By protecting your information, make sure that TOS doesn't find out what you don't want them to find out. If you are the head of your negotiating team, control the flow of information within your team – members should know whom they may or may not talk to. Try to keep a tight control over information not only within your organization, but without it – it is amazing how bits of information travel around within the industry.[57]

Here are several ways to handle probes made by TOS. You can ignore TOS and quickly shift to another topic. You can refuse to answer and explain your reason. You might want to delay your response to the question. You perhaps give only a partial answer or answer vaguely. Pre-empt TOS by asking the question yourself. Let TOS interrupt your attempts to answer. Try admitting certain minor points, or conceding minor things, to TOS to avoid more probing. Finally, you might want to postpone negotiations until you're ready to divulge more information.[58]

Countermeasures   Plan ahead: do a lot of research on TOS and its organization a long time before the negotiation begins.

If you need to be sophisticated about your search for information about TOS, and if the nature of your transaction with TOS warrants such a search, use some of the ethically acceptable methods of industrial espionage found in the following books: (1) M.E. Porter, *Competitive Strategy: Techniques for Analyzing Industries and Competitors* (New York: The Free Press, 1980), and (2) W.L. Sammon, M. Kurland and R. Spitalnic, *Business Competitor Intelligence: Methods for Collecting, Organizing, and Using Information* (New York: Wiley, 1984).

Establish contacts with members of TOS's organization way ahead of time – they may provide you with useful information.

Use minor concessions to extract information from TOS.

If you are involved in a law suit, use modern discovery and pre-trial disclosure rules to your advantage. These rules make it almost impossible to hide vital information from the parties involved.[59] Here are some other countermeasures, which are found elsewhere in this chapter:

Stick to your plan/be committed

If you're convinced you're right (and you should be), stick to your plan and ignore TOS's counterproductive activities.

You best weapon is a well-thought-out plan of action outlining your goals and objectives. Always look for weaknesses in your plan, for instance, possible areas through which TOS can penetrate your defences and divert you with counter-proposals that don't meet your objectives.

Keep track of the course of the negotiations – use a secretary to record the proceedings.

TOS may try to use unprofessional pressure tactics to force you towards their desired direction. Learn how to deal with dirty tricks.

Countermeasures Don't underestimate TOS's capabilities. Always assume they come to the negotiating table well prepared.

Expect TOS to be as committed to obtaining their goals as you are to yours. Convince them to be flexible and open about the means they use to achieve their goals while they remain firm about their goals. Other countermeasures you may use include:

The well is dry: 'I'm ethically constrained from going any further...'

This is different from limited authority, in that you actually *do* have the power to decide on the matter at hand – but you don't believe TOS's proposal is ethically acceptable. Or you may pretend it is not ethically acceptable to you. By pretending, of course, you're trying to put off TOS's rallying efforts by summoning an excuse instead of rejecting their proposal directly. This tactic can have one of two effects: first, it might work; and secondly, it could reinvigorate TOS, who will take even greater efforts to persuade you that their proposal is ethically acceptable. TOS usually quotes success stories here.

Countermeasures As long as there's no blatant violation of your values, tell TOS that ethics is a highly relative matter. You may have to get into a philosophical exchange with TOS to dislodge their objections.

Tell TOS your own success stories to show them how acceptable your proposal is under certain conditions. Other countermeasures include:

1.	Keep the pressure on	132
2.	Let an expert negotiate for you	155

The well is dry: 'I'm financially constrained...'

Again, this tactic is different from limited authority since you *do* have the authority to decide the matter. You may or may not have enough money to accept TOS's proposal, but the excuse may work because it tries to stop TOS's efforts without putting the blame on you.

You also force TOS to lower the cost of the proposed project and bring it down to your desired level.

Countermeasures At the opening of the negotiations, immediately find out the size of the budget TOS is working with. This will save you the trouble of presenting proposals way above TOS's means.

Find out if TOS's budget constraint is temporary or permanent. If it is temporary, re-sell them on your proposal later at an opportune time, say, at the beginning of their fiscal year, or perhaps at the very end of their current fiscal year in preparation for the next.

Convince TOS of the value of your proposal using a payback period chart, showing them how the monetary benefits of your proposal outstrip its costs.

If their budget constraint is indefinite, persuade TOS to seek a budget increase from their superiors. Show them how the cost-saving potential of your proposal will pay back their investment within a specific period. Other countermeasures include:

Wet noodle

You may have to use this tactic if you believe your relationship with TOS has deteriorated to a level where you're going to have to use more competitive tactics to defend yourself.

When you use the Wet Noodle, you give no emotional or verbal response to TOS. Don't respond to their force or pressure. Sit impassively – like a wet noodle – and assume a poker face.

If you are an honest, open person, you will need some practice to be able to maintain a poker face when under pressure. It takes energy to keep your body language under control.

If TOS insists on getting a verbal response from you, then use the methods suggested earlier in this chapter under 'Secrecy'.

Countermeasures Once information between you and TOS stops flowing freely within the boundaries set by mutual trust, then you know your relationship has deteriorated.

You may have good reasons to use pressure tactics on TOS if they refuse to respond to you, but this is strictly a matter of personal judgement on your part. Their lack of response is obviously intended to keep you off balance, while they maintain the appearance of being unpredictable. Other countermeasures you may use are:

1.	Keep the pressure on	132
2.	Let an expert negotiate for you	155
3.	Get an ally	148
4.	Get a prestigious ally	150
5.	Remind TOS of the competition	146
6.	Issues surprise	212
7.	Put TOS on the defensive	216
8.	Threaten to take the problem to TOS's boss	191
9.	Acting crazy	195
10.	Do the opposite	187
11.	Intimidate by size	197
12.	Intimidate by legitimacy	198
13.	Intimidate by reward or punishment	199
14.	Intimidate by guilt	200
15.	Threaten to withdraw by requesting a transfer or bringing in another negotiator	201
16.	Make TOS feel guilty	220
17.	Phoney body language	221
18.	Doomsday	203
19.	Apparent withdrawal	222

Admit your mistakes

Instead of defending yourself when you're wrong, admit you're wrong. This will make TOS feel you're honest, and it may lead to an honest, partnering, consultant–client relationship, which is the basis of a successful negotiation.

Countermeasures When TOS admits their mistakes to you honestly, this is a signal that your relationship has progressed to a more co-operative mode. Reinforce TOS's behaviour by responding in a positive way – i.e. show more openness, trust, and initiate an information exchange that will promote both your interests. Other countermeasures you may use include:

1.	Be patient	176
2.	Go beyond the call of duty	178
3.	Lay your cards on the table	179
4.	Listen well	181

Say, 'Yes, and...'

When you use this tactic, you gain two advantages: First, you appear more agreeable to TOS even under the pressure of their attack. Secondly, since the word 'and' is reassuring, this tactic prevents any disagreement at all from entering the discussion: 'And' *amplifies* TOS's viewpoint, it doesn't *challenge* it. This may convert TOS's offensive confrontation into a defensive interrogation or protestation since TOS will often feel compelled to defend themselves by using a 'Yes, but...' rejoinder.

Countermeasures Likewise, when TOS says this to you, you know your relationship is improving and becoming a more amicable one. At least, TOS is showing you that they would like your relationship to take a more positive turn, in spite of the pressures you may be putting on them at the moment. It is a signal that you've got something to offer to TOS that would be to their advantage.

Support TOS by responding positively in your future transactions. Other countermeasures you may use include:

Say, 'Yes, but...'

If you admit TOS is right and you're wrong, say, 'Yes, but...' This offers TOS an agreement first and then lets you state your own case under more congenial circumstances. You are responding to TOS's attack with a congenial defensive argument.

Countermeasures Recognize that TOS has acknowledged you are in the right, although they're still emphasizing their own side of the story. If you firmly believe you're right, don't allow their determination to have you reconsider deflect you from what you want to do. It is a good sign that they are honest enough to recognize that they have the shorter end of the stick. Listen to their additional pleas and counter-arguments – but do not give in. On the other hand, you may discover as they explain their side that not only have you erred somewhere, but also that both of you have missed some important insights. Don't hesitate to correct yourself. This might even be the right time to concede reasonably. Other countermeasures include:

Buy time

Don't promise TOS to do something right away. Instead promise to study the matter, conduct a test or a study, come up with a new plan, and so forth. However, don't just stall for time – doing one or more of those things is buying time constructively.

Countermeasures When TOS is buying time, you know that they are reconsidering your proposal and are probably working on some counter-proposal to keep negotiations rolling. Use this time out period, then, to strengthen *your* position, to caucus with your team members if you're negotiating as a group and to re-think the issues taken up in past meetings. Other countermeasures from this chapter are:

Learn when to leave well enough alone

You never get everything you want all the time. The ideal solution may be impossible – no matter how hard you try. It is not easy, though, to figure out what policy you can use to help you decide when to take what TOS gives you. Obviously, much depends on the situation, your personal needs, your organization's needs and the timing.

There is one specific situation where the 'walk-out' is almost always appropriate, however. When TOS is obviously giving you a hard time, bypass those people and negotiate with their superiors.[60]

Countermeasures Don't let TOS use the walk-out ploy to get you to lower your aspirations or give up major concessions, especially if their demands are unreasonable. If you think they are bluffing, call their bluff by ending your transactions diplomatically.

One expert negotiator suggest this as a graceful way of exiting whenever an impasse is reached and a decision is made to end things: 'Let him go, but make sure you repair as much as you can of the personal relationship between you.... Admit you have been too hard. Appreciate his position. Congratulate him on standing up to you. Tell him that while he is sleeping on it, you will do the same. Perhaps something can be worked out, who knows?'[61] Other countermeasures include:

Turn the other cheek

Allow TOS to get off their chest whatever it is that is bothering them. Let TOS confront you without you confronting them, so hold your tongue and temper, or the situation will get worse. Act interestedly and sympathetically. Probe. Take notes. Try to show interest in what TOS is saying.

Countermeasures When it is your turn to tell TOS how strongly you feel about certain issues, exercise as much self-control as you can while TOS is turning the other cheek. Unabated anger (with or without valid reasons) can easily give you away and destroy your relationship with TOS. The problem may simply be an inadvertent mistake somewhere that has not yet been spotted. And always avoid vulgarities when you express your feelings. Other countermeasures include:

Be patient

If you can afford to outwait TOS, you'll probably win through most successfully. This is why the patient Japanese love to negotiate with impatient Americans. They feel if they stall for long enough, the Americans will accept almost anything.

Remember that a patient person has time to understand the issues, to evaluate risks, to test TOS's strength and the urgency of their need to settle, to think of alternatives and to solve pending problems.[62]

Countermeasures Make sure TOS is not just taking an extended time out. Even if your need to settle may not be urgent, unjustified delays by TOS might work against you. Negotiate reasonable deadlines.

Take advantage of TOS's patience by reviewing your position and unravelling snags, in order to strengthen your position when you meet again. These are some of the other countermeasures you may use:

Divide and conquer

If you're negotiating with TOS's team, sell at least one member of that team on your proposal. They will help you to sell the rest of their members.

Don't go too far and alienate those who are sympathetic to you from the rest of their team. All you really need to do is to spend more time with those who are open to what you have to say.

Countermeasures   If you're the head of your negotiating team, make sure you caucus often and maintain constant communication with your members. Closely watch those who may be sympathetic towards TOS's proposal. It is crucial that you project an image of unity during negotiation sessions, so spend enough time with these wavering members so you can put up a unified front. Iron out all differences in your team. You must come out of these sessions fully resolved to work together as a team. Other countermeasures include:

1.	Communication limits	152
2.	Control the agenda	153
3.	Deadlines	137
4.	Keep the pressure on	132
5.	Let an expert negotiate for you	155
6.	Trump TOS's ace	142
7.	Anticipate TOS's objections	162
8.	Counterattack	211

Go beyond the call of duty

Show so much extra effort that TOS *knows* you've *really* got their best interests at heart. This works better when TOS has a serious problem that you can help solve. However, do not expect too much in return. What this move achieves is to predispose TOS to treat your case more favourably at the time and, perhaps, remember your help sometime in the future when you negotiate again. After you and TOS discuss things, and you both find out that your proposal does not best serve their needs, then be first to recognize this and recommend someone else. It is extremely hard to do this, and many negotiators don't use this tactic. It can pay long-run dividends, however, so try it sometime.

On the other hand, don't undermine your own interests in the course of doing favours for TOS. Even though you're earning TOS's goodwill, try not to appear overly ingratiating. People sense this at once, most don't like it.[63]

Countermeasures Always show your appreciation of TOS's efforts without committing yourself to their proposal. Even though you're inclined to favour TOS because of what they have done for you, you should take hold of yourself and objectively evaluate their offer to ensure that it serves you best. If it does, consider yourself fortunate to have a helpful counterpart. If it does not, pass on TOS's helpfulness to others who come your way. You may still be negotiating with TOS in the future – favours offered then could ensure a more positive re-acquaintance later. Other countermeasures are:

Lay your cards on the table

Being honest with TOS helps establish the trust and rapport which you need so much in your relationship. When you honestly reveal yourself, you make it easy for TOS to be more comfortable with you.[64] But you must find a way of doing this without even subtly pressuring TOS to do the same thing. It would be nice, of course, if they reciprocated. In the process of impressing TOS with your openness and concern for their interests, it is easy to slip into the fault of appearing to be ingratiating. Don't use superficial displays of solicitousness to win their favour – for instance, don't appear too eager to be their friend. Show them you are genuinely concerned by putting substantive matters up front: discuss serious problems, explore solutions, review issues and reveal your uneasiness about their views.[65]

People handle the matter of openness rather differently. A lot depends on the quality of your past and present relationship with TOS, your perceived sense of control over your case and the nature of the transaction itself. (Some business transactions are required by law to involve full disclosure.) Here are a range of options: you may choose to give TOS total freedom to inspect your books and documents.

You may limit the amount of information you want TOS to know. You may simply answer their questions and reveal no more. You may allow third parties to look into your records on behalf of TOS. Finally, you may choose not to share any information at all with TOS.[66]

You'll have to use your own judgement in deciding how much, and what, when and how, you will share information with TOS. Too little information revealed will not inspire the confidence that you seek to build. On the other hand, too much information may arouse suspicion and cause embarrassment. Information revealed too early may strike TOS as being manipulative; information revealed too late may give the impression you're reluctant to share things with them. Past experience and the situation itself will dictate how you share your information with TOS. But you *should* share. Be brave enough and let down your defences. You'll find that being honest with TOS will bring you rewards that you perhaps didn't think possible. For instance, a study made in the USA, in the mid-1980s, by the prestigious Duke University Medical Centre shows that openness is even good for your health! People who are mistrustful, cynical and hostile are 50 per cent more likely to have clogged arteries. They run a higher risk of coronary disease and heart attacks. This kind of person produces more 'fight-or-flight' hormones, which accelerate plaque build-up on artery walls. So will those of you who have already made a career of disbelief and mistrust be persuaded by these findings to adopt a change of heart? You'll be healthier if you open up to TOS!

Countermeasures Don't feel compelled to reveal as much information as TOS has done, especially if they happen to be new business clients or partners.

Before revealing information, cross-check the accuracy and reliability of the information TOS gave you. You may do this in various ways: check with trusted friends in the business who know them; check company records; or check the data of third parties.

If TOS is an old client or business partner, you will have to make your own judgement based on the facts of the situation and calculate the risks and benefits corresponding to the amount of information you may want to reveal to TOS. Other countermeasures you may use are discussed elsewhere in this chapter:

Listen well

Only by listening well can you first learn about and then evaluate the interests and concerns of TOS. Knowledge of these is essential if you're going to reach a mutually satisfactory solution. If you do all the talking, you unduly expose yourself to TOS and you make yourself more vulnerable.[67] Not only that, you won't pick up the clues to concerns that genuinely affect TOS's interests. By being self-preoccupied and insensitive during discussions, you also lose the opportunity to watch out for weaknesses in TOS's reasoning, which could be detrimental to your position.[68] To assess the case in hand, we can never really have too much information about TOS. We should always try to get a perfect reading of TOS's thoughts and intentions. But to be able to do this, we must free ourselves from our own preconceptions and prejudicial blind spots. It's natural to have a narrow focus, but to become a good negotiator, you will need to make a sustained effort to widen your focus. When you do that, you will assess reality more objectively and accurately.[69] Eventually we would also want TOS to listen to us when we make our presentations. Why not listen well to them first and initiate a mutually reinforcing climate of trust and openness?[70]

Here are some things you should *not* do: don't focus on your own preconceived notions of what TOS's team is like or what they are saying. Don't approach the negotiating table with a preoccupied, closed mind. Remember that you too can make mistakes in your arguments. Don't be too eager to argue with TOS or to belittle them. Don't be impatient with the minute details of the discussion, especially when your negotiations involve highly technical material. Don't be too suspicious of TOS and suppose they are manipulating you.[71]

Now here are some of the *dos* of listening: take notes – you can even hire a permanent secretary/stenographer/'official listener' for your team. Give TOS feedback by re-stating or summarizing what you heard and confirming its correctness. Try to create environmental conditions conducive to a undisturbed discussion. Respect TOS and value the self-esteem of the members of their team. Maintain eye contact with TOS.[72]

Countermeasures Plan ahead about the kind and amount of information you want to reveal to TOS to achieve optimal results at this stage of your business relationship.

Remember that – just like you – TOS may be greedy for information to improve their bargaining position. So always consider the risks involved in the amount of information you reveal. Also remember whatever you say, whether in meetings or in informal sessions, may be 'on the record'.

When TOS is listening well, you have a solid opportunity to create a win–win relationship. Take advantage of their receptiveness and share information that will project your needs and interests in the best light. You may look up these countermeasures in this chapter:

Make TOS look good

Show TOS how coming to an agreement with your team will help their team look good in the eyes of their company and bosses. Help TOS to optimize what they already have going for them. Help TOS overcome their weaknesses through the use of your product or service.

Countermeasures Be aware of the fact that TOS is slanting the sale of their product or service to you in a way that will make you appear good before your own bosses. Re-evaluate the merits of their presentation and see if their product or service is really what your company needs.

Don't forget to consider the products or services of other vendors. You may be overlooking features of other products or services that may be more useful. Other countermeasures you may use are discussed elsewhere in this chapter:

Make TOS an ally

Your chances of success in negotiating with TOS will increase if you see your relationship as a co-operative endeavour rather than a game where one wins and the other loses.[73] Treat TOS as an equal who – just like you – is interested in getting the best deal for their side.[74]

Convince TOS of your sincerity in treating them as an ally by the way you approach the substantive aspects of your negotiation. Don't make the people involved the problem, instead focus your attention on the conflicting issues at hand. Highlight *both* your interests rather than specific positions you may both be hard-nosed about achieving. By uncovering the interests being served by the positions you have presented, you may both come up with other solutions which are mutually satisfactory. Increase your options through practical means like brainstorming together. Or widen both your perceptions of the problem by asking for the advice of different experts. Use such objective criteria as third party (expert) advice or research results as your way of settling conflicts.[75]

Use these practical dos in nurturing your partnership with TOS: avoid surprises by making sure you discuss all details of your plans together. Be honest and open, especially about doubts, problems and apprehensions. Follow through with your promises in order to increase your credibility with TOS.

Be sensitive to TOS as individual human beings – respect their team and protect their self-esteem by not being eager to prove them wrong, or by being condescending. Do all you can to make your meetings pleasant and pleasurable. Review the tips on listening well (see pp. 181–3) and practise them. Avoid subjecting TOS to pressure tactics that will cloud their ability to perform optimally. Always try to look at your relationship with TOS as a long-term one. Remember that every successful negotiation together cements your partnership even more.[76]

Countermeasures   If you have reason enough to trust TOS, and if you think you have enough to gain from the relationship, then give it a go. Other countermeasures you may use are:

1.	Admit your mistake	171
2.	Be patient	176
3.	Go beyond the call of duty	178
4.	Let an expert negotiate for you	155
5.	Lay your cards on the table	179
6.	Listen well	181
7.	Make promises	151
8.	Make TOS look good	183
9.	Make TOS an ally	184
10.	Stick to your plan/be committed	167

One-step fall back

This tactic concerns concessions (Review what we have already said in Chapter 2, 'How to make concessions', pp. 26–34).

There will always be times in the negotiation process when you will have to concede to TOS, and when you will have to step back or fall back. On these occasions always make the least valuable concession first – in fact try to develop a wide range of concessions. That way, you will have more room in which to manoeuvre, and you'll avoid having to trade off more valuable items.

You can trade one step at a time, each time that you are obliged to do so. When you're doing this, though, be persistent in getting something from TOS in exchange for the concession you have made.

Make sure you give up only those terms which will do the least harm to your interests by their absence.[77]

Countermeasures Do not allow TOS to get you to be soft on other issues just because they have conceded to you. Remember, you deserved that concession, and so it shouldn't be the basis for an automatic reciprocal concession on your part. Always keep a tally sheet of all concessions made by both sides. Don't be taken in by TOS's persistence. Any future concessions you make must be based on equivalent concessions made by TOS. Here are some other countermeasures from elsewhere in this chapter:

Do the opposite

Go against popular trends – be unpredictable. For instance, buy stock when everybody is pessimistic and prices are low, and sell when everybody is optimistic and prices are high. This is very easy to say, but quite hard to do.

Countermeasures   Don't assume you know TOS well. Always be prepared for surprises. Have contingency plans just in case they announce a sudden change of strategy – or if they back out of previously agreed-upon commitments.

Watch TOS's movements all the time. Document their moves and any sudden turns they may make occasionally. Other countermeasures you may use are:

Faking

Leading TOS to believe something which is not quite true about you, or 'faking', is commonly practised, especially during the initial stages of the negotiation when you and TOS are still weighing each other up. At this stage, this kind of dissembling is understandable, and may even be expected. But don't make a habit of it, it goes quite counter to the openness and honesty that is necessary to a win–win conclusion.[78]

You may have other reasons for faking your scenarios: you may not want to be too predictable. You may need extra time to consider other options. You may not want to be pushed to concluding your negotiation right away. You may want TOS to be put just off-balance so you'll have the upper hand in the relationship. You may not be ready to reveal your real intentions to TOS.[79]

The thing about faking or bluffing is not to get caught. This is easier at the initial stages of the negotiation when TOS as yet doesn't know you very well. Later on, as TOS gets to know you better, the burden of believability and not getting caught becomes greater, especially if you're faking threats. You'll need to ask yourself three questions before bluffing over a threat: is your objective worth all the trouble the bluff will entail?; can you afford the worst consequence that will occur if you're found out?; and do you have the acting ability to pull it off? Think very carefully before faking a threat because the consequences are more grievous and can seriously backfire on you.[80]

Countermeasures Try to develop contacts and sources of information against which to check TOS's claims and behaviour. It would be good to befriend someone in TOS's company.

If you notice something strange and out of line in TOS's behaviour, perhaps there's too much drama in their pronouncements or the issues they bring up are irrelevant to the main issues, then it could be that something underhand is going on. Be sceptical and extra observant at this point. Does TOS's body language match what they're saying?

If the matter at hand is important enough and TOS is threatening retaliation if you don't agree to a concession, then you may want to call TOS's bluff. Do this only when the consequences aren't serious on your side, just in case TOS is not bluffing. This may be worth trying, especially if you're eyeing TOS as a long-time partner and you wish to test their integrity and reliability. Other countermeasures you may use are:

Take-it-or-leave-it

Here you present TOS with only one firm choice, or else the deal is off. Often this tactic is used as a bluff and as a short cut to get closer to your desired position.

People often use this tactic deliberately to deadlock negotiations which no longer hold any promise, that is as a slow means of killing it.[81]

If you are not interested in a long-term relationship with TOS, you may use this tactic. Remember, however, that it can easily rouse hostility if it is done in a nonchalant manner.[82]

Many Western supermarkets and department stores use this tactic by charging fixed prices.

There are five conditions when this tactic is not objectionable: (1) when lowering the price for a single customer would mean cutting the price for all others; (2) when the customer obviously likes the item; (3) when the marked price is the lowest reduced price you can allow; (4) when you do not wish to waste time haggling; and (5) when the law stipulates a certain price range for the product or service.[83]

Countermeasures You can pretend not to hear TOS when they give you that one firm offer. Pre-empt them by offering other ways of settling the matter.[84]

Talk to the manager in a department store and find out for sure if the marked price is fixed. If it *is* fixed, try other ways of repackaging the item: maybe bring the item home yourself; the reduction in delivery costs could be credited to you. Or maintain the tractor mower yourself, so you won't have to pay for the store's maintenance service and thereby lower the price.[85]

Re-examine what the item is worth to you. After thinking about it, and if you decide you can live without it, simply reject the offer and walk out.[86] Other countermeasures include:

1.	Get an ally	148
2.	Get a prestigious ally	150
3.	Remind TOS of the competition	146
4.	Learn when to leave well enough alone	174
5.	Pull rank	215
6.	We're the greatest!	141

Trial balloon

When you use this variation of faking, you release your decision through a so-called 'reliable source' to TOS before you inform them what your decision is. This lets you test their reaction to your decision. A simpler variation of this is simply to ask TOS, 'What if...?' The reply, 'How?', is their buying signal.[87]

When you use 'what if?' questions, you're actually giving TOS the chance of first refusal. You are also letting them know you are flexible, in that you're not pinning yourself down to a firm offer that may not even meet TOS's needs. It also helps them because your hypothetical offers give them an idea of what you're capable of offering.

Countermeasures If TOS asks you a 'what if?' question, take advantage of this opportunity by letting them know something about you without completely revealing your needs and objectives. How much you reveal depends on what stage of the relationship you have reached. However, if TOS is a trusted partner, use 'what if?' questions to express your needs and to find out more about TOS – i.e. their needs, objectives, limitations, etc.

If you don't know TOS too well yet and you feel they are making phoney final offers, then call their bluff: simply don't give in. Other countermeasures you may use are:

1..	Big pot	129
2.	Keep the pressure on	132
3.	Nibbling away	156
4.	Trump TOS's ace	142
5.	You've got to do better than that	160
6.	Don't give in	144
7.	Secrecy	165
8.	Remind TOS of the competition	146
9.	Stick to your plan/be committed	167
10.	Wet noodle	170
11.	Lay your cards on the table	179
12.	Listen well	181
13.	Make TOS an ally	184
14.	Deadlines	137
15.	Let an expert negotiate for you	155
16.	The power of powerlessness	145

Threaten TOS: threaten to take the problem to their bosses

Here you think TOS has not handled the negotiation effectively, and you see no reason for dealing with these people any further. During the course of discussions your interests have been continually undermined by them. There is some value in negotiating with TOS's entire organization, but the people you've been dealing with so far are getting in the way. So you say you will deal instead with their bosses, or terminate the entire matter.

This tactic is a serious threat to their image as it directly reflects their inability to handle matters.

Countermeasures If you are an effective negotiator, matters should not get so out of hand that TOS should have to resort to dealing with your bosses. It could happen, though, that TOS has unreasonable requests and cannot be pacified with what your company's policies allow. In such cases, you don't have any choice when TOS takes the matter to your bosses. When they do, explain the situation clearly to your bosses and protect your name by showing them that you did your best within the limits imposed on your position and as company policies allowed. If this is a buy–sell situation and TOS is the customer, your bosses will most likely end up placating them through some token means, anyway. The customer is always right! Other countermeasures you may use are discussed elsewhere in this chapter:

1.	Anticipate TOS's objections	162
2.	Admit your mistakes	171
3.	Buy time	173
4.	Be patient	176
5.	Communication limits	152
6.	Control the agenda	153
7.	Counterattack	211
8.	Don't give in	144
9.	Deadlines	137
10.	Get an ally	148
11.	Get a prestigious ally	150
12.	Go beyond the call of duty	178
13.	Intimidate by legitimacy	198
14.	Intimidate by reward or punishment	199
15.	Intimidate by guilt	200
16.	Threaten to withdraw by requesting a transfer or by bringing in another negotiator	201
17.	Keep the pressure on	132

Leak information to TOS

Arrange to have TOS receive the information that you want them to know. Use the 'grapevine' or 'rumour-mill' to increase the credibility of the information in TOS's eyes. This is different from the Trial Balloon, in that here *information* is leaked, not decisions; this tactic will make you look good in TOS's eyes. If you release information about your accomplishments through people whom TOS associate with, you increase your chances of improving your visibility and reputation in their company.

Countermeasures   Don't believe all that is said about TOS, especially if the material is coming from *their* grapevine or rumour-mill. Talk directly with TOS, and make an eyeball-to-eyeball assessment of the people concerned. Be very critical of the sources of information. Make sure the people are reliable and that you can counter-check the information's validity. Other countermeasures you may use are:

Protective defence mechanism: seek sympathy

This tactic is good to use if you are in somewhat bad shape, and need to ask TOS to give you extra consideration in the light of your plight. For instance, to get generous concessions on price or payment terms, you can tell TOS your business is in a bad shape – e.g. your cash flow is slow and your accounts payable are piling up. You may be faking, or your situation may unfortunately be real. If you're bluffing, you'll have to be prepared for the consequences of being found out.

Countermeasures   Whenever TOS puts on a 'poor-little-me' act to disarm you, immediately turn on your scepticism. If they say their company is going under to get special considerations from you, tap some other sources to confirm or refute what they're claiming about their company (perhaps friends in government agencies or trade associations).

Above all, don't fall for sympathy ploys or do something purely out of pity for TOS. If they are in bad shape, they are not in a position to negotiate, you have all the power. Always think of what you'll get out of a situation in business terms. Remember that you run a business, not a charitable institution. Some other countermeasures are:

Aggressive tactics[88]

Acting crazy

Most people usually can't stand to see or hear other people making a scene, which is why Acting Crazy puts TOS under duress to give in to your demands, just to get you to stop doing what you're doing! You'll need good acting abilities and a keen sense of timing and good judgement – and the guts to pull it off. Normally, when the situation does not call for it, it may well seem rather awkward to have to put on such a show. The need for this, though, may arise naturally in cases where you have a valid claim for the product or service, and TOS simply ignores your right to the service you're entitled to. When really angry, and for good reasons, there may well be no problem acting crazy; go ahead and do it. Report TOS to their bosses or picket in front of their main offices. However, if you insist on acting crazy just to have your way on an irrelevant issue, you're pulling a dirty trick.[89]

Countermeasures Always stay calm when TOS is acting crazy – view the scene with some suspicion and disbelief; don't be intimidated by their flamboyant display. Don't budge if they badger you. Know that this is merely a ploy to wear you down to a point of unconditional surrender. Continue to act rationally and conserve your energy. Later on, when they have worn themselves out, ask them what precisely is causing them to be so upset.[90] Here are other countermeasures you may use from this chapter:

The 'call-girl' principle

The call-girl says, 'Pay me first', because she knows the value of her services dramatically decreases after they've been performed. So act first, reach your goal, and see what TOS will do about it. But appraise the consequences in case you fail. An example of this tactic is to cross out part of a written contract you received in the mail, sign it and send it back.

Countermeasures Don't pay for the services of TOS before they are rendered. Always insist that you reserve the right to re-evaluate the job after it's done. Other countermeasures you may use are:

1.	Big pot	129
2.	Keep the pressure on	132
3.	You've got to do better than that	160
4.	Counterattack	211
5.	Don't give in	144
6.	Stall for time	164
7.	Rely on policy	163
8.	The well is dry: 'I'm financially constrained...'	169
9.	The well is dry: 'I'm ethically constrained from going any further...'	168
10.	Buy time	173
11.	Learn when to leave well enough alone	174
12.	Remind TOS of the competition	146

Intimidate by size

Whales very easily swallow up the small fish in the sea: take huge conglomerates buying out small companies. Or take your every-day case of the neighbourhood tough bullying the smaller boys just to have his way.

Countermeasures If you are the puny boy in the neighbourhood, you may well call on a bigger fellow or your gang to work on the notorious local toughie. If you're the small company that refuses to be bought out by the conglomerate, you'd use the media or your trade association to state your case and defend your company – feeble though that attempt may be. The point is, you should air your protests anyway, even if you know it is merely a matter of time before the other company has its way. Other countermeasures are:

1.	Don't give in	144
2.	Get an ally	148
3.	Get a prestigious ally	150
4.	The power of powerlessness	145
5.	Make TOS an ally	184
6.	Trump TOS's ace	142
7.	You've got to do better than that	160
8.	Remind TOS of the competition	146

Intimidate by legitimacy

Intimidation by legitimacy can take a variety of forms: the printed application forms for bank loans are things which most people don't question, but simply sign.[91] Charisma and self-confidence confer an air of legitimacy in much the same way that official titles do.[92] A plush, towering office building can speak of a corporations's overwhelming power in the business world. Power symbols like a Rolls-Royce motorcar, a mink coat, a sergeant's stripes, a policeman's uniform and condominiums in exclusive residential areas all announce the owner's claim to power as defined by the trappings that society prescribes.[93]

Countermeasures Don't be distracted by displays of ostentation. These are intended to play on your vulnerability to a symbol's material power. Keep your mind focused sharply on your own interests. Don't question TOS's credentials, for instance, as represented by their titles. But at the same time, make it known to them that you are not about to be taken in by their seemingly official superiority. Remember, what really counts are the issues involved and the possibility of finding solutions that serve both your mutual interests.[94] Other countermeasures are discussed elsewhere in this chapter:

Intimidate by reward or punishment

We have all known this tactic since childhood. We had to pick up our discarded clothes or else we would lose a week's allowance, or we wouldn't be able to watch TV for a week. As grown-ups, we continue to confront the ugly head of this tactic when we deal, for instance, with a boss who imposes an unreasonably high sales quota. If we don't meet the quota, we're fired: the carrot and the stick. We are all familiar with the image.

Threats used in situations that do not warrant them lead relationships into a downward spiral.[95] Usually people who are unskilled in human relations and who lack perception of other people as equals resort to such crude means. Be sure that when you make threats, you can indeed follow through, lest TOS calls your bluff and causes you to lose face.

Countermeasures If you have been threatened, always make use of the room available to manoeuvre. Never be taken in by the threat itself. Even if your chances of winning are minimal, don't fail to make your protests known, especially if you feel you're being treated unjustly. For example, trade unions strike even if management threatens them with immediate expulsion.

Before responding to threats, you'll need to consider two things: the credibility of TOS in actually carrying out the threat, and the potential damage to you that may result if TOS really isn't bluffing.[96] Other countermeasures in this chapter are:

Intimidate by guilt

Usually you can use guilt if you and TOS have a fairly good personal relationship and you have already done them a number of favours. If TOS insists on taking a particular course of action which you think will jeopardize your interests and your relationship, tell them that you're afraid things may come to a head if you're pushed too far.[97]

Beware when you go beyond the call of duty to look after the interests of TOS. If you've announced the fact that you have a disinterested concern for TOS, then live up to your words. Later on, when TOS takes an action that is prejudicial to your interests, don't bemoan the fact that you've helped them in the past.

Countermeasures Be careful about accepting special favours from TOS. Vested interests may be lurking behind pronouncements of 'no strings attached'.[98]

You'll need to be clear about the actions that you need to take and the consequences they bear on all parties involved. If you are really convinced that unwanted consquences on TOS are just tangential and not your fault, then stay firm, stick to your plan and don't give in to TOS's ploy of making you feel guilty about what you want to do. Other countermeasures you may use are:

1.	Communication limits	152
2.	Keep the pressure on	132
3.	Let an expert negotiate for you	155
4.	Anticipate TOS's objections	162
5.	Counterattack	211
6.	Don't give in	144
7.	Get an ally	148
8.	Get a prestigious ally	150
9.	Stall for time	164
10.	Remind TOS of the competition	146
11.	Stick to your plan/be committed	167
12.	The well is dry: 'I'm ethically constrained from going any further...'	168
13.	The well is dry: 'I'm financially constrained...'	169

•

Threaten TOS: threaten to withdraw by requesting a transfer or by bringing in another negotiator

This is tantamount to saying, 'I don't want to deal with you any more. I'm fed up. Try your luck with the next person.'

Countermeasures The action you take will depend on the ultimate result of TOS's threat to withdraw. If their action makes you look bad to your superiors, then you must make a serious effort to iron out your relationship with TOS. However, if you find that your have substantial differences in perceptions and style which are actually irreconcilable, it may be a good thing to bring in a fresh face. Other countermeasures you may use can be looked up in this chapter:

Destroy a straw man

Pad your high-priority goals with others which have a much lower priority, while making TOS think these padded goals are most important to you. Then you can give some of them away, ostensibly in a begrudging manner, and still have what you wanted in the first place. Here, of course, you need to be a good actor.[99]

Countermeasures Don't be too quick to assume that TOS has in fact made substantial concessions when they do concede. Keep pushing for even more concessions and remain protective of your 'bottom line'. Try to do this without being inflexible. Always try to find mutually agreeable solutions. You will have to really know TOS well, and what their real interests are, in order to distinguish the true concessions from the straw ones they make. You will, however, be able to make this distinction, once you know TOS well enough. Other countermeasures include:

1.	Big pot	129
2.	Nibbling away	156
3.	Trump TOS's ace	142
4.	You've got to do better than that	160
5.	Don't give in	144
6.	Stick to your plan/be committed	167
7.	Wet noodle	170
8.	Intimidate by size	197
9.	Intimidate by legitimacy	198
10.	Use a shotgun	214

Doomsday

When should you threaten TOS that the worst will befall them if they don't comply with your proposal? That depends on a number of things: if external conditions are involved which control their future, they may see the light with your warning and give in to your proposal; however, if you have full control over the worst-case scenario that you paint to TOS, they may not believe you.

You may choose to issue a genuine warning when things will indeed become worse for TOS if they don't follow a certain course of action. Or you may do a little bluffing to precipitate the kind of reaction you want. Before you bluff, though, think about the following: are your goals worth the trouble involved? What's the worst thing that can happen if they call your bluff? Are you a good enough actor or actress to carry it off? Do you think TOS will see through you?[100]

Countermeasures Even if you have a strong suspicion that TOS is only bluffing, plan for the eventuality that they are not. Tell TOS you recognize their intent to carry out their threat, and you realize the consequences. Instead of challenging TOS's intention to go through with their bluff, acknowledge that they're capable of pulling it off. This alone minimizes their inclination to manoeuvre you any further. Re-state your interest in settling the matter using more constructive means. Make sure, though, that TOS understands that you do not intend to be intimidated that way, and that you're prepared to live with the worst results of their threat.[101] Other countermeasures include these:

Five smokescreens

If you want to change the subject, delay a decision or cloud an issue, use a smokescreen. The following are five smokescreens you may use.

Smokescreen no. one: Put a new person in charge

If you are the current negotiator and you can gain a lot by a lengthy delay, then step down for a time and have someone take over meanwhile. Tell TOS that your replacement is only filling in temporarily and that the final decisions still rest with you.

Countermeasures   TOS may tell you they are stepping down as head negotiator temporarily due to conditions beyond their control. Then they introduce you to the 'acting' negotiator, who will not have the final say, anyway. If this new person isn't going to have some measure of authority even over small issues, then you can be sure TOS is using him or her as a smokescreen. What can you do about this?

First, express your discontent with both the old and new negotiator and tell them that you're under pressure to come to a final agreement. Remind them of the concessions you've made and that you may not be able to honour them for too long if final agreement cannot be reached within a certain deadline.[102]

Prepare to abandon the negotiations altogether if TOS is taking an inordinate amount of time delaying the proceedings. Tell them that you soon will look at other alternatives considering the obvious lack of urgency on their part to participate in the negotiations.[103] Here are some other countermeasures you may use:

1.	Keep the pressure on	132
2.	Deadlines	137
3.	Don't give in	144
4.	Remind TOS of the competition	146
5.	Stick to your plan/be committed	167
6.	Big pot	129
7.	Communication limits	152
8.	Control the agenda	153
9.	Let an expert negotiate for you	155
10.	Trump TOS's ace	142
11.	You've got to do better than that	160
12.	Anticipate TOS's objections	162
13.	Counterattack	211
14.	Get an ally	148
15.	Get a prestigious ally	150
16.	Stall for time	164
17.	Rely on policy	163
18.	The well is dry: 'I'm ethically constrained from going any further...'	168
19.	The well is dry: 'I'm financially constrained...'	169
20.	Wet noodle	170
21.	Learn when to leave well enough alone	174
22.	Be patient	176
23.	Lay your cards on the table	179

Smokescreen no. two: Generate a bigger issue

Create false issues that divert TOS's attention from problems which you're not prepared to solve at that moment: do this when you're cornered. When you are cornered and you have to make any reasonable progress, you may have to make concessions which you cannot afford to do at that time, so generate a bigger issue.

Countermeasures Scrutinize the new issues that TOS brings up and point out their irrelevancy to the original objectives of your negotiations.

  If you notice that interruptions, such as new issues, are being brought up just at the point where you are approaching some kind of resolution, then you're probably right in suspecting it is merely a delaying ploy. Impose strict deadlines and take control of the agenda. Other countermeasures are:

Smokescreen no. three: Broaden the problem, for instance, by creating an equal but opposite issue

See guidelines and countermeasures given for generating a bigger issue (p. 206).

Smokescreen no. four: Provide detailed information

A less obvious way of derailing discussions over current issues would be to spend a considerable time scrutinizing and discussing information that you want to make appear relevant but which is really unnecessary.

Countermeasures See to it that you and TOS agree, in principle, over the salient issues at the beginning. Impose a timetable within which to work, and tell TOS that any extraneous information will simply be ignored. Be firm about your deadlines. If they continue to delay, be prepared to consider other alternatives.

If TOS is overloading you with technical data because weighty technical issues are involved in the product or service you're discussing, have a technical expert look over their data to see if it's relevant and valid. Other countermeasures are:

Smokescreen no. five: Stall for time until interest falls

Here what you are doing, in effect, is to kill the negotiation slowly if you pursue this tactic to the extreme. The other four smokescreens are also ways of stalling for time. Now, in complex negotiations involving a lot of details, it is easy to skip over or even lose track of problem issues if you and TOS neglect discussing them, or if you don't follow-up on their status. If your intention is simply to eliminate a few issues through your stalling, it may work, that is if TOS isn't sharp enough to detect the oversight and is no more interested in the issues than you are.

Countermeasures See the countermeasures suggested for the four previously discussed smokescreens (pp. 204–7).

Use flattery and charm

People who want to gain TOS's favour through oblique means, such as the feeding of egos, will have to judge correctly what the ego-needs really are. Sometimes the slightest compliment about how you look or how your house is decorated can easily disarm you. But flattery can also mean unqualified deference to TOS' judgement, opinions, views and predilections. For instance, you could express how impressed you are with TOS's insightful analysis during your discussions. These tricks will work if TOS has a need for such stroking.

Countermeasures Your best defence against flattery is a solid sense of your own self-worth. Nobody's opinion of you, good or bad, should add or detract from your own self-esteem. There is nothing wrong with being grateful when others are sincerely appreciative of you – but you will need to put this firmly into perspective. Don't allow it to influence you during the negotiations. Other countermeasures from this chapter include:

Half-step fall back

Tell TOS you're yielding. But you're not actually doing so because you're making a contingent offer. This only half-commits you since the offer depends on the approval of your boss. This buys time and creates the impression you're helping TOS. If you come through on your contingent offer, you give TOS added value by relieving tension and suspense. If you don't deliver, though, TOS may feel that 'at least you've tried', and they will credit you with a concession you didn't really give to them.[104]

Countermeasures Be sceptical every time TOS makes a quasi-concession which is good only when their boss approves. Only concessions that deliver the goods should be considered real concessions. Other countermeasures you may use are:

Let's split the difference

Ever since we were children, we thought that splitting something down the middle was the fairest way of solving dilemmas. You and your friend want to meet some time tonight but can't agree on the time: 'Will we meet at 6.00 or 7.00 p.m tonight? Okay, let's split the difference and meet at 6.30 instead.' The assumption here, of course, is that splitting things right down the middle is 'equal' and therefore necessarily 'equitable' or 'fair' to both sides. Not so. Splitting things down the middle can be most unfair to the person who has more to lose by going 50–50.

Countermeasures Remember that the first one who offers this arrangement has more to gain. For example, you're a sales rep in a computer store and a customer is interested in a personal computer tagged at $2,000. The customer bargains for $1,500, and you respond with a $1,800. She makes her final bid by saying, 'Okay. Why not split the difference? $1,650 is my last offer.' As the sales rep, you know the store is breaking even at $1,750. Although the arrangement appears fair, it really is inequitable because the store won't break even, much less earn a minimum profit out of the deal. In this case, simply say 'no'.[105] Other countermeasures are:

1.	Big pot	129
2.	Keep the pressure on	132
3.	Nibbling away	156
4.	You've got to do better than that	160
5.	Don't give in	144
6.	Rely on policy	163
7.	Remind TOS of the competition	146
8.	The well is dry: 'I'm financially constrained...'	169
9.	Wet noodle	170
10.	Trump TOS's ace	142
11.	Destroy a straw man	202
12.	Funny money	218

Counterattack

Have a few issues in reserve to use when TOS is on the attack. Expose just enough of them to create a diversion. Don't go too far, though, for this can be counterproductive and put TOS on the defensive. Here timing is of the essence. You need to be skilful enough to keep your discussions from deteriorating into debating sessions.

Countermeasures   A situation will have to be very extreme for you to decide to mount a counterattack against TOS. Otherwise it is not the best scenario for you to create or support if your goal is to get cool and rational discussions started again. Other countermeasures you may decide to use on occasion when more drastic action is called for are discussed elsewhere in this chapter:

Dirty 'unfair' tactics

The reason for studying the following tactics here is largely because the participants in our seminar, 'How You Can Negotiate and Win', expressed a preference for them and may already have been using them in their business transactions. We think it is good to know how dirty tricks are pulled on you, to give you at least an equal chance with TOS. However, you must think very carefully before using these tactics, either as your main offensive or as countermeasure, as they may be very counterproductive. You may in fact lose more than you have already put into the negotiations.

Issues surprise

If you want to delay settling matters for some reason or other, you can introduce problem issues that are tangential to your mutual objectives. For instance, let's say you are the merchandising manager of a huge department store and are getting ready to place your orders with an exclusive Paris fashion designer. All the designs have been submitted, and a mini-fashion show has already been organized. You are close to signing a purchase order when one of your buyers informs you of an Italian designer who produces clothes of a very similar style and quality for much less money. As the manager, you are obliged to save the store money, so you put your decision to place the order with the Parisian designer on hold, even though all arrangements short of signing the contract have been made. The next day, you call the Paris designer and tell her that you've learned through the grapevine that 100 per cent cotton material will be in great demand in two months. Since her spring/summer collection uses all synthetic fibres, you've decided to withhold the purchase order until much later in the year, perhaps, towards autumn.

Surprise issues have the same effect as smokescreens. They give you more time to reconsider your decision in the light of new information received. They put you in a very uncomfortable spot, though, if you and TOS have already orally agreed.

Countermeasures   The surprise may tip your balance for the moment, but don't allow it to bother you during subsequent sessions. If you have contacts in TOS's organization, find out if there have been unwelcome new developments that may have caused TOS to change their mind. Probe if TOS is hiding behind smokescreens.

Reaffirm the contents of the original agenda and the issues outlined in it. Protest the introduction of new issues that may be unrelated to this original list. Start working on your alternative because TOS, after all, may not be all that interested in closing the deal with you. In the meantime push until you get TOS to tell you what the real problem is.[106] Other countermeasures from this chapter are:

1.	Communication limits	152
2.	Control the agenda	153
3.	Deadlines	137
4.	Keep the pressure on	132
5.	Counterattack	211
6.	Don't give in	144
7.	Remind TOS of the competition	146
8.	Learn when to leave well enough alone	174
9.	Do the opposite	187
10.	Intimidate by size	197
11	Intimidate by legitimacy	198
12.	Intimidate by reward or punishment	199
13.	Threaten TOS: threaten to withdraw by requesting a transfer or by bringing in another negotiator	201
14.	Take-it-or-leave-it	189
15.	Phoney body language	221
16.	Apparent withdrawal	222

Good guy–bad guy

Sometimes this is called 'Good Cop–Bad Cop' in the USA and elsewhere. You'll need a partner to do this. One behaves rudely ('bad buy'), while the other keeps a quiet, reasonable profile ('good guy'). The bad guy imposes his terms on you, and when you refuse, he gets angry and leaves the room. At this point, the good guy enters and tells you he can offer you a better deal.[107]

You play-act this routine to get TOS to reduce their expectations in dealing with you. Also you do this to enhance the position of the good guy in the eyes of TOS, so you can get a fast concession.[108]

Sometimes the bad guy isn't even a person – it can be an unreasonable requirement in the loan application form, for instance, or in the terms of sale of telephone equipment.[109]

Countermeasures Don't react to the bad guy's routine. This is one of the easiest tactics to spot, so you'll discover it immediately, anyway, and know what TOS is up to.

Smile and tell TOS, 'That's the best good guy–bad guy act I've ever seen'. Or smile and say, 'That was the worst good guy–bad guy act I've ever seen'.

If you decide to deal with the good guy, don't evaluate his offer in terms of what the bad guy offered you. Stick to your guns. Keep thinking about your 'bottom line', bargain hard just the same.[110] Here are some other countermeasures:

Use a shotgun

This is an intimidating tactic in which you demand so many things all at once that TOS is overwhelmed and loses their focus on their own objectives and demands. Another variation of this is bombarding TOS with a great deal of information, so that they are unable to keep track of the essential issues. (See 'Smokescreen number four: Provide detailed information', p. 207.)

Countermeasures You and TOS meet for the first time and they unload a barrage of demands. Don't take their demands too seriously. If your reading of TOS is that they are hard bargainers, then realize that they are merely using a common ploy.

Later on, as you and TOS get down to business and review the objectives and priorities involved in the transaction, insist on having them prioritize their demands. If they don't do so very explicitly, then you'll have to deduce these priorities indirectly from the rest of your discussions. Here are other countermeasures you may use:

Pull rank

If you have a prestigious occupation (e.g. doctor, professor, lawyer, etc.) or you are an acknowledged expert in your field or are TOS's boss, use your position to keep TOS from even starting to bargain with you. For instance, you can say: 'Who do you think you are, anyway, challenging me this way? You've got some nerve!' This ploy usually happens as a spontaneous outburst when arguments get heated between you and TOS, and they're starting to challenge your credibility or qualifications.

If you value your relationship with TOS, try to check your temptation to make this kind of outburst when they challenge you. However, if you think TOS isn't really worth all the effort you're making for a successful relationship and if your transactions have gone sour, give in and pull rank – vent your anger, but in an acceptable way.

There may be times when you are not angry, and all you are trying to do is to intimidate TOS. You don't come out too well, though, after using this tactic. The chances are that you will lose TOS altogether.

Countermeasures Don't be overwhelmed by TOS, even if they are a well-established authority in their field. You still have the right to challenge them, especially if your welfare is at stake. If you are going to see a doctor or dentist, for instance, you have a right to discuss their methods. If they resent your efforts, report them to the appropriate professional association if you have to.

If there is a good reason to deal with TOS despite their display of superiority, hire an expert who can even things up. Other countermeasures include:

1.	Remind TOS of the competition	146
2.	Counterattack	211
3.	Get an ally	148
4.	Get a prestigious ally	150
5.	Wet noodle	172
6.	Intimidate by size	197
7.	Intimidate by legitimacy	198
8.	Intimidate by reward or punishment	199
9.	Intimidate by guilt	200
10.	Threaten TOS: threaten to withdraw by requesting a transfer or by bringing in another negotiator	201
11.	Threaten TOS: threaten to take the problem to TOS's bosses	191
12.	Make TOS feel guilty	220
13.	Apparent withdrawal	222

Put TOS on the defensive

Start off with accusative questions and continue with negative statements. Do this for brief periods only. Use other tactics in between. Don't use it too long or hard, unless you want to humiliate TOS. And if that's your purpose, why negotiate in the first place?

Countermeasures Don't accept TOS's offensive behaviour – remain calm, and remind yourself that this is unacceptable behaviour in professional negotiations. When TOS tries to put you on the defensive, they must have something up their sleeve. This is a deliberate attempt to confuse and disorient you. If you are well aware that TOS's histrionics have nothing to do with your self-esteem and self-worth, then you'll come out of this unscathed.

Reiterate your position briefly and emphatically, if appropriate. Do not over-explain or get defensive or you will walk right into TOS's trap. Don't feel you have to have the last word. End the discussion promptly, and tell TOS you'll meet again when they are in a better mood and can act rationally once again.[111] Here are other countermeasures from this chapter:

1.	Counterattack	211
2.	Don't give in	144
3.	Get an ally	148
4.	Get a prestigious ally	150
5.	Stall for time	164
6.	Stick to your plan/be committed	167
7.	Wet noodle	170
8.	Intimidate by size	197
9.	Intimidate by legitimacy	198
10.	Intimidate by reward or punishment	199
11.	Intimidate by guilt	200
12.	Threaten TOS: threaten to withdraw by requesting a transfer or bringing in another negotiator	201
13.	Phoney body language	221
14.	Apparent withdrawal	222

Who, me?

Deny your involvement in an issue and pretend you don't know what's going on.

A typical scene is one in which a motorist is caught by the traffic police officer for speeding. The officer asks the motorist to pull to the side and the latter says, 'Who, me?' We learned this trick in childhood when we denied it was us when our mother asked who ate the cake on the kitchen table.

The thing, of course, is not to get caught. In this case, we know that the motorist was foolish in denying his or her speeding offence – the police have radar that can infallibly indicate your driving speed.

Countermeasures If you are the police officer, simply ignore the denials and present the speeding motorist with the ticket. Your radar tells you that they exceeded the speed limit.

But what if you got involved in a situation where there is no foolproof way of checking TOS's behaviour? If TOS are good actors, you may give them the benefit of the doubt and resolve that you'll keep an eye on them in the future. If you know TOS well enough and you smell something fishy, you won't believe their bluff, anyway. Other countermeasures are:

Funny money

When it is to your advantage, concentrate on percentage figures ('funny money'), not absolute figures ('real money'); or on costs per unit (funny), not total costs (real); or on rounded figures (funny) instead of exact figures (real). Funny money diverts TOS's attention.

Example one: *(Funny Money)* You are the contractor for a house, and you're convincing the owner to spend a little extra on an added feature. You say, 'Why make such a big thing out of adding an extra den at the back of the house? The construction cost will amount to only 2 per cent of your total cost.' *(Real money)* You are the owner of the house, and you know that total construction cost is already running a little over $500,000, excluding added features like the den, lawn and garden. You've overrun your budget by $100,00 as it is. That den, which you'll use only every so often, will cost you $25,000. That's what you should be thinking.

Example Two: *(Funny money)* You are the buyer, and you're wondering why this wholesaler of handbags won't sell the entire lot to you for $6.00 per bag instead of $6.50 per bag. After all, you'll be ordering 1 million bags. You find the seller's attitude to be somewhat haughty. What a small concession for the size of the order you intend to give them! *(Real money)* You are the seller and you don't understand why this buyer does not see that if you granted the 50 cent concession, you stand to lose $500,000, which is what you need barely to break even as it is.

Countermeasures If TOS is presenting you with figures, spend extra time examining them. Examine them with an expert, especially when technical data is involved. Do this because there are ways in which quantitative data can be 'window-dressed' and made to look very attractive.

Brush up on your basic mathematics and financial terms and concepts – things like average, median, mode, simple annual interest, annual compound interest, and so forth. We encounter these concepts in our daily lives, but too often we forget about them.[112] Other countermeasures include:

1. Let an expert negotiate for you   155
2. Let's look at the record   139
3. Don't give in   144
4. Big pot   129
5. Buy time   173
6. Faking   187
7. Keep the pressure on   132
8. Leak information to TOS   193
9. Nibbling away   156
10. The power of powerlessness   145
11. Pull rank   215
12. Remind TOS of the competition   146
13. Rely on policy   163
14. Stick to your plan/be committed   167
15. The well is dry: 'I'm ethically constrained 168
    from going any further...'
16. The well is dry: 'I'm financially constrained...' 169
17. Wet noodle   170

Make TOS feel guilty

Sometimes TOS will do something negative to you without being aware of it. Use this opportunity to make them feel guilty, especially if you've done them some favours. Say, 'I'm surprised at you', 'Shame on you', 'How can you do this to me after all I've done for you!', etc. You may even use harsher language.

Of course, what's objectionable about your approach, even if you have valid reasons to get angry, is that you don't give TOS the chance to realize what they have done and to apologize. They may have committed this act unwittingly, unaware of what it did to you. You are more likely to arouse hostility and contempt when you impose the guilt on them without giving them time to review what has happened.

When you and TOS have a good relationship, it is better to point out to them that their oversight cost you some inconvenience and trouble. Here let TOS know how you feel in a more discrete and acceptable manner. Here making them feel guilty is not as unfair as before, when you denied TOS a chance to explain. The previous way was a quick-and-dirty way of gaining the upper hand.[113]

Countermeasures   Analyse TOS's accusations first to see if they have valid reasons for being angry. Don't accept the guilt that TOS is trying to make you feel.

While you're getting to know TOS, don't accept any favours which may later be used to make you feel obligated in any way. Be sceptical about their pronouncements of 'no strings attached' when they offer you favours.[114]

Once you have gained an insight into what actually happened, explain your position clearly, without apologizing for what you've done. Tell TOS that you did not intend for your actions to cause them so much inconvenience or harm. Assure them that you will take their situation into consideration from now on. Other countermeasures include:

1.	Communication limits	152
2.	Keep the pressure on	132
3.	Counterattack	211
4.	Don't give in	144

Phoney body language

Body language is explained in Chapter 6, 'Nonverbal communication'. Use your knowledge of body language to lie to TOS, for instance, when you want to disarm them. Give TOS the appearance of being open, friendly and honest by not crossing your arms and legs, by sitting right next to them, by smiling frequently, by keeping your eyes wide open in order to feign interest, etc.

Countermeasures At the stage of still getting to know TOS, be sceptical of everything – both of what they say and their body language. About the only way of really finding out what they are like is by watching them closely at the bargaining-table and comparing their behaviour to the actions they take afterwards. It is only against such actions, decisions and concessions that you can check the veracity of both their verbal and nonverbal behaviour. There are no other gauges of their sincerity and integrity, except of course what trusted people have to say about them. Other countermeasures you may use are:

Apparent withdrawal

Tell TOS you've withdrawn from the negotiations, when you're still working behind the scenes (without their knowledge) to accomplish your goals, for example, through your temporary substitute in the negotiations. Do this when the situation has so much deteriorated that it is best to put in a new face to revive faith in the transactions. All alone, you know of course that you may come back still and bargain with TOS as you did before. You are waiting for the opportune time to again enter negotiations. If it appears that there are no improvements with your substitute, you should start working on other options. In the meantime you haven't broken off negotiations with TOS – they are still there, talking with your side. When you do decide to come back, though, you don't necessarily have to start where your substitute left off. Find reasons to rehash some issues if you think it is important.

Countermeasures Be suspicious the moment there's a change in leadership in TOS's team. Do not think that just because the leader is away, his or her influence has also disappeared. Don't back down. Bargain as hard as you did before. Stick to your plan, and let the new negotiator know how steadfast you are.

Be prepared to line up other alternatives for yourself, just in case the original negotiator returns and revives the problems you were confronted with before he/she left. That impasse may still exist, and *you* may have to withdraw the next time. Other countermeasures include the following:

Shills

A shill is somebody who works for you without TOS knowing it. You use shills to stimulate interest in the product or service you're selling, to establish a market price, to create competition and to test a low offer, among other things. The following are six tactics your shill can use.

Shill no. one: Whipsaw/auction

Let your shill bring together in your reception room all the vendors (or buyers) you're dealing with. The idea is to make the feeling of competition more intense among these people, to motivate them to give you a better deal.

Countermeasures If you are in the reception room and you see many of your competitors, take advantage of this opportunity to learn what they are offering TOS. Do not rely solely on your interview with TOS in order to find out. Talk to your competitors, some may be more than willing to tell you.

Just because TOS has contacted your biggest competitors, it doesn't mean you have to adjust your 'bottom line'. Stick to your offer. Do not concede if you don't have anything to gain. Other countermeasures you may use are:

Shill nos. two to six

These shills are often used by sellers. They are substantially the same in essence, although different in form. Once again, remember that the shill does or says the following even though it's not true.

Shill number two: show your prospects that other buyers are already touring your plant and are ready to buy your open capacity.

Shill number three: tell the prospective buyer, 'Our inventory is in short supply and has been subject to prior sale'.

Shill number four: tell your prospective buyer, 'I've only got one more left, and it'll take a month to get new ones in'.

Shill number five: Tell the buyer, 'Prices are likely to rise as soon as shortages develop'.

Shill number six: show your prospective buyer that other clients have already placed their orders. (One way of doing this is tagging the items on display with a sign that says 'Sold'.)

Countermeasures In response to shill number two, you can contact any of the buyers you know who had supposedly toured the plant and confirm if in fact they *are* buying up TOS's products.

With regard to shill number three, what TOS is telling you, in effect, is that they are not really interested in your business. If you want to buy their products, you will have a great deal of trouble, and you will have to give in to their terms. Our advice is to forget it. Withdraw and deal with somebody else. TOS is not really negotiating: TOS is dictating.

Shill numbers four and five are very similar, and both are commonly used to get you to buy right away. Ask yourself just how important the item is to you and how much time it is worthwhile to spend in looking for this item. If it is dispensable, forget it for now. And if you still care about it, come back next month. Of course, you must remember to check with other sources of the same item. They may have it too, and you may not have to play games with them.

Regarding shill number six, do not be taken in just because many items have been sold, if in fact they are sold. Remember that the seller may still have more inventory to unload, thus you still have room for bargaining. Also try finding other sources for the same item, or think of an equivalent or better substitute.

Appendix: Favourite tactics of eleven nations

This appendix sets out in summary form the favourite negotiating tactics chosen by groups of managers from eleven countries in five situations: (1) asking a seller for a lower price; (2) asking a buyer to pay more; (3) asking the boss for a rise; (4) asking the boss for a promotion; and (5) asking the boss if they could change their holiday dates.

The USA

1 These were the 12 favourite tactics chosen by American executives when they asked the seller for a lower price; these accounted for 51.7 per cent of all tactics picked here by Americans. They are listed in descending order of importance:

Take-it or-leave-it	189
You've got to do better than that	160
Remind TOS of the competition	146
Big pot	129
Be patient	176
Don't give in	144
Nibbling away	156
The well is dry: 'I'm ethically constrained from going any further...'	168

Keep the pressure on	132
The well is dry: 'I'm financially constrained...'	169
Deadlines	137
Funny money	218

2 These were the 15 favourite tactics chosen by American executives when they asked the buyer to pay more; these accounted for 55.5 per cent of all tactics picked here by Americans. They are listed in descending order of importance:

Big pot	129
You've got to do better than that	160
Be patient	176
Let's look at the record	139
Keep the pressure on	132
Remind TOS of the competition	146
Don't give in	144
Take-it-or-leave-it	189
Funny money	218
Turn the tables on TOS	158
Deadlines	137
We're the greatest!	141
Let's split the difference	210
Buy time	173
The well is dry: 'I'm financially constrained...'	169

3 These were the nine favourite tactics chosen by American executives when they asked their boss for a rise; these accounted for 51.3 per cent of all tactics picked here by Americans. They are listed in descending order of importance.

Let's look at the record	139
We're the greatest!	141
Control the agenda	153
Go beyond the call of duty	178
Keep the pressure on	132
Funny money	218
Anticipate TOS's objections	162
Be patient	176
Lay your cards on the table	179

4 These were the 12 favourite tactics chosen by American executives when they asked their boss for a promotion; these accounted for 60.1 per cent of all tactics picked here by Americans. They are listed in descending order of importance:

Let's look at the record	139
We're the greatest!	141
Go beyond the call of duty	178
Keep the pressure on	132
Lay your cards on the table	179
Be patient	177
Big pot	129
Get an ally	148
Make TOS an ally	184
Make TOS look good	183
Use flattery and charm	208
Anticipate TOS's objections	162

5 These were the 14 favourite tactics chosen by American executives when they asked their boss to change their holiday dates; these accounted for 53.6 per cent of all tactics picked by Americans. They are listed in descending order of importance:

Let's look at the record	139
Anticipate TOS's objections	162
Lay your cards on the table	179
Keep the pressure on	132
Make TOS feel guilty	220
Go beyond the call of duty	178
Use flattery and charm	208
Don't give in	144
Intimidate by legitimacy	198
Rely on policy	163
Get an ally	148
Pull rank	215
Acting crazy	195
Big pot	129

Canada

1 These were the four favourite tactics chosen by Canadian executives when they asked the seller for a lower price; these accounted for 50.0 per cent of all tactics picked here by Canadians. They are listed in descending order of importance:

Let's split the difference	210
Big pot	129
You've got to do better than that	160
Shill number one: Whipsaw/auction	223

2 These were the three favourite tactics chosen by Canadian executives when they asked the buyer to pay more; these accounted for 44.4 per cent of all tactics picked here by Canadians. They are listed in descending order of importance:

Big pot	129
Let's split the difference	210
Escalation (NB: This was not included in Chapter 7: escalation means that even after you and TOS have agreed on the settlement terms, you ask for more just before the signing of the contract.)	

3 These were the four favourite tactics chosen by Canadian executives when they asked their boss for a rise; these accounted for 47.1 per cent of all tactics picked here by Canadians. They are listed in descending order of importance:

Big pot	129
Let's look at the record	139
We're the greatest!	141
Make TOS feel guilty	220

4 These were the four favourite tactics chosen by Canadian executives when they asked their boss for a promotion; these accounted for 68.8 per cent of all tactics picked here by Canadians. They are listed in descending order of importance:

We're the greatest!	141
Let's look at the record	139
Get a prestigious ally	150
Use flattery and charm	208

5   These were the three favourite tactics chosen by Canadian executives when they asked their boss to change their holiday dates; these accounted for 38.9 per cent of all tactics picked by Canadians. They are listed in descending order of importance:

The power of powerlessness	145
Anticipate TOS's objections	162
Make TOS feel guilty	220

Hong Kong

1   These were the nine favourite tactics chosen by Hong Kong executives when they asked the seller for a lower price; these accounted for 44.4 per cent of all tactics picked here by Hong Kong executives. They are listed in descending order of importance:

Remind TOS of the competition	146
Big pot	129
Let's look at the record	139
Funny money	218
Deadlines	137
Take-it-or-leave-it	189
The power of powerlessness	145
Nibbling away	156
The well is dry: 'I'm financially constrained...'	169

2   These were the eight favourite tactics chosen by Hong Kong executives when they asked the buyer to pay more; these accounted for 36.7 per cent of all tactics picked here by Hong Kong executives. They are listed in descending order of importance:

Let's look at the record	139
Funny money	218
Remind TOS of the competition	146
Be patient	176
Big pot	129
Keep the pressure on	132
Faking	187
Get a prestigious ally	150

3   These were the six favourite tactics chosen by Hong Kong executives when they asked their boss for a rise; these accounted for 41.6 per cent of all tactics picked here by Hong Kong executives. They are listed in descending order of importance:

Let's look at the record	139
Big pot	129
Keep the pressure on	132
Be patient	176
The power of powerlessness	145
We're the greatest!	141

4   These were the eight favourite tactics chosen by Hong Kong executives when they asked their boss for a promotion. These eight tactics accounted for 43.7 per cent of all tactics picked here by Hong Kong executives. They are listed in descending order of importance:

Let's look at the record	139
Keep the pressure on	132
Big pot	129
Leak information to TOS	193
Lay your cards on the table	179
We're the greatest!	141
Be patient	176
Make promises	151

5   These were the 13 favourite tactics chosen by Hong Kong executives when they asked their boss to change their holiday dates; these accounted for 45.2 per cent of all tactics picked by Hong Kong executives. They are listed in descending order of importance:

Keep the pressure on	132
The power of powerlessness	145
Acting crazy	195
Rely on policy	163
Admit your mistakes	171
Lay your cards on the table	179
Big pot	129
Let's look at the record	139
Nibbling away	156

Trial balloon	190
Get an ally	148
Let's split the difference	210
Make promises	151

Taiwan

1 These were the ten favourite tactics chosen by Taiwan executives when they asked the seller for a lower price; these accounted for 50.9 per cent of all tactics picked here by Taiwan executives. They are listed in descending order of importance:

Take-it-or-leave-it	189
Remind TOS of the competition	146
Shill number one: Whipsaw/auction	223
You've got to do better than that	160
Big pot	129
Funny money	218
Faking	187
Keep the pressure on	132
Nibbling away	156
Put TOS on the defensive	216

2 These were the 13 favourite tactics chosen by Taiwan executives when they asked the buyer to pay more; these accounted for 47.5 per cent of all tactics picked here by Taiwan executives. They are listed in descending order of importance:

We're the greatest!	141
Big pot	129
Shill no. three: Tell the prospective buyer, 'Our inventory is in short supply and has been subject to prior sale'	224
Shill no. five: Tell the buyer, 'Prices are likely to rise as soon as shortages develop'	224
Deadlines	137
Funny money	218
Leak information to TOS	193
Be patient	176
Go beyond the call of duty	178
Keep the pressure on	132

Let's look at the record	139
Shill no. two: Show your prospects that other buyers are already touring your plant and are ready to buy up your open capacity	224
Make TOS an ally	184

3 These were the nine favourite tactics chosen by Taiwan executives when they asked their boss for a rise; these accounted for 47.8 per cent of all tactics picked here by Taiwan executives. They are listed in descending order of importance:

Keep the pressure on	132
Let's look at the record	139
Trial balloon	190
Funny money	218
We're the greatest!	141
You've got to do better than that	160
Destroy a straw man	202
Leak information to TOS	193
Make TOS look good	183

4 These were the ten favourite tactics chosen by Taiwan executives when they asked their boss for a promotion; these accounted for 51.9 per cent of all tactics picked here by Taiwan executives. They are listed in descending order of importance:

Let's look at the record	139
Keep the pressure on	132
We're the greatest!	141
Be patient	176
Remind TOS of the competition	146
Say, 'Yes, but...'	172
Make TOS look good	183
Trial balloon	190
Leak information to TOS	193
Make TOS feel guilty	183

5 These were the ten favourite tactics chosen by Taiwan exectives when they asked their boss to change their holiday dates; these accounted for 44.4 per cent of all tactics picked by Taiwan executives. They are listed in descending order of importance:

Admit your mistakes	171
Anticipate TOS's objections	162
Use flattery and charm	208
Say, 'Yes, but...'	176
Destroy a straw man	202
Make promises	151
Make TOS an ally	184
Trial balloon	190
You've got to do better than that	160
Make TOS feel guilty	220

Singapore

1 These were the ten favourite tactics chosen by Singapore executives when they asked the seller for a lower price; these accounted for 48.1 per cent of all tactics picked here by Singapore executives. They are listed in descending order of importance:

Remind TOS of the competition	146
Take-it-or-leave-it	189
Keep the pressure on	132
Funny money	218
Big pot	129
Use a shotgun	214
You've got to do better than that	160
Stall for time	164
The power of powerlessness	145
Buy time	173

2 These were the eight favourite tactics chosen by Singapore executives when they asked the buyer to pay more; these accounted for 48.6 per cent of all tactics picked here by Singapore executives. They are listed in descending order of importance:

Turn the tables on TOS	158
You've got to do better than that	160
Big pot	129
Keep the pressure on	132
Remind TOS of the competition	146

Shill no. three: Tell your prospective buyer, 'Our 224
inventory is in short supply and has been subject to
prior sale'

Shill no. four: Tell your prospective buyer, 'I've got only 224
one more left, and it'll take a month to get new ones in'

The well is dry: 'I'm ethically constrained from going 168
any further...'

3 These were the nine favourite tactics chosen by Singapore
executives when they asked their boss for a rise; these
accounted for 60.0 per cent of all tactics picked here by
Singapore executives. They are listed in descending order of
importance:

Let's look at the record	139
Keep the pressure on	132
You've got to do better than that	160
Acting crazy	195
Make TOS feel guilty	220
Rely on policy	163
Go beyond the call of duty	178
Funny money	218
Make TOS look good	183

4 These were the nine favourite tactics chosen by Singapore
executives when they asked their boss for a promotion; these
accounted for 62.2 per cent of all tactics picked here by
Singapore executives. They are listed in descending order of
importance:

Let's look at the record	139
Keep the pressure on	132
Be patient	176
Remind TOS of the competition	146
Go beyond the call of duty	178
Lay your cards on the table	179
We're the greatest!	141
Leak information to TOS	193
Make promises	151

5 These were the ten favourite tactics chosen by Singapore
executives when they asked their boss to change their holiday
dates; these accounted for 48.6 per cent of all tactics picked by

Singapore executives. They are listed in descending order of importance:

Use flattery and charm	208
Be patient	176
Anticipate TOS's objections	162
Go beyond the call of duty	178
Acting crazy	195
Keep the pressure on	132
Leak information to TOS	193
Rely on policy	163
Admit your mistakes	171
One-step fall back	185

Malaysia

1   These were the four favourite tactics chosen by Malaysian executives when they asked the seller for a lower price; these accounted for 33.3 per cent of all tactics picked here by Malaysian executives. They are listed in descending order of importance:

Keep the pressure on	132
Take-it-or-leave-it	189
Funny money	218
Apparent withdrawal	222

2   These were the seven favourite tactics chosen by Malaysian executives when they asked the buyer to pay more; these accounted for 29.2 per cent of all tactics picked here by Malaysian executives. They are listed in descending order of importance:

Big pot	129
Do the opposite	187
Keep the pressure on	132
Let an expert negotiate for you	155
Nibbling away	156
Turn the tables on TOS	158
You've got to do better than that	160

3   These were the four favourite tactics chosen by Malaysian executives when they asked their boss for a rise; these accounted for 33.3 per cent of all tactics picked here by Malaysian executives. They are listed in descending order of importance:

Let's look at the record	139
You've got to do better than that	160
Be patient	176
Lay your cards on the table	179

4   This was the one favourite tactic chosen by Malaysian executives when they asked their boss for a promotion; this accounted for 8.7 per cent of all tactics picked here by Malaysian executives.

Go beyond the call of duty	178

5   These were the two favourite tactics chosen by Malaysian executives when they asked their boss to change their holiday dates; these accounted for 19.0 per cent of all tactics picked here by Malaysian executives. They are listed in descending order of importance:

Smokescreen no. four: Create an equal but opposite issue	224

Escalation (NB: This was not included in Chapter 7: escalation means that even after you and TOS have agreed on the settlement terms, you ask for more just before the signing of the contract.)

Indonesia

1   These were the seven favourite tactics chosen by Indonesian executives when they asked the seller for a lower price; these accounted for 43.8 per cent of all tactics picked here by Indonesian executives. They are listed in descending order of importance:

Escalation (NB: This was not included in Chapter 7: escalation means that even after you and TOS have agreed on the settlement terms, you ask for more just before the signing of the contract.)

Shill no. one: Whipsaw/Auction   223
Low-balling (NB: This was not included in Chapter 7:
low-balling means you come in with such minimal
demands that TOS thinks you're an easy mark.
Actually, you've built in a few clauses like inflation
protection or cost-plus, etc. to protect yourself.)
We're the greatest!   141
You've got to do better than that   160
Stall for time   164
Be patient   176

2   These were the nine favourite tactics chosen by Indonesian
executives when they asked the buyer to pay more; these
accounted for 52.1 per cent of all tactics picked here by
Indonesian executives. They are listed in descending order of
importance:

Big pot   129
Shill no. one: Whipsaw/auction   223
Let's look at the record   139
Nibbling away   156
Turn the tables on TOS   158
Remind TOS of the competition   146
Say, 'Yes, and...'   172
Learn when to leave well enough alone   174
Let's split the difference   210

3   These were the three favourite tactics chosen by Indonesian
executives when they asked their boss for a rise; these
accounted for 22.9 per cent of all tactics picked here by
Indonesian executives. They are listed in descending order of
importance:

Trial balloon   190
Funny money   218
Make TOS feel guilty   220

4   These were the three favourite tactics chosen by Indonesian
executives when they asked their boss for a promotion; these
accounted for 20.8 per cent of all tactics picked here by
Indonesian executives. They are listed in descending order of
importance:

Let's look at the record	139
Pull rank	215
Leak information to TOS	193

5 These were the ten favourite negotiating tactics chosen by Indonesian executives when they asked their boss to change their holiday dates; these accounted for 58.3 per cent of all tactics picked here by Indonesian executives. They are listed in descending order of importance:

Be patient	177
Go beyond the call of duty	178
Make TOS look good	183
Trial balloon	190
Let's look at the record	139
Nibbling away	156
Reposition TOS	159
Take-it-or-leave-it	189
Smokescreen no. one: Put a new person in charge	223
Apparent withdrawal	222

Philippines

1 These were the seven favourite tactics chosen by Filipino executives when they asked the seller for a lower price; these accounted for 54.3 per cent of all tactics picked here by Filipino executives. They are listed in descending order of importance:

Take-it-or-leave-it	189
Funny money	218
Let's split the difference	210
Nibbling away	156
You've got to do better than that	160
Remind TOS of the competition	146
The well is dry: 'I'm ethically constrained from going any further...'	168

2 These were the four favourite tactics chosen by Filipino executives when they asked the buyer to pay more; these accounted for 38.5 per cent of all tactics picked here by

Filipino executives. They are listed in descending order of importance:

Funny money	218
Remind TOS of the competition	146
Shill no. one: Whipsaw/auction	223
Let's split the difference	210

3 These were the ten favourite tactics chosen by Filipino executives when they asked their boss for a rise; these accounted for 66.7 per cent of all tactics picked here by Filipino executives. They are listed in descending order of importance:

Let's look at the record	139
We're the greatest!	141
Big pot	129
Trial balloon	190
Acting crazy	195
Keep the pressure on	132
Use a shotgun	214
Anticipate TOS's objections	162
Get an ally	148
Leak information to TOS	193

4 These were the five favourite tactics chosen by Filipino executives when they asked their boss for a promotion; these accounted for 45.8 per cent of all tactics picked here by Filipino executives. They are listed in descending order of importance:

Make TOS feel guilty	220
Keep the pressure on	132
Let's look at the record	139
We're the greatest!	141
Use flattery and charm	208

5 These were the four favourite tactics chosen by Filipino executives when they asked their boss to change their holiday dates; these accounted for 33.3 per cent of all tactics picked by Filipino executives. They are listed in descending order of importance:

Acting crazy	195
Issues surprise	212
Let an expert negotiate for you	155
Make TOS an ally	184

Australia

1 These were the nine favourite tactics chosen by Australian executives when they asked the seller for a lower price; these accounted for 53.0 per cent of all tactics picked here by Australian executives. They are listed in descending order of importance:

Remind TOS of the competition	146
You've got to do better than that	160
The well is dry: 'I'm financially constrained...'	169
Faking	187
Keep the pressure on	132
Take-it-or-leave-it	189
Don't give in	144
Doomsday	203
Be patient	176

2 These were the ten favourite tactics chosen by Australian executives when they asked the buyer to pay more; these accounted for 53.7 per cent of all tactics picked here by Australian executives. They are listed in descending order of importance:

Be patient	176
Big pot	129
Let's look at the record	139
Remind TOS of the competition	146
Turn the tables on TOS	158
We're the greatest!	141
Anticipate TOS's objections	162
Don't give in	144
Funny money	218
Stall for time	164

3   These were the seven favourite tactics chosen by Australian executives when they asked their boss for a rise; these accounted for 63.2 per cent of all tactics picked here by Australian executives. They are listed in descending order of importance:

Let's look at the record	139
Big pot	129
We're the greatest!	141
Anticipate TOS's objections	162
Keep the pressure on	132
Lay your cards on the table	179
Get an ally	148

4   These were the ten favourite tactics chosen by Australian executives when they asked their boss for a promotion; these accounted for 60.6 per cent of all tactics picked here by Australian executives. They are listed in descending order of importance:

Let's look at the record	139
Keep the pressure on	132
We're the greatest!	141
Turn the tables on TOS	158
Reposition TOS	159
Anticipate TOS's objections	162
Don't give in	144
Be patient	176
Go beyond the call of duty	178
Lay your cards on the table	179

5   These were the six favourite tactics chosen by Australian executives when they asked their boss to change their holiday dates; these accounted for 47.5 per cent of all tactics picked here by Australian executives. They are listed in descending order of importance:

Anticipate TOS's objections	162
Don't give in	144
Make TOS feel guilty	220
Keep the pressure on	132
Admit your mistakes	171
Lay your cards on the table	179

New Zealand

1 These were the seven favourite tactics chosen by New Zealand executives when they asked the seller for a lower price; these accounted for 47.9 per cent of all tactics picked here by New Zealand executives. They are listed in descending order of importance:

Remind TOS of the competition	146
Be patient	176
Take-it-or-leave-it	189
You've got to do better than that	160
Funny money	218
The well is dry: 'I'm financially constrained...'	169
Buy time	173

2 These were the eight favourite tactics chosen by New Zealand executives when they asked the buyer to pay more; these accounted for 39.7 per cent of all tactics picked here by New Zealand executives. They are listed in descending order of importance:

Big pot	129
Be patient	176
Keep the pressure on	132
Take-it-or-leave-it	189
You've got to do better than that	160
Anticipate TOS's objections	162
Remind TOS of the competition	146
Make promises	151

3 These were the six favourite tactics chosen by New Zealand executives when they asked their boss for a rise; these accounted for 47.1 per cent of all tactics picked here by New Zealand executives. They are listed in descending order of importance:

Let's look at the record	139
Lay your cards on the table	179
Big pot	129
Keep the pressure on	132
We're the greatest!	141
Get an ally	148

4 These were the seven favourite tactics chosen by New Zealand executives when they asked their boss for a promotion; these accounted for 64.8 per cent of all tactics picked here by New Zealand executives. They are listed in descending order of importance:

Go beyond the call of duty	178
Let's look at the record	139
We're the greatest!	141
Be patient	176
Big pot	129
Keep the pressure on	132
Lay your cards on the table	179

5 These were the nine favourite tactics chosen by New Zealand executives when they asked their boss to change their holiday dates; these accounted for 51.4 per cent of all tactics picked by New Zealand executives. They are listed in descending order of importance:

Lay your cards on the table	179
Admit your mistakes	171
Anticipate TOS's objections	162
Use flattery and charm	208
Keep the pressure on	132
Half-step fall back	209
Learn when to leave well enough alone	174
Go beyond the call of duty	178
Make TOS an ally	184

South Africa

1 These were the ten favourite tactics chosen by South African executives when they asked the seller for a lower price; these accounted for 46.7 per cent of all tactics picked here by South African executives. They are listed in descending order of importance:

Remind TOS of the competition	146
You've got to do better than that	160
Keep the pressure on	132
Take-it-or-leave-it	189

Big pot	129
Faking	187
Turn the tables on TOS	158
Trump TOS's ace	142
Don't give in	144
Be patient	176

2 These were the 12 favourite tactics chosen by South African executives when they asked the buyer to pay more; these accounted for 56.5 per cent of all tactics picked here by South African executives. They are listed in descending order of importance:

Big pot	129
Keep the pressure on	132
Turn the tables on TOS	158
Don't give in	144
Let's look at the record	139
Funny money	218
You've got to do better than that	160
Anticipate TOS's objections	162
Get angry at TOS on purpose (NB: This tactic is not included in Chapter 7. One way of making TOS angry is to say something like, 'Your offer is an insult' and then walk away.)	
Good guy/bad buy	213
Trump TOS's ace	142
Shill no. five: Tell the buyer, 'Prices are likely to rise as soon as shortages develop'	224

3 These were the ten favourite tactics chosen by South African executives when they asked their boss for a rise; these accounted for 57.4 per cent of all tactics picked here by South African executives. They are listed in descending order of importance:

Let's look at the record	139
Keep the pressure on	132
Big pot	129
Lay your cards on the table	179
Acting crazy	195
Make TOS feel guilty	220

Remind TOS of the competition	146
We're the greatest!	141
Don't give in	144
Go beyond the call of duty	178

4 These were the ten favourite tactics chosen by South African executives when they asked their boss for a promotion; these accounted for 58.1 per cent of all tactics picked here by South African executives. They are listed in descending order of importance:

Let's look at the record	139
Keep the pressure on	132
Stick to your plan/be committed	167
We're the greatest!	141
Anticipate TOS's objections	162
Go beyond the call of duty	178
Remind TOS of the competition	146
Don't give in	144
Make TOS feel guilty	220
Make promises	151

5 These were the six favourite tactics chosen by South African executives when they asked their boss to change their holiday dates; these accounted for 37.5 per cent of all tactics picked here by South African executives. They are listed in descending order of importance:

Lay your cards on the table	179
Keep the pressure on	132
The power of powerlessness	145
Acting crazy	195
Control the agenda	153
Anticipate TOS's objections	162

References

Introduction to Part I

1. The materials for the section, 'The changing international business environement' were synthesized from: William A. Dymsza, 'Trends in multinational business and global environments: a Perspective', *Journal of International Business Studies*, Winter 1984, 37; John D. Daniels and Lee H. Radebaugh, *Internatinal Business: Environments and Operations* (Menlo Park, Calif. Addison-Wesley, 1986), pp. 15, 16, 826, 829.
2. The materials for the section, 'Increased foreign presence in the USA' were adapted from: Charles W. Stevens, 'Multinational firms still expect dollar to fall further', *Wall Street Journal*, 11 January 1988, p. 6; Blanca Riemer *et al.*, 'A cash-rich Europe finds the US ripe for picking', *Businessweek*, 25 January 1988, pp. 48, 49; Michael R. Sesit, 'Japanese acquisitions in US jumped to $5.9 billion in '87; strong yen cited', *Wall Street Journal*, 21 January 1988, p. 14; 'Firestone Purchase Completed', *Wall Street Journal*, 6 May 1988, p. 35; 'Japanese management "magic" expected to give Firestone boost', *Chattanooga Times*, 23 February 1988, p. C-7.
3. The materials for the previous three paragraphs were combined from: Steven Solomon, 'Europe's quiet revolution', *Forbes*, 14 December 1987, p. 52; Joyce Heard *et al.*, 'How business is creating Europe Inc.', *Businessweek*, 7 September 1987, p. 40; Shawn Tully, 'Europe gets ready for 1992', *Fortune*, 1 February 1988, p. 84.
4. Heard *et al.*, 'How business is creating Europe Inc.', *op. cit.*, p. 40; John Rossant, 'Can France's great sell-off sell Chirac as president?, *Businessweek*, 25 May 1987, p. 76.
5. Riemer, 'Europe: taking the sting out of the plunging dollar', *op. cit.*, pp. 72, 73.
6. The material for the previous two paragraphs were taken from: Tully, 'Europe gets ready for 1992', *op. cit.*, pp. 81, 82, 84.

7. Materials for the section 'The growing significance of Japan in international business' were combined from: Dymsza, 'Trends in multinational business and global environments: a perspective', *op. cit.*, pp. 27, 28; Kenichi Ohmae, *Triad Powers: The Coming Shape of Global Competition* (New York: The Free Press, 1985), pp. 64, 68, 69, 81, 118, 119.

8. The materials for the section 'Competition made steeper by industrializing Third World countries' were consolidated from: Dymsza, 'Trends in multinational business and global environments: a perspective', *op. cit.*, pp. 29, 30, 41.

9. The materials for the section 'Peculiar problems in developing countries' was taken from: *ibid.*, pp. 31, 33.

10. The materials for the section 'Race for the lead in high-tech industries forges alliances' were incorporated from: Kenichi Ohmae, *Triad Power, op. cit.*, pp. 14, 15, 19, 20.

11. Materials for the section 'Increased modernization, education, and technological diffusion improve business practices' were gathered from: Dymsza, 'Trends in multinational business and global environments: a perspective' *op. cit.*, p. 39; Heard *et al.*, 'How business is creating Europe Inc.', *op. cit.*, p. 41; 'A special report: technology in the workplace: a tower of babble', *Wall Street Journal*, 12 June 1987, p. 30.

12. The material for the section 'Shift to the short-term perspective' was taken from: Dymsza, 'Trends in multinational business and global environments: a perspective', *op. cit.*, p. 38.

Chapter 1 The six stages

1. The introduction to 'Stage 1: prenegotiation' was adapted from: J.B. McCall and M.B. Warrington, *Marketing by Agreement: a Cross-Cultural Approach to Business Negotiations* (New York: Wiley, 1984), p. 30; Roy J. Lewicki and Joseph A. Litterer, *Negotiation* (Homewood, Ill.: Richard D. Irwin, 1985), pp. 45–73; Robert B. Maddux, *Successful Negotiation* (Los Altos, Calif.: Crisp Publications, 1986), pp. 22–23, 31; Gordon F. Shea, *Creative Negotiating* (Boston, Mass.: CBI Publishing, 1983), pp. 54–9.

2. Materials for 'Stage 1: prenegotiation' were synthesized from: Douglas Henne, Marvin J. Levine, W.J. Usery, Jr and Herbert Fishgold, 'A case study in cross-cultural mediation: the General Motors–Toyota Joint Venture', *Cross-Cultural Mediation*, 41(3), September 1986, 6–8; 'GM, Toyota agree to explore joint output of small car, a proposal rejected by Ford', *Wall Street Journal*, 9 March 1982, pp. 2–3; J. Koten, 'GM "90% sure" of joint venture accord with Toyota in US as the talks drag on', *Wall Street Journal*, 24 January 1983, pp. 2, 14; R.D. Hershey, Jr, 'Toyota warned by FTC', *New York Times*, 19 October 1983, pp. D-I and D-24; A. Fleming, 'GM–Toyota: blazing topic', *Automotive News*, 21 February 1985; John Graham and Yoshihiro Sano, *Smart Bargaining: Doing Business with the Japanese* (Cambridge, Mass.: Ballinger, 1984), pp. 113–15; Stephen E. Weiss, 'Creating the GM–Toyota joint venture: a case in complex negotiation', *Columbia Journal of World Business*, Summer 1987, 32; 'How GM–Toyota deal buys time', *Businessweek*, 28 February 1983, p. 32; J. Koten, 'GM, Toyota Pact is expected soon on joint output', *Wall Street Journal*, 31 January 1983, p. 2.

3. Materials for the section 'Stage 2: entry' were taken from: Weiss, 'Creating the GM–Toyota joint venture', *op. cit.,* p. 32, 33; N.B. Thayer and S.E. Weiss, 'Japan: the changing logic of a former minor power', in Hanss Binnendijk (ed.), *National Negotiating Styles* (Foreign Service Institute, US Department of State, 1987) pp. 45–74; Henne, Levine, Usery, and Fishgold, 'A case study in cross-cultural mediation', *op. cit.,* pp. 9–11.
4. Materials for the section 'Stage 3: establishing effective relationships with TOS' were adapted from: Henne, Levine, Usery, and Fishgold, 'A case study in cross-cultural mediation', *op. cit.,* p. 11; Weiss, 'Creating the GM–Toyota joint venture', *op. cit.,* p. 33.
5. The section 'Stage 4: Learning more about TOS and reformulating your earlier strategies' was written from: Henne, Levine, Usery and Fishgold, 'A case study in cross-cultural mediation', *op. cit.,* pp. 12–13; Weiss, 'Creating the GM–Toyota joint venture', *op. cit.,* p. 33.
6. Materials for the section 'Stage 5: bargaining and concession-making' were adapted from: Roger Fisher and William Ury, *Getting To Yes* (Harrisonburg, Va: Penguin Books/R.R. Donnelley, 1983), pp. 21, 22, 45, 61, 86; Henne, Levine, Usery, and Fishgold, 'A case study in cross-cultural mediation', *op. cit.,* pp. 12–13; Weiss, 'Creating the GM–Toyota joint venture', *op. cit.,* pp. 29, 33; Shea, *Creative Negotiating,* pp. 82–4.
7. The section Stage 6: reaching agreement' was written from materials gathered from: Hershey, Jr, 'Toyota warned by FTC', *op. cit.;* Henne, Levine, Usery, and Fishgold, 'A case study in cross-cultural mediation', *op. cit.,* pp. 14–15; Weiss, 'Creating the GM–Toyota joint venture', *op. cit.,* pp. 29, 33.

Chapter 3 The ideal negotiator

1. The first section was adapted from the following sources: Jagdish N. Sheth, 'Cross-cultural influences on the buyer–seller interaction negotiation process', *Asia Pacific Journal of Management,* September 1983, 51; David N. Burt, 'The nuances of negotiating overseas', *Journal of Purchasing and Materials Management,* Winder 1984, 5, 6; Glen Fisher, *International Negotiation: A Cross-Cultural Perspective* (Chicago: Intercultural Press, 1980) pp. 28–30; Ashok Kapoor, 'MNC negotiations: characteristics and planning implications', *Columbia Journal of World Business,* Winter 1974, 125; John Fayerweather and Ashok Kapoor, *Strategy and Negotiation for the International Corporation: Guidelines and Cases* (Cambridge, Mass.: Ballinger, 1976), p. 38; Louis T. Wells, Jr, 'Negotiating with Third World governments', *Harvard Business Review,* January–February 1977, 55(1), 73, 79.
2. The second section was synthesized from the following: Jeffrey A. Fadiman, 'Special report: a traveller's guide to gifts and bribes', *Harvard Business Review,* July–August 1986, 4, 124, 125, 126, 130; Farouk I. Heiba, 'International business negotiations: a strategic planning model', *International Marketing Review,* Autumn–Winter 1984, 9; Douglas Lamont, 'International bribery: cases involving Pacific rim nations and recommended actions', paper presented at Academy of International Business Conference, Southeast Region, New Orleans, Louisiana, USA, 4–7 November 1987; 'How to speak basic baksheesh: a palm-greasing primer', *Trips,* Spring 1988, 1, 53–6.

3. Materials for the third section were taken from: John A. Reeder, 'When West meets East: cultural aspects of doing business in Asia', *Business Horizons*, January–February 1987, 71–4; Heiba, 'International business negotiations: a strategic planning model', *op. cit.*, p. 8; Burt, 'The nuances of negotiating overseas', *op. cit.*, pp. 3, 5.

4. The fourth section was taken from McCall and Warrington, *Marketing by Agreement*, *op. cit.*, pp. 42–5, 47, 48; Albert Mehrabian, 'Communication without words', *Psychology Today*, September 1968, 2, 53–5; Fisher, *International Negotiation*, *op. cit.*, pp. 25, 53–4; Lennie Copeland and Lewis Griggs, *Going International: How to Make Friends and Deal Effectively in the Global Marketplace* (New York: Random House, 1985), p. 112.

5. Materials for the fifth section were taken from: Burt, 'The nuances of negotiating overseas', *op. cit.*, p. 5; Fisher, *International negotiation*, *op. cit.*, p. 39; Lucian W. Pye, 'The China trade: making the deal', *Harvard Business Review*, July–August 1986, 4, 77.

6. Phyllis Birnbaum, 'Humoring the Japanese', *Across the Board*, October 1986, p. 11.

7. Material for the sixth section was taken from: Phyllis Birnbaum, 'Humoring the Japanese', *Across the Board*, October 1986, 23 (11), 10.

8. Materials for the seventh section were adapted from: M.W. Searls, Jr., 'Business negotiations with the People's Republic of China', in American Chamber of Commerce, *Doing Business in China* (Hong Kong: South China Morning Post, 1980), pp. 138–40; Richard H. Solomon, *Chinese Political Negotiating Behaviour: A Briefing Analysis* (Santa Monica, Calif.: Rand Corporation, December 1985), pp. vi, 2, 5, 8; Business International Corporation, *Business Strategies for the People's Republic of China* (New York: Business International Corporation, November 1980), p. 310; Lucian W. Pye, *Chinese Commercial Negotiating Style* (Cambridge, Mass.: Oelgeschlager, Gunn, and Hain, 1982), p. 35.

9. Materials for the last section were synthesized from: James A. McCaffrey and Craig R. Hafner, 'When two cultures collide: doing business overseas', *Training and Development Journal*, October 1985, 39(10), 28; Fadiman, 'Special report: a traveler's guide to gifts and bribes', *op. cit.*, p. 124; Henry H. Calero and Bob Oskam, *Negotiate the Deal You Want* (New York: Dodd, Mead, 1983), pp. 108–9.

Introduction to Part II

1. 'Where the jobs are', *Newsweek*, 2 February 1987, p. 44
2. Stephen Bochner (ed.), *Cultures in Contact: Studies in Cross-Cultural Interaction* (New York: Pergamon, 1982), p. 48.
3. Richard W. Brislin, Kenneth Cushner, Craig Cherrie and Mahealani Yong, *Intercultural Interactions: A Practical Guide* (Beverly Hills, Calif.: Sage, 1986), pp. 305, 308.
4. Bochner, *Cultures in Contact*, *op. cit.*, p. 35.
5. Brislin *et al.*, *Intercultural Interactions*, *op. cit.*, p. 314.
6. Bernard Wysocki, Jr, 'Despite global role, many Japanese try to avoid foreigners', *Wall Street Journal*, 13 November 1986, p. 1.
7. Brislin, *et al.*, *Intercultural Interactions*, *op. cit.*, p. 319.
8. Bochner, *Cultures in Contact*, *op. cit.*, pp. 19–20.

9. Wysocki, 'Despite global role, many Japanese try to avoid foreigners', *op. cit.*, p. 1.
10. Brislin *et al.*, *Intercultural Interactions*, *op. cit.*, p. 262.
11. *Ibid.*, p. 263.
12. Wysocki, 'Despite global role, many Japanese try to avoid foreigners', *op. cit.*, p. 25.
13. Bochner, *Cultures in Contact*, *op. cit.*, p. 50.

Chapter 6 Nonverbal communications

1. JoAnn Craig, *Culture Shock! What Not to Do in Malaysia and Singapore, How and Why Not to Do It* (Singapore: Times Books International, 1979), p. 9.
2. Mark L. Knapp, *Essentials of Nonverbal Communication* (New York: Holt, Rinehart and Winston, 1980), pp. 29–30; Marjorie Fink Vargas, *Louder than Words: An Introduction to Nonverbal Communication* (Ames, Iowa: Iowa State University Press, 1986), pp. 39–40; Peter Bull, *Body Movement and Interpersonal Communication* (New York: Wiley, 1983), p. 41.
3. Paul Ekman, *Telling Lies: Clues to Deceit in the Marketplace, Politics, and Marriage* (New York: W.W. Norton, 1985), p. 126; Sheila J. Ramsey, 'Nonverbal behavior: an intercultural perspective', in Molefi Kete Asante, Eileen Newmark and Cecil A. Blake (eds), *Handbook of Intercultural Communication* (Beverly Hills, Calif.: Sage, 1975), p. 107; Robert Rosenthal, Judith A. Hall, M. Robin DiMatteo, Peter L. Rogers and Dan Archer, *Sensitivity to Nonverbal Communication: The PONS Test* (Baltimore, Md: Johns Hopkins University Press, 1979), p. 206.
4. SRI International, *Doing Business in The Philippines* (Menlo Park, Calif.: SRI International, 1987), pp. 8–9, *Doing Business in Thailand,* (1987), p. 12, and, *Doing Business in Malaysia,* (1987), p. 20.
5. SRI International, *Doing Business in France* (Menlo Park, Calif.: SRI International, 1987), p. 14; Sondra Snowdon, *The Global Edge: How Your Company Can Win in the International Marketplace* (New York: Simon and Schuster, 1986), p. 184.
6. Cathie Draine and Barbara Hall, *Culture Shock! Indonesia* (Singapore: Times Books International, 1986), p. 73; Lennie Copeland and Lewis Griggs, *Going International: How to Make Friends and Deal Effectively in the Global Marketplace* (New York: Random House, 1985), p. 110.
7. Neil Chesanow, *The World-Class Executive: How to Do Business Like a Pro around the World* (New York: Rawson Associates, 1985), p. 199; Adam Kendon, Richard M. Harris and Mary Ritchiekey (eds), *Origin of Behavior in Face-to-Face Interaction* (Chicago: Mouton, 1975), pp. 448–9.
8. Roger E. Axtell (Parker Pen Co.), *A Guide to International Behavior: Dos and Taboos around the World* (New York: Benjamin Co. Inc., 1985), p. 43; Bull, *Body Movement and Interpersonal Communication, op. cit.*, pp. 61–2; Desmond Morris, *The Pocket Guide to Manwatching* (London: Triad/Granada, 1982), pp. 51–2.
9. Axtell, *Dos and Taboos around the World, op. cit.*, p. 44. Morris, *The Pocket Guide to Manwatching, op. cit.*, pp. 51–2.
10. Axtell, *Dos and Taboos around the World, op. cit.*, p. 43.
11. *ibid.*, p. 44.
12. *loc. cit.*, p. 44.
13. Copeland and Griggs, *Going International, op. cit.* p. 111.

14. Joseph A. DeVito, *The Interpersonal Communication Book* (New York: Harper and Row, 1986), p. 194; Allan Pease, *Body Language: How to Read Others' Thoughts by Their Gestures* (Australia: Camel, 1981), p. 87.

15. Chesanow, *The World-Class Executive, op. cit.*, p. 258.

16. *ibid.*, p. 142; Vargas, *Louder Than Words, op, cit.*, p. 62.

17. Robert and Nanthapa Cooper, *Culture Shock! Thailand* (Singapore: Times Books International, 1982), p. 22.

18. SRI International, *Doing Business in Scandinavia* (Menlo Park, Calif.: SRI International, 1978), p. 7.

19. Vargas, *Louder than Words, op. cit.* p. 47; Mark L. Knapp, *Nonverbal Communication in Human Interaction* (New York: Holt, Rinehart and Winston, 1978), p. 308.

20. Copeland and Griggs, *Going International, op. cit.*, p. 112.

21. *ibid.*, p. 111; Vargas, *Louder than Words, op. cit.*, p. 62; Snowdon, *The Global Edge, op. cit.*, p. 105.

22. Vargas, *Louder than Words, op. cit.*, p. 47.

23. Loretta A. Malandro and Larry L. Barker, *Nonverbal Communication* (New York: Newberry Award Records, Inc., 1983), p. 170.

24. Copeland and Griggs, *Going International, op. cit.*, p. 109. SRI International, *Doing Business in Spain* (Menlo Park, Calif.: SRI International, 1978), p. 21, *Doing Business in the Soviet Union* (1978), p. 20, *Doing Business in Mexico* (1980), p. 15, *Doing Business in Indonesia* (1987), p. 23, *Doing Business on the Arabian Peninsula* (1978), p. 25, and *Doing Business in Thailand* (1987), p. 25; Chesanow, *The World-Class Executive, op. cit.*, p. 286.

25. SRI International, *Doing Business on the Arabian Peninsula, op. cit.*, p. 24; Bull, *Body Movement and Interpersonal Communication, op. cit.*, p. 78; DeVito, *The Interpersonal Communication Book, op. cit.*, pp. 212–13. Vargas, *Louder than Words, op. cit.*, p. 90.

26. SRI International, *Doing Business in Mexico, op. cit.*, p. 15; Axtell, *Dos and Taboos around the World, op. cit.*, p. 96.

27. SRI International, *Doing Business in Thailand, op. cit.*, p. 25.

28. SRI International, *Doing Business in France, op. cit.*, p. 16.

29. Copeland and Griggs, *Going International, op. cit.*, p. 109; Vargas, *Louder than Words, op. cit.*, p. 89.

30. SRI International, *Doing Business in Spain, op. cit.*, p. 21.

31. Chesanow, *The World-Class Executive, op. cit.*, p. 286; Bull, *Body Movement and Interpersonal Communication, op. cit.*, p. 78; DeVito, *The Interpersonal Communication Book, op. cit.*, p. 213; Vargas, *Louder than Words, op. cit.*, pp. 89–90; Albert Mehrabian, *Silent Messages* (Belmont, Calif.: Wadsworth, 1971), p. 71; Knapp, *Nonverbal Communication in Human Interaction, op. cit.*, pp. 257–8; Ramsey, 'Nonverbal behavior: an intercultural perspective', *op. cit.*, pp. 126–8.

32. SRI International, *Doing Business in Great Britain,* (Menlo Park, Calif.: SRI International, 1978), p. 17, *Doing Business in India* (1979), p. 18, *Doing Business in Korea* (1980), p. 21, *Doing Business in Singapore* (1987), p. 21, *Doing Business in Taiwan* (1979), p. 19, *Doing Business in Scandinavia* (1978), p. 15, and *Doing Business in the People's Republic of China* (1979), p. 47; Axtell, *Dos and Taboos around the World, op. cit.*, p. 31; Copeland and Griggs, *Going International, op. cit.*, p. 109; Malandro and Barker, *Nonverbal Communication, op. cit.*, p. 252.

33. SRI International, *Doing Business in Thailand, op. cit.*, p. 23, and *Doing Business in Taiwan, op. cit.*, p. 19; Craig, *Culture Shock! What Not to Do in Malaysia and Singapore, op. cit.*, p. 134.

34. SRI International, *Doing Business in Scandinavia, op. cit.,* p. 15.
35. SRI International, *Doing Business in the United States* (Menlo Park, Calif.: SRI International, 1978), p. 21; Bull, *Body Movement and Interpersonal Communication, op. cit.,* p. 78; Vargas, *Louder than Words, op. cit.,* pp. 85–6; Malandro and Barker, *Nonverbal Communication, op. cit.,* p. 249; DeVito, *The Interpersonal Communication Book, op. cit.,* pp. 211–13.
36. SRI International, *Doing Business in India, op. cit.,* p. 18.
37. SRI International, *Doing Business in the Philippines, op. cit.,* p. 18, *Doing Business in Thailand, op. cit.,* p. 33, *Doing Business in Korea, op. cit.,* p. 21, *Doing Business in Malaysia, op. cit.,* p. 20, and *Doing Business in Indonesia, op. cit.,* p. 21; Cooper, *Culture Shock! Thailand, op. cit.,* p. 16; Axtell, *Dos and Taboos around the World, op. cit.,* p. 46.
38. Craig, *Culture Shock! What Not to Do in Malaysia and Singapore, op. cit.,* p. 89. SRI International, *Doing Business on the Arabian Peninsula, op. cit.,* p. 22; *Doing Business in Indonesia, op. cit.,* p. 21; and *Doing Business in India, op. cit.,* p. 18.
39. Vargas, *Louder than Words, op. cit.,* pp. 37–8; Copeland and Griggs, *Going International, op. cit.,* pp. 109–11.
40. Chesanow, *The World-Class Executive, op. cit.,* p. 199; Axtell, *Dos and Taboos around the World, op. cit.,* p. 45; Desmond Morris, *The Pocket Guide to Manwatching* (London: Triad/Granada, 1982), p. 99; SRI International, *Doing Business in Singapore, op. cit.,* p. 20, and, *Doing Business in Thailand, op. cit.,* p. 24.
41. SRI International, *Doing Business in Scandinavia, op. cit.,* p. 6, *Doing Business in Mexico, op. cit.,* p. 14, *Doing Business on the Arabian Peninsula, op. cit.,* p. 23, and *Doing Business in Singapore, op. cit.,* p. 19.
42. SRI International, *Doing Business in India, op cit.,* p. 18, *Doing Business in Taiwan, op. cit.,* p. 19, *Doing Business in Malaysia, op. cit.,* p. 20, and *Doing Business in Thailand, op. cit,* p. 23.
43. Copeland and Griggs, *Going International, op. cit.,* p. 112. SRI International, *Doing Business in Korea, op. cit.,* p. 21, *Doing Business in Indonesia, op. cit.,* p. 21 and *doing Business in Taiwan, op. cit.* p. 19.
44. SRI International, *Doing Business in the United States, op. cit.,* pp. 17–18, *Doing Business in Korea, op. cit.,* p. 21, and *Doing Business on the Arabian Peninsula, op. cit.,* p. 23.
45. Cooper, *Culture Shock! Thailand, op. cit.,* pp. 1–7; SRI International, *Doing Business in Thailand, op. cit.,* p. 12.
46. Craig, *Culture Shock! What Not to Do in Malaysia and Singapore, op. cit.,* p. 82. SRI International, *Doing Business in Malaysia, op. cit.,* pp. 10–11.
47. Boye de Mente, *The Japanese Way of Doing Business: The Psychology of Management in Japan* (Englewood Cliffs, NJ: Prentice-Hall, 1981), pp. 58–9; SRI International, *Doing Business in Japan, op. cit.,* p. 28.
48. Axtell, *Dos and Taboos around the World, op. cit.,* p. 32; SRI International, *Doing Business in Taiwan, op. cit.,* p. 19.
49. Axtell, *Dos and Taboos around the World, op. cit.,* pp. 33–5; Bull, *Body Movement and Interpersonal Communication, op. cit.,* p. 78; DeVito, *The Interpersonal Communication Book, op. cit.,* pp. 212–13; Vargas, *Louder Than Words, op. cit.,* p. 89; Mehrabian, *Silent Messages, op. cit.,* p. 71, Ramsey, 'Nonverbal behavior: an intercultural perspective', *op. cit.,* p. 126.
50. Chesanow, *The World-Class Executive, op. cit.,* pp. 79–80; SRI International, *Doing Business in Federal Republic of Germany, op. cit.,* p. 7.
51. Vargas, *Louder than Words, op. cit.,* p. 109; Chesanow, *The World-Class Executive, op. cit.,* p. 97. SRI International, *Doing Business in the United States, op. cit.,* p. 21.

52. Vargas, *Louder than Words, op. cit.,* p. 109. Chesanow, *The World-Class Executive, op. cit.,* pp. 97–8, 287. SRI International, *Doing Business in Great Britain, op. cit.,* p. 15; and *Doing Business in the Federal Republic of Germany, op. cit.,* p. 7.

53. De Mente, *The Japanese Way of Doing Business, op. cit.,* p. 69; SRI International, *Doing Business in Japan, op. cit.,* p. 5.

54. Chesanow, *The World-Class Executive, op. cit.,* p. 120; SRI International, *Doing Business in the Arabian Peninsula, op. cit,* pp. 24–5.

55. Glenn E. Littlepage, Julie Maddox and Martin A. Pineault, 'Recognition of discrepant nonverbal messages and detection of deception', *Perceptual and Motor Skills,* 60, 1985, 119; Paul Ekman and W.V. Friesen, 'Nonverbal leakage and clues to deception', *Psychiatry,* 32, 1969, 88–106; Paul Ekman and W.V. Friesen, 'Detecting deception from the body or face', *Journal of Personality and Social Psychology,* 29(2), 1974, 288–9; Paul Ekman, 'Facial signs, fantasies and possibilities', in Thomas A. Sebeok (ed.), *Sight, Sound, and Sense* (Bloomington, Ind.: Indiana University Press, 1978); Glenn Littlepage and Martin A. Pineault, 'Detection of deception of planned and spontaneous communication', *Journal of Social Psychology,* 125 (2), April 1985, 195, 'Detection of deceptive factual statements from the body and face', *Personality and Social Psychology Bulletin,* 5, 1979, 325–8, and 'Detection of truthful and deceptive interpersonal communication across information transmission modes', *Journal of Social Psychology,* 114, 1981, 57–68; Albert Mehrabian, *Silent Messages* (New York: Aldine-Atherton, 1972), p. 85; Ekman, *Telling Lies, op. cit.,* p. 81.

56. A Meihlke, *Surgery of the Facial Nerve* (Philadelphia, Pa: Saunders, 1973); R.E. Myers, 'Comparative neurology of vocalization and speech: proof of a dichotomy', *Annals of the New York Academy of Sciences,* 280, 1976, 745–57. K. Tschiasshy, 'Eight syndromes of facial paralysis and their significance for locating the lesion', *Annals of Otology, Rhinology, and Laryngology,* 62, 1953, 677–91; Paul Ekman, Gowen Roper and Joseph C. Hager, 'Deliberate facial movement', *Child Development,* 51, 1980, 886; Ekman, *Telling Lies, op. cit.,* pp. 81, 84.

57. L. Kwint, 'Ontogeny of motility of the face', *Child Development,* 5, 1934, 1–12; Paul Ekman, Gowen Roper and Joseph C. Hager, 'Deliberate facial movement', *Child Development,* 51, 1980, 887, 889; Ekman, *Telling Lies, op. cit.,* pp. 132–3.

58. Judith A. Hall, *Nonverbal Sex Differences* (Baltimore, Md: Johns Hopkins University Press, 1984), pp. 60, 63, 66, 71; D.N. Stern and E.P. Bender, 'An ethological study of children approaching a strange adult: sex differences', in R.C. Friedman, R.M. Richart and R.L. Vande Wiele (eds), *Sex Differences in Behavior* (New York: Wiley, 1974), pp. 233–258; Ekman, *Telling Lies, op. cit.,* p. 127.

59. Mark L. Knapp, *Nonverbal Communication in Human Interaction, op. cit.,* p. 270–1; E.A. Haggard and F.S. Isaacs, 'Micromomentary facial expressions as indicators of ego mechanisms in psychotherapy', in L.A. Gottschalk and A.H. Auerbach (eds), *Methods of Research in Psychotherapy* (New York: Appleton-Century-Crofts, 1966), pp. 154–165; De Vito, *The Interpersonal Communication Book, op. cit.,* p. 205; Paul Ekman, W.V. Friesen and S.S. Tomkins, 'Facial affect scoring technique: a first validity study', *Semiotica,* 3, 1971, 37–58; Paul Ekman and W.V. Friesen, 'Measuring facial movement', *Environmental Psychology and Nonverbal Behavior,* 1976, 56–75; 'Detecting deception from the body or

face', *Journal of Personality and Social Psychology,* Vol. 29 (3), 1974, 289; and *Unmasking the Face* (Palo Alto, Calif.: Consulting Psychologists Press, 1984); Ekman, *Telling Lies, op. cit.,* pp. 129–30.

60. Morris, *The Pocket Guide to Manwatching, op. cit.,* p. 169; Robert G. Harper, Arthur N. Wiens and Joseph D. Matarazzo, *Nonverbal Communication: The State of the Art* (New York: Wiley, 1978), p. 102; Ekman, *Telling Lies, op. cit.,* p. 131.

61. Harper, Wiens, and Matarazzo, *Nonverbal Communication, op. cit.,* pp. 105–6; Ekman, *Telling Lies, op. cit.,* p. 144; Harold Sackeim, Ruben C. Gur and Marcel C. Saucy, 'Emotions are expressed more intensely on the left side of the face', *Science,* 202, 1978, 434.

62. Paul Ekman, Joseph C. Hager and Wallace V. Friesen 'The symmetry of emotional and deliberate facial actions', *Psychophysiology,* 18(2), 1981, 101–6; Ekman, *Telling Lies, op. cit.,* p. 146.

63. Knapp, *Nonverbal Communication in Human Interaction, op, cit.,* pp. 231, 268; Ekman, *Telling Lies, op. cit.,* pp. 148–9; Morris, *The Pocket Guide to Manwatching, op. cit.,* pp. 172–3.

64. D.E. Bugental, J.W. Kaswan, L.R. Love and M.N. Fox, 'Child versus adult perception of evaluative messages in verbal, vocal, and visual channels', *Developmental Psychology,* 2, 367–75; D.E. Bugental, L.R. Love and R.M. Gianetto, 'Perfidious feminine faces', *Journal of Personality and Social Psychology,* 17, 314–18; P. Noller, 'Channel consistency and inconsistency in the communications of married couples', *Journal of Personality and Social Psychology,* 43, 732–41; Hall, *Nonverbal Sex Differences, op. cit.,* p. 68; Ekman, *Telling Lies, op. cit.* p. 158.

65. Morris, *The Pocket Guide to Manwatching, op. cit.,* p. 173; Ekman, *Telling Lies, op. cit.,* p. 149.

66. Knapp, *Nonverbal Communication in Human Interaction, op. cit.,* pp. 309–10; E.H. Hess, 'The role of pupil size in communication', *Scientific American,* 233, November 1975, 110–12, 116–19; E.H. Hess, *The Tell-Tale Eye* (New York: Van Nostrand Reinhold, 1975); B. Rice, 'Rattlesnakes, French fries and pupillometric oversell', *Psychology Today,* 7, 1974, 55–9; M.P. Janisse and W.S. Peavler, 'Pupillary reasearch today: emotion in the eye', *Psychology Today,* 7, 1974, 60–3; DeVito, *The Interpersonal Communication Book, op. cit.,* pp. 207–8; Ekman, *Telling Lies, op. cit,* p. 142.

67. Sigmund Freud, 'The psychopathology of everyday life [1901]', in James Strachey, Jr. (ed.), *The Complete Psychological Works* (New York: W.W. Norton, 1976), Vol. 6, p. 86; Ekman, *Telling Lies, op. cit.,* p. 88.

68. Albert Mehrabian, *Nonverbal Communication* (New York: Aldine-Atherton, 1972), p. 100; S.V. Kasl and G.F. Mahl, 'The relationship of disturbances and hesitations in spontaneous speech to anxiety', *Journal of Personality and Social Psychology,* 1, 1965, 425–33; Knapp, *Essentials of Nonverbal Communication, op. cit.,* p. 141; Knapp, *Nonverbal Communication in Human Interaction, op. cit.,* p. 232; Ekman, *Telling Lies, op. cit.,* p. 90.

69. John Weisman, 'The truth will out', *TV Guide,* 3 September, 1977, p. 13; Ekman, *Telling Lies, op. cit.,* pp. 90, 92.

70. Klaus Scherer, 'Methods of research on vocal communication: paradigms and parameters', in Klaus Scherer and Paul Ekman (eds), *Handbook of Methods in Nonverbal Behavior Research* (New York: Cambridge University Press, 1982); Paul Ekman, Wallace V. Friesen and Klaus Scherer, 'Body movement and voice pitch in deceptive

interaction', *Semiotica*, 16, 1976, pp. 23–7; John Sirica, *To Set the Record Straight* (New York: W.W. Norton, 1979), pp. 99–100; Ekman, *Telling Lies, op. cit.*, pp. 93–4.

71.   DeVito, *The Interpersonal Communication Book, op. cit.*, p. 201; Knapp, *Nonverbal Communication in Human Interaction, op. cit.*, pp. 13–15, 202–3; Fernando Poyatos, *Man Beyond Words: Theory and Methodology of Nonverbal Communication* (New York: NYSEC Monographs, 1976)), p. 41; Bull, *Body Movement and Interpersonal Communication, op. cit.*, pp. 61–3; Vargas, *Louder than Words*, pp. 33–6; Harold G. Johnson, Paul Ekman and Wallace V. Friesen, 'Communicative body movements: American emblems', *Semiotica*, 15, 1975, 335–53. Paul Ekman, 'Movements with precise meanings', *Journal of Communication*, 26, 1976, 14–26; Ekman, *Telling Lies, op. cit.*, pp. 101–2.

72.   Knapp, *Nonverbal Communication in Human Interaction, op. cit.*, pp. 14–15; Ekman, *Telling Lies, op. cit.*, pp. 102–3.

73.   DeVito, *The Interpersonal Communication Book, op. cit.*, p. 201; Knapp, *Nonverbal Communication in Human Interaction, op. cit.*, pp. 15–16, 203, 208–10; Poyatos, *Man beyond Words, op. cit.*, pp. 41–2; Bull, *Body Movement and Interpersonal Communication, op. cit.*, pp. 63–8, 155; Vargas, *Louder than Words, op. cit.*, pp. 37–8; Ekman, *Telling Lies, op. cit.*, pp. 104, 105, 107.

74.   DeVito, *The Interpersonal Communication Book, op. cit.*, pp. 202–3; Knapp, *Nonverbal Communication in Human Interaction, op. cit.*, pp. 17–18; Poyatos, *Man beyond Words, op. cit.*, pp. 43–6; Malandro and Barker, *Nonverbal Communication, op. cit.*, pp. 126–8; Vargas, *Louder than Words, op. cit.*, pp. 48–9; Ekman, *Telling Lies, op. cit.*, pp. 109, 110, 112; Paul Ekman and Wallace V. Friesen, 'Nonverbal behavior and psychopathology', in R.J. Friedman and M.N. Katz (eds), *The Psychology of Depression: Contemporary Theory and Research* (Washington, DC: J. Winston, 1974).

75.   Ekman, *Telling Lies, op. cit.*, p. 187.

76.   Glenn E. Littlepage and Martin A. Pineault, 'Detection of deception of planned and spontaneous communication', *Journal of Social Psychology*, 125 (2), April 1985, 196 and 201; Albert Mehrabian, *Nonverbal Communication* (New York: Aldine-Atherton, 1972), p. 86; John Dean, *Blind Ambition* (New York: Simon and Schuster, 1976), p. 304.

77.   Ekman, *Telling Lies, op. cit.*, pp. 185, 188.

78.   Knapp, *Essentials of Nonverbal Communication. op. cit.*, pp. 141–2. Bull, *Body Movement and Interpersonal Communication. op. cit.*, pp. 55–6. Ekman, *Telling Lies, op. cit.*, p. 189.

Chapter 7 Tactics and countermeasures

1.   Philip Sperber, *Fail-Safe Business Negotiating: Strategies and Tactics for Success* (Englewood Cliffs, NJ: Prentice-Hall, 1983), pp. 40–1; Chester L. Karrass, *Give and Take: The Complete Guide to Negotiating Strategies and Tactics* 1(New York: Thomas Y. Crowell, 1974), pp. 14–16; Michael Schatzki, *Negotiation: The Art of Getting What You Want* (New York: New American Library, 1981), pp. 44–6, 51–2; Roy J. Lewicki and Joseph A. Litterer, *Negotiation* (Homewood, Ill.: Richard D. Irwin, 1985), pp. 75–9.

2.   Roger Fisher and William Ury, *Getting to Yes: Negotiating Agreement without Giving In* (New York: Penguin, 1983), pp. 103–4; Gordon F. Shea,

Creative Negotiating: Developing Innovative Win–Win Agreements that Work in your Business, Organizational, and Personal Life (Boston, Mass.: CBI Publishing, 1983), p. 83.

3.   Schatzki, *Negotiation, op. cit.,* pp. 37, 41; Sperber, *Fail-Safe Business Negotiating, op. cit.,* pp. 40–1; Karrass, *Give and Take, op. cit.,* pp. 191–2; Fisher and Ury, *Getting to Yes, op. cit.,* pp. 102–5; Chester L. Karrass, *The Negotiating Game* (New York: World, 1970), p. 188.

4.   Karrass, *Give and Take, op. cit.,* p. 191; Sperber, *Fail-Safe Business Negotiating, op. cit.,* pp. 40–1; Lewicki and Litterer, *Negotiation, op. cit.,* pp. 75–9.

5.   Henry H. Calero and Bob Oskam, *Negotiate the Deal You Want* (New York: Dodd, Mead, 1983), p. 270; Lewicki and Litterer, *Negotiation, op. cit.,* pp. 134, 284; Sperber, *Fail-Safe Business Negotiating, op. cit.,* pp. 20, 104.

6.   Sperber, *Fail-Safe Business Negotiating, op, cit.,* p. 41; Schatzki, *Negotiation, op. cit.,* pp. 50–2; John Winkler, *Bargaining for Results* (New York: Facts On File, 1984), p. 15.

7.   Calero and Oskam, *Negotiate the Deal You Want, op. cit.,* p. 270; Lewicki and Litterer, *Negotiation, op. cit.,* p. 138. Sperber, *Fail-Safe Business Negotiating, op. cit.,* pp. 38, 41, 47.

8.   Karrass, *The Negotiating Game, op. cit.,* p. 188; Karrass, *Give and Take, op. cit.,* pp. 39–40.

9.   Mack Hanan, James Cribbin and Howard Berrian, *Sales Negotiation Strategies* (New York: Amacom, 1977) pp. 140–1; Shea, *Creative Negotiating, op. cit.,* p. 38; Lewicki and Litterer, *Negotiation, op. cit.,* pp. 46, 280, 290; Sperber, *Fail-Safe Business Negotiating, op. cit.,* pp. 42, 155, 157; Calero and Oskam, *Negotiate the Deal You Want, op. cit.,* pp. 250–7.

10. Chester L. Karrass, 'Effective negotiation: the strategy of planning continued', *Pacific Purchaser,* December 1983, 10–11; Robert B. Maddux, *Successful Negotiation* (Los Altos, Calif.: Crisp Publications, 1986), p. 19; Karrass, *Give and Take, op. cit.,* pp. 86–7; Hanan, Cribbin, and Berrian, *Sales Negotiation Strategies, op. cit.,* p. 32; Juliet Nierenberg and Irene S. Ross, *Women and the Art of Negotiating* (New York: Simon and Schuster, 1985), pp. 109–10; Sperber, *Fail-Safe Business Negotiating, op. cit.,* p. 27; Lewicki and Litterer, *Negotiation, op. cit.,* pp. 183, 266; Calero and Oskam, *Negotiate the Deal You Want, op. cit.,* pp. 134–5, 152–4.

11. I. William Zartman and Maureen R. Berman, *The Practical Negotiator* (New Haven, Conn.: Yale University Press, 1982), pp. 20–1. Jim Murray, *The Art of Negotiating: Or How to Negotiate Practically Anything with Anyone* (Guelph, Ontario: Jay Gibson Creative Ltd, 1981), p. 27; Maddux, *Successful Negotiation, op. cit.,* p. 19; Dean G. Pruitt, *Negotiation Behavior* (New York: Academic Press, 1981), p. 139; Sperber, *Fail-Safe Business Negotiating, op. cit.,* p. 39; Shea, *Creative Negotiating, op. cit.,* pp. 44–5; Calero and Oskam, *Negotiate the Deal You Want, op. cit.,* pp. 133–5, 163.

12. Jerry Richardson and Joel Margulis, *The Magic of Rapport: The Business of Negotiation* (New York: Avon Books, 1984), p. 99; Gerard I. Nierenberg, *Fundamentals of Negotiating* (New York: Harper and Row, 1987), p. 114; Sperber, *Fail-Safe Business Negotiating, op. cit.,* p. 8; Lewicki and Litterer, *Negotiation, op. cit.,* pp. 177, 186; Pruitt, *Negotiation Behavior, op. cit.,* pp. 139–40; Calero and Oskam, *Negotiate the Deal You Want, op. cit.,* pp. 76, 94, 109–10.

13. Roy J. Lewicki and Joseph A. Litterer, *Negotiation: Readings, Exercises, and Cases* (Homewood, Ill.: Richard D. Irwin, 1985), pp. 112–13; John Ilich, *The Art and Skill of Successful Negotiation* (Englewood Cliffs, NJ:

Prentice-Hall, 1973), pp. 105–6; Richardson and Margulis, *The Magic of Rapport, op. cit.,* p. 130; Karrass, *Give and Take op. cit.,* pp. 8, 81–82; Calero and Oskam, *Negotiate the Deal You Want, op. cit.,* pp. 315–16.

14. Hanan, Cribbin and Berrian, *Sales Negotiation Strategies, op. cit.,* pp. 111–12, 123–4; Herb Cohen, *You Can Negotiate Anything* (New York: Bantam Books, 1980), pp. 58–9; Karrass, *Give and Take, op. cit.,* pp. 121–3, 147–8; Nierenberg, *Fundamentals of Negotiating, op. cit.,* pp. 158–9; Lewicki and Litterer, *Negotiation: Readings, Exercises, and Cases, op. cit.,* pp. 112–13; Calero and Oskam, *Negotiate the Deal You Want, op. cit.,* pp. 265–72.

15. Tessa Albert Warshaw, *Winning by Negotiation* (New York: Berkley Books, 1980), pp. 179–80; Nierenberg and Ross, *Women and the Art of Negotiating, op. cit.,* pp. 46, 96; Sperber, *Fail-Safe Business Negotiating op. cit.,* pp. 45–6; Calero and Oskam, *Negotiate the Deal You Want, op. cit.,* pp. 125–6.

16. Lewicki and Litterer, *Negotiation: Readings, Exercises, and Cases, op. cit.,* 76–7, 203, 205, 208; Nierenberg and Ross, *Women and the Art of Negotiating, op. cit.,* pp. 81–2; Richardson and Margulis, *The Magic of Rapport, op. cit.,* pp. 109–10; Karrass, *Give and Take, op. cit.,* pp. 131–3; Calero and Oskam, *Negotiate the Deal You Want, op. cit.,* pp. 91–6, 326.

17. Sperber, *Fail-Safe Business Negotiating, op. cit.,* p. 1, 39, 48–9; Ilich, *The Art and Skill of Successful Negotiation, op. cit.,* p. 183; Murray, *The Art of Negotiating, op. cit.,* pp. 38, 39; Shea, *Creative Negotiating, op. cit.,* pp. 42–3, 56–8; Karrass, *Give and Take, op, cit.,* p. 68; Calero and Oskam, *Negotiate the Deal You Want, op. cit.,* pp. 165–7, 252–7.

18. Fred E. Jandt, *Win–Win Negotiating: Turning Conflict into Agreement* (New York: John Wiley, 1985), pp. 263–4; Lewicki and Litterer, *Negotiation, op. cit.,* pp. 45–6, 55–6, 59–60; Lewicki and Litterer, *Negotiation: Readings, Exercises, and Cases, op. cit.,* pp. 30–1; Calero and Oskam, *Negotiate the Deal You Want, op. cit.,* pp. 189–91, 231.

19. Ilich, *The Art and Skill of Successful Negotiation, op. cit.,* pp. 62–4; Nierenberg, *Fundamentals of Negotiating, op. cit.,* pp. 49–50; Calero and Oskam, *Negotiate the Deal You Want, op. cit.,* p. 197.

20. Neil Chesanow, *The World-Class Executive: How To Do Busines Like A Pro around The World* (New York: Rawson Associates, 1985), pp. 21, 273–4; Andrew Kupfer, 'How to be a global manager', *Fortune,* 14 March 1988, p. 58; Vern Terpstra and Kenneth David, *The Cultural Environment of International Business* (Dallas, Tex: South-Western Publishing, 1985), pp. 121–6; Calero and Oskam, *Negotiate the Deal You Want, op. cit.,* p. 329; Karrass, *Give and Take, op. cit.,* p. 46; Sperber, *Fail-Safe Business Negotiating, op. cit.,* p. 155; Edward Levin, *Negotiating Tactics; Bargain Your Way to Winning* (New York: Fawcett Columbine, 1980), pp. 118–20.

21. Jandt, *Win–Win Negotiating,* p. 289; Karrass, *Give and Take, op. cit.,* pp. 46–8.

22. Bill Scott, *The Skills of Negotiating* (London: Gower, 1981), p. 52.

23. Schatzki, *Negotiation, op. cit.,* p. 114; Karrass, *Give and Take, op. cit.,* pp. 47–8.

24. Cohen, *You Can Negotiate Anything, op. cit.,* pp. 92–5; Schatzki, *Negotiation, op. cit.,* p. 113.

25. Andrew Kupfer, 'How to be a global manager', *Fortune,* 14 March 1988, p. 58; Calero and Oskam, *Negotiate the Deal You Want, op. cit.,* p. 329.

26. Karrass, *Give and Take, op. cit.,* pp. 44–7; Cohen, *You Can Negotiate Anything, op. cit.,* pp. 92–5; Schatzki, *Negotiation, op. cit.,* p. 114.

27. Lewicki and Litterer, *Negotiation, op. cit.,* pp. 151–4; Karrass, *Give and Take, op. cit.,* pp. 44–6; Calero and Oskam, *Negotiate the Deal You Want, op. cit.,* p. 202.

28. Hanan, Cribbin and Berrian, *Sales Negotiation Strategies, op. cit.*, pp. 107–9; Cohen, *You Can Negotiate Anything, op. cit.*, pp. 101–13; Lewicki and Litterer, *Negotiation, op. cit.*, pp. 249, 255.

29. Mack Hana, James Cribbin and Herman Heiser, *Consultative Selling* (New York: AMACOM, 1973), pp. 108–9; Lewicki and Litterer, *Negotiation, op. cit.*, pp. 249–51; Hanan, Cribbin and Berrian, *Sales Negotiation Strategies, op. cit.*, pp. 57–77, 107–9, 148–9; Karrass, *Give and Take, op. cit.*, pp. 198–9.

30. Lewicki and Litterer, *Negotiation, op. cit.*, pp. 190–1; Richardson and Margulis, *The Magic of Rapport, op. cit.*, pp. 109–10; Calero and Oskam, *Negotiate the Deal You Want, op. cit.*, pp. 98, 136–7.

31. Warschaw, *Winning by Negotiation, op. cit.*, pp. 179–80; Sperber, *Fail-Safe Business Negotiating, op. cit.*, pp. 45–6. Calero and Oskam, *Negotiate the Deal You Want, op. cit.*, p. 124.

32. Earl Brooks and George S. Odiorne, *Managing by Negotiations*, (New York: Van Nostrand Reinhold, 1984), p. 115.

33. Murray, *The Art of Negotiating, op. cit.*, p. 37; Schatzki, *Negotiation, op. cit.*, pp. 106–8; Calero and Oskam, *Negotiate the Deal You Want, op. cit.*, pp. 257–8.

34. Sperber, *Fail-Safe Business Negotiating, op. cit.*, 48–50; Cohen, *You Can Negotiate Anything, op. cit.*, pp. 55–8.

35. Hanan, Cribbin and Heiser, *Consultative Selling, op. cit.*, p. 44; Karrass, *Give and Take, op. cit*, pp. 138–40.

36. Sperber, *Fail-Safe Business Negotiating, op. cit.*, p. 34; Calero and Oskam, *Negotiate the Deal You Want, op. cit.*, pp. 209–12.

37. Joseph A. Folger and Marshall Scott Poole, *Working through Conflict: A Communication Perspective* (Glenview, Ill.: Scott, Foresman, 1984), p. 126; Calero and Oskam, *Negotiate the Deal You Want, op. cit.*, p. 172.

38. Calero and Oskam, *Negotiate the Deal You Want, op. cit.*, pp. 174–5; Folger and Poole, *Working through Conflict, op. cit.*, pp. 124–6.

39. Sperber, *Fail-Safe Business Negotiating, op. cit.*, p. 160; Calero and Oskam, *Negotiate the Deal You Want, op. cit.*, p. 176.

40. Karrass, *Give and Take, op. cit.*, pp. 164–5.

41. David Lewis, *Power Negotiating Tactics and Techniques* (New York: Prentice-Hall, 1981), pp. 78–9; Schatzki, *Negotiation, op. cit.*, pp. 133–4.

42. Hanan, Cribbin and Berrian, *Sales Negotiation Strategies, op. cit.*, pp. 127–44, 146; Karrass, *Give and Take, op. cit.*, pp. 63–4, 112; Schatzki, *Negotiation, op. cit.*, p. 133.

43. Lewis, *Power Negotiating, op. cit.*, p. 79.

44. Gerard I. Nierenberg, *Fundamentals of Negotiating* (New York: Hawthorn Books, 1973), p. 172; Lewicki and Litterer, *Negotiation, op. cit.*, pp. 308–9.

45. Hanan, Cribbin and Berrian, *Sales Negotiation Strategies, op. cit.*, pp. 144–6; Schatzki, *Negotiation, op. cit.*, pp. 133–4; Karrass, *Give and Take, op. cit.*, p. 112.

46. Karrass, *Give and Take, op. cit.*, pp. 112–13; Schatzki, *Negotiation, op. cit.*, p. 134.

47. Hanan, Cribbin and Berrian, *Sales Negotiation Strategies, op. cit.*, p. 127.

48. Nierenberg, *Fundamentals of Negotiation, op. cit.*, pp. 169–70; Hanan, Cribbin and Berrian, *Sales Negotiation Strategies, op. cit.*, pp. 112–13.

49. Schatzki, *Negotiation, op. cit.*, pp. 115–16.

50. Karrass, *Give and Take, op. cit.*, pp. 14–16; Sperber, *Fail-Safe Business Negotiating, op. cit.*, pp. 39–40; Calero and Oskam, *Negotiate the Deal You Want, op. cit.*, pp. 133–4.

51. Schatzki, *Negotiation, op. cit.,* pp. 35–6; Lewicki and Litterer, *Negotiation, op. cit.,* pp. 76–7; Calero and Oskam, *Negotiate the Deal You Want, op. cit.,* p. 134.

52. Karrass, *Give and Take, op. cit.,* pp. 91–2; Sperber, *Fail-Safe Business Negotiating, op. cit.,* pp. 40–1; Calero and Oskam, *Negotiate the Deal You Want, op. cit.,* pp. 270, 250–7.

53. Karrass, *Give and Take, op. cit.,* p. 92; Hanan, Cribbin and Berrian, *Sales Negotiation Strategies,op. cit.,* p. 136.

54. Ilich, *The Art and Skill of Successful Negotiation, op. cit.,* pp. 158–60; Richardson and Margulis, *The Magic of Rapport, op. cit.,* pp. 157–62; Karrass, *Give and Take, op. cit.,* pp. 132–3.

55. Richardson and Margulis, *The Magic of Rapport, op. cit.,* p. 161.

56. Hanan, Cribbin and Berrian, *Sales Negotiation Strategies, op. cit.,* p. 135; Charles M. Futrell, *Fundamentals of Selling* (Homewood, Ill.: Richard D. Irwin, 1984), p. 344; Richard T. Hise, *Effective Salesmanship* (Hinsdale, Ill.: Dryden Press, 1980), pp. 275–6.

57. Nierenberg, *Fundamentals of Negotiation, op. cit.,* pp. 49–50; Karrass, *Give and Take, op. cit.,* p. 83.

58. Roger Haydock, *Negotiation Practice* (New York: Wiley, 1984), p. 68; Murray, *The Art of Negotiating, op. cit.,* pp. 18–21; Nierenberg, *Fundamentals of Negotiation, op. cit.,* pp. 133–8.

59. Haydock, *Negotiation Practice, op. cit.,* p. 56.

60. Ilich, *The Art and Skill of Successful Negotiation, op. cit.,* p. 183; Calero and Oskam, *Negotiate the Deal You Want, op. cit.,* p. 256.

61. Winkler, *Bargaining For Results, op. cit.,* pp. 116–7.

62. Haydock, *Negotiation Practice, op. cit.,* p. 131; Karrass, *Give and Take, op. cit.,* pp. 142–3.

63. Ilich, *The Art of Skill of Successful Negotiation, op. cit.,* p. 161; Calero and Oskam, *Negotiate the Deal You Want, op. cit.,* pp. 105–6.

64. Hanan, Cribbin and Heiser, *Consultative Selling, op. cit.,* p. 60; Calero and Oskam, *Negotiate the Deal You Want, op. cit.,* pp. 106–7.

65. Lewicki and Litterer, *Negotiation, op. cit.,* pp. 72–3; Lewicki and Litterer, *Negotiation: Readings, Exercises, and Cases, op. cit.,* pp. 221–2; Calero and Oskam, *Negotiate the Deal You Want, op. cit.,* pp. 105–6.

66. Karrass, *The Negotiating Game op. cit.,* pp. 175–6; Hanan, Cribbin and Heiser, *Consultative Selling, op. cit.,* pp. 59–61; Murray, *The Art of Negotiating, op. cit.,* pp. 18–21; Calero and Oskam, *Negotiate the Deal You Want, op. cit.,* pp. 103, 154–6, 254.

67. Haydock, *Negotiation Practice, op. cit.,* p. 60; Murray, *The Art of Negotiating, op. cit.,* pp. 15–17; Lewicki and Litterer, *Negotiation op. cit.,* pp. 179–81; Margulis and Richardson, *The Magic of Rapport, op. cit.,* pp. 83–6.

68. Karrass, *Give and Take, op. cit.,* pp. 100–3; Sperber, *Fail-Safe Business Negotiating, op. cit.,* p. 119; Lewicki and Litterer, *Negotiation, op. cit.* pp. 179–80; Calero and Oskam, *Negotiate the Deal You Want, op. cit.,* p. 99.

69. David D. Seltz and Alfred J. Modica, *Negotiate Your Way to Success* (New York: New American Library, 1980), p. 23; Lewicki and Litterer, *Negotiation, op. cit.,* p. 180; Calero and Oskam, *Negotiate the Deal You Want, op. cit.,* p. 101.

70. Washington State Bar Association, *Negotiation Techniques: An Overview of Negotiation Techniques with Applications to Specific Subject Areas* (Washington: Washington State Bar Association, 1981), p. 80; Murray, *The Art of Negotiating, op. cit.,* pp. 15–17; Lewicki and Litterer, *Negotiation, op. cit.,* pp. 179–81; Margulis and Richardson, *The Magic of Rapport, op. cit.,* pp. 83–6.

71. Haydock, *Negotiation Practice op. cit.*, pp. 60–1; Karrass, *Give and Take, op. cit.*, p. 101; Calero and Oskam, *Negotiate the Deal You Want, op. cit.*, pp. 101–3.

72. Nierenberg and Ross, *Women and the Art of Negotiating op. cit.*, p. 157; Washington State Bar Association, *Negotiation Techniques, op. cit.*, pp. 81–2; Seltz and Modica, *Negotiate Your Way to Success, op. cit.*, pp. 131–4; Karrass, *Give and Take, op. cit.*, pp. 102–3; Richardson and Margulis, *The Magic of Rapport*, pp. 84–5; Calero and Oskam, *Negotiate the Deal You Want, op. cit.*, pp. 104–5.

73. Nierenberg, *Fundamentals of Negotiating, op. cit.*, pp. 22–4; Nierenberg, *The Art of Negotiating, op. cit.*, pp. 20–2.

74. Hanan, Cribbin and Berrian, *Sales Negotiation Strategies, op. cit.*, p. 84; Calero and Oskam, *Negotiate the Deal You Want, op. cit.*, p. 234.

75. Lewicki and Litterer, *Negotiation, op. cit.*, pp. 103, 107, 114; Fisher and Ury, *Getting to Yes, op. cit.*, pp. 41–58, 65, 67, 71, 73, 84.

76. Hanan, Cribbin and Berrian, *Sales Negotiation Strategies, op. cit.*, p. 85; Sperber, *Fail-Safe Business Negotiating, op. cit.*, p. 49; Chester L. Karrass, 'Effective negotiation: the strategy of planning, part three,' *Pacific Purchaser*, February 1984, p. 16; Joe Sutherland Gould, *The Negotiator's Problem Solver* (New York: Wiley, 1986), pp. 53–5; Calero and Oskam, *Negotiate the Deal You Want, op. cit.*, pp. 105–10, 113, 210–11.

77. Karrass, *Give and Take, op. cit.*, p. 39; Hanan, Cribbin and Berrian, *Sales Negotiation Strategies, op. cit.*, pp. 119–21.

78. Nierenberg and Ross, *Women and the Art of Negotiating, op. cit.*, p. 64; Nierenberg, *Fundamentals of Negotiating, op. cit.*, pp. 159–60; Maddux, *Successful Negotiation, op. cit.*, p. 49.

79. Nierenberg and Ross, *Women and the Art of Negotiating, op. cit.*, p. 63; Nierenberg, *Fundamentals of Negotiating, op. cit.*, pp. 159–60; Calero and Oskam, *Negotiate the Deal You Want, op. cit.*, pp. 270–2.

80. Levin, *Negotiating Tactics, op. cit.*, pp. 109–11; Karrass, *The Negotiating Game, op. cit.*, pp. 192–3; Fisher and Ury, *Getting to Yes, op. cit.*, pp. 142–3; Sperber, *Fail-Safe Business Negotiating, op. cit.*, p. 49; Karrass, *Give and Take, op. cit.*, p. 23; Jandt and Gillette, *Win–Win Negotiating, op. cit.*, p. 268; Calero and Oskam, *Negotiate the Deal You Want, op. cit.*, pp. 160–3.

81. Levin, *Negotiating Tactics, op. cit.*, pp. 138–9; Haydock, *Negotiation Practice, op. cit.*, p. 88.

82. Murray, *The Art of Negotiating, op. cit.*, p. 33; Karrass, *Give and Take, op. cit.*, p. 218.

83. Karrass, *Give and Take, op. cit.*, p. 219.

84. Fisher and Ury, *Getting to Yes, op. cit.*, p. 148.

85. Gould, *The Negotiator's Problem Solver, op. cit.*, pp. 148–9; Larry Carlson, 'The art of negotiating', *Pacific Purchaser*, 65 (10), October 1983, 11; Karrass, *Give and Take, op. cit.*, pp. 219–20.

86. Levin, *Negotiating Tactics, op. cit.*, p. 139.

87. Hanan, Cribbin and Berrian, *Sales Negotiation Strategies, op. cit.*, pp. 104–5; Calero and Oskam, *Negotiate the Deal You Want, op. cit.*, p. 168.

88. Aggressive tactics are defined as those tactics which impose pressure in various forms, mostly of a less acceptable nature on account of the threat or negative actions involved, that serve only to hinder or cloud TOS's chances of obtaining positive outcomes in the negotiation.

89. Jandt and Gillette, *Win–Win Negotiating, op. cit.*, p. 267; Levin, *Negotiating Tactics, op. cit.*, p. 118; Karrass, *Give and Take, op. cit.*, p. 243.

90. Washington State Bar Association, *Negotiation Techniques, op. cit.*, p. 95; Karrass, *Give and Take, op. cit.*, p. 244.

91. Karrass, *Negotiate to Close*, *op. cit.*, p. 71; Cohen, *You Can Negotiate Anything*, *op. cit.*, p. 58.

92. John Ilich, *Power Negotiating: How to Get the Upper Hand Every Time!* (New York: Playboy, 1980), pp. 125–6; Nierenberg and Ross, *Women and the Art of Negotiating*, *op. cit.*, pp. 109–11; Calero and Oskam, *Negotiate the Deal You Want*, *op. cit.*, p. 107.

93. Gavin Kennedy, *Everything Is Negotiable: How to Negotiate and Win*, *op. cit.*, pp. 250, 260.

94. Schatzki, *Negotiation*, *op. cit.*, p. 132–3; Cohen, *You Can Negotiate Anything*, *op. cit.*, pp. 58–60, 66–8.

95. Kennedy, *Everything Is Negotiable*, *op. cit.*, p. 268.

96. Lewicki and Litterer, *Negotiation*, *op. cit.*, pp. 333–4; Fisher and Ury, *Getting to Yes*, *op. cit.*, p. 143; Sperber, *Fail-Safe Business Negotiating*, *op. cit.*, p. 156; Karrass, *Give and Take*, *op. cit.*, pp. 227–30; Calero and Oskam, *Negotiate the Deal You Want*, *op. cit.*, p. 272.

97. Schatzki, *Negotiation*, *op. cit.*, p. 132; Ilich, *Power Negotiating*, *op. cit.*, pp. 81–3; Calero and Oskam, *Negotiate the Deal You Want*, *op. cit.*, pp. 244–5.

98. Calero and Oskam, *Negotiate the Deal You Want*, *op. cit.*, p. 272.

99. P.D.V. Marsh, *Contract Negotiation Handbook* (London: Gower, 1984), p. 381; Schatzki, *Negotiation*, *op. cit.*, pp. 104–5.

100. Levin, *Negotiating Tactics*, *op. cit.*, pp. 109–10; Karrass, *The Negotiating Game*, *op. cit.*, pp. 192–3; Fisher and Ury, *Getting to Yes*, *op. cit.*, pp. 142–3; Sperber, *Fail-Safe Business Negotiating*, *op. cit.*, p. 49; Karrass, *Give and Take*, *op. cit.*, p. 23; Jandt and Gillette, *Win–Win Negotiating*, *op. cit.*, p. 268; Calero and Oskam, *Negotiate The Deal You Want*, *op. cit.*, pp. 161–2.

101. Karrass, *The Negotiating Game*, *op. cit.*, pp. 192–3; Fisher and Ury, *Getting to Yes*, *op. cit.*, pp. 142–3; Sperber, *Fail-Safe Business Negotiating*, *op. cit.*, p. 156; Karrass, *Give and Take*, *op. cit.*, p. 23; Calero and Oskam, *Negotiate the Deal You Want*, *op. cit.*, p. 247.

102. Scott, *The Skills of Negotiating*, *op. cit.*, p. 52; Schatzki, *Negotiation*, *op. cit.*, pp. 113–5; Calero and Oskam, *Negotiate the Deal You Want*, *op. cit.*, p. 271.

103. Donald B. Sparks, *The Dynamics of Effective Negotiation* (Houston, Tex.: Gulf Publishing, 1982), p. 134; Calero and Oskam, *Negotiate the Deal You Want*, *op. cit.*, p. 271.

104. Hanan, Cribbin and Berrian, *Sales Negotiation Strategies*, *op. cit.*, p. 120.

105. Levin, *Negotiating Tactics*, *op. cit.*, pp. 124–5; Karrass, *Give and Take*, *op. cit.*, p. 200.

106. Sperber, *Fail-Safe Business Negotiating*, *op. cit.*, p. 159; Lewis, *Power Negotiating Tactics and Techniques*, *op. cit.*, p. 134; Calero and Oskam, *Negotiate the Deal You Want*, *op. cit.*, pp. 132, 150, 252, 267, 293–4.

107. Scott, *The Skills of Negotiating*, *op. cit.*, p. 141; Marsh, *Contract Negotiation Handbook*, *op. cit.*, p. 347; Fisher and Ury, *Getting to Yes*, *op. cit.*, pp. 141–2, Ilich, *Power Negotiating*, *op. cit.*, pp. 47–9. Karrass, *Negotiate to Close*, *op. cit.*, pp. 189–90; Schatzki, *Negotiation*, *op. cit.*, p. 105, Karrass, *Give and Take*, *op. cit.*, p. 79.

108. Schatzki, *Negotiation*, *op. cit.*, pp. 105–6; Fisher and Ury, *Getting to Yes*, *op. cit.*, pp. 141–2; Karrass, *Negotiate to Close*, *op. cit.*, p. 191.

109. Cohen, *You Can Negotiate Anything*, *op. cit.*, pp. 58–9; Karrass, *Give and Take*, *op. cit.*, p. 80.

110. Fisher and Ury, *Getting to Yes*, *op. cit.*, pp. 141–2; Sperber, *Fail-Safe Business Negotiating*, *op. cit.*, p. 151; Karrass, *Give and Take*, *op. cit.*, pp. 79–80; Maddux, *Successful Negotiation*, *op. cit.*, p. 50; Schatzki, *Negotation*, *op. cit.*, pp. 105–6.

111. Richardson and Margulis, *The Magic of Rapport, op. cit.,* pp. 175–7; Fisher and Ury, *Getting to Yes, op. cit.,* pp. 142–3; Calero and Oskam, *Negotiate the Deal You Want, op. cit.,* pp. 125–6, 157–8, 236, 259.
112. Lewis, *Power Negotiating Tactics and Techniques, op. cit.,* p. 115; Karrass, *Give and Take, op. cit.,* pp. 75–7;
113. Ilich, *Power Negotiating, op. cit.,* pp. 81–3; Calero and Oskam, *Negotiate the Deal You Want, op. cit.,* pp. 244–5.
114. Calero and Oskam, *Negotiate the Deal You Want, op. cit.,* p. 272.

Index

Assertiveness for Managers

Terry Gillen

Do you, asks Terry Gillen, want to be the kind of manager who:

- motivates his or her team to achieve their objectives?
- inspires loyalty in subordinates?
- has the respect of colleagues?
- is highly regarded by senior management?
- feels self-confident at work?

Today's business environment is changing dramatically – and so is our understanding of management effectiveness, especially when dealing with people. A major requirement of successful managers is personal credibility; it helps them motivate staff, work better with colleagues and impress their 'superiors'. Personal credibility depends on the way managers interact with other – where they do so assertively they naturally exhibit the characteristics we value in other people and which staff admire particularly in a manager.

Terry Gillen's practical book opens with an assertiveness profile to help you assess your own skills. In Part One the foundations of assertiveness theory are related to the workplace. Workout pages assist skill development.

Part Two is a ready reference of how to behave assertively in a range of typical managerial situations.

1994   260 pages   0 566 07613 6

A Gower Paperback

The Creative Negotiator

Stephen Kozicki

Negotiation is understanding other people, and knowing how to communicate with them to achieve agreement - the classic win/win solution. Most of us negotiate every day, both at work and in our private lives. In *The Creative Negotiator*, Kozicki persuades us that successful negotiation need not be about conflict, and provides a step-by-step process for negotiating success. This revolves around:

- A flexible negotiating style
- Carefully planned outcomes: realistic, acceptable, 'worst possible'
- Four basic principles: There are no rules
  Everything is negotiable
  Ask for a better deal
  Learn to say 'no'

Effective negotiating should be a creative process, but also a simple one if his principles are followed.

Kozicki was persuaded to write the book by peers impressed by his ability to make good negotiation appear simple.

Contents

Introduction • The Columbus Technique • Are You a Motivated Negotiator? • The Negotiation Model • The Investigative Phase • The Presentation Phase • The Bargaining Phase •The Agreement Phase • Team Negotiations • The Creative Negotiator! • Bibliography.

1994   214 pages   0 566 07492 3

A Gower Paperback

Customer First
A Strategy for Quality Service

Denis Walker

How did British Airways turn a loss of £69.9 million into a profit of over £250 million in under 10 years?

The secret was in its approach to customer service, and that strategy was devised by the author of this book. Walker argues that improving customer service is no longer a matter of choice – the future of your organization depends on it. Drawing on his experience as a senior manager at British Airways during the 1980s and subsequently as a management consultant, he sets out a model for planning, implementing and maintaining a service improvement programme designed to give your company competitive advantage.

Customer First is concise and easy to read, offering a complete strategy that is easy to implement. It includes an audit to allow you to assess your organization's strengths and weaknesses, and a complete training programme designed to take you through the first 12 to 18 months of your new strategy.

Contents

Part I The "Customer First" Concept • What is service? • Service as strategy • Knowing your customers • Knowing your competitors • Developing a vision • Organizing for service • Auditing material service • Auditing personal service • What went wrong? • Part II Planning and Running a Service Programme • The importance of ownership • Where are we now? • Visions and values • Launching a service programme • Keeping up the momentum • Managing a service business • Marketing customer service • Handling customer complaints • Part III The British Airways Story • The background • The "Customer First" campaign • The second phase • Holding the gains • Summary of Part III • Conclusion: Pitfalls and payoffs • Index.

1994   168 pages   0 566 07543 1

A Gower Paperback

A Systematic Approach to
Getting Results

Surya Lovejoy

'Getting Results is a practical handbook for making things happen', explains Surya Lovejoy. 'Today's managers are offered training in everything from understanding management accounts to power dressing, yet they are often left on their own when it comes to setting and meeting management objectives.'

Every manager has to produce results. This book is designed to equip managers with effective project management tools without drowning them in jargon. And whether the project is a conference, a sales target, or an office re-location, the principles are the same. You need a systematic approach for working out:

- exactly what has to happen
- when everything has to happen
- how to ensure that it does
- what could go wrong – and the implications
- how you will remain sane during the process

Contents

Introduction • Turning a task into a project • Turning a project into an action plan • Creating and managing the budget • Creating project maps • Creating a winning team • Turning the action plan into action • Outwitting the paperwork • Remaining sane • Avoiding the technology trap • Crisis projects • Help! • After the project • Index.

1994   192 pages   0 566 07541 5

A Gower Paperback

The Goal
Beating the Competition
Second Edition

Eliyahu M Goldratt and Jeff Cox

Written in a fast-paced thriller style, *The Goal* is the gripping novel which is transforming management thinking throughout the Western world.

Alex Rogo is a harried plant manager working ever more desperately to try to improve performance. His factory is rapidly heading for disaster. So is his marriage. He has ninety days to save his plant – or it will be closed by corporate HQ, with hundreds of job losses. It takes a chance meeting with a colleague from student days – Jonah – to help him break out of conventional ways of thinking to see what needs to be done.

The story of Alex's fight to save his plant is more than compulsive reading. It contains a serious message for all managers in industry and explains the ideas which underlie the Theory of Constraints (TOC) developed by Eli Goldratt – the author described by Fortune as 'a guru to industry' and by Businessweek as a 'genius'.

As a result of the phenomenal and continuing success of *The Goal*, there has been growing demand for a follow-up. Eliyahu Goldratt has now written ten further chapters which continues the story of Alex Rogo as he makes the transition from Plant Manager to Divisional Manager. Having achieved the turnround of his plant, Alex now attempts to apply all that Jonah has taught him, not to crisis management, but to ongoing improvement.

These new chapters reinforce the thinking process utilised in the first edition of *The Goal* and apply them to a wider management context with the aim of stimulating readers into using the technique in their own environment.

1993   352 pages   0 566 07418 4

A Gower Paperback

How to Write Effective Reports

Second Edition

John Sussams

In business, administration and research, the report is an indispensable tool and all managers or specialists need to master the skills involved in writing one. John Sussams' book covers all aspects of the subject in a thoroughly practical fashion. It not only discusses language and style but also explains how to structure and organize material to facilitate understanding. In addition it deals with planning, presentation and production.

The text is enlivened by examples and illustrations and there are a number of exercises designed to improve the reader's report-writing ability. This new edition reflects recent developments and includes a section on the latest word-processing and desktop publishing techniques.

Contents

Why a Report?: Working papers; Other means of communication • Structure: The summary; The main body of the report; Complex ideas; Appendices; Charts and diagrams; Presentation of statistical data • Layout: Margins; Paragraphs; Headings; Numbering of diagrams, tables, and appendices; Spacing; When to print on both sides of the paper; Summary • Language • Spelling and Punctuation: Spelling; Punctuation; Italics; Numbers; Abbreviations • Materials and Equipment: Covers; Binding; Paper; Typefaces; Reprographic methods; Charts and diagrams • Planning: The schedule; The skeleton report; Assembling the raw material; Drafting; Timing; Editorial control • Exercises • Suggested further reading.

1993   144 pages   0 566 07476 1

A Gower Paperback

What Maastricht Means for Business
Opportunities and regulations in the EC Internal Market

Brian Rothery

A businessman's guide to the opportunities presented by the Maastricht Agreement, together with information on the implications of the resulting legislation for anyone managing a company in Europe, or trading with the European Community.

Contents

1993   272 pages   0 566 07431 1

A Gower Paperback